S0-FIQ-444

FRAMINGHAM STATE COLLEGE
3 3014 00020 3085

THE UNITED STATES AS A WORLD POWER

THE MACMILLAN COMPANY
NEW YORK · BOSTON · CHICAGO
ATLANTA · SAN FRANCISCO

MACMILLAN & CO., Limited
LONDON · BOMBAY · CALCUTTA
MELBOURNE

THE MACMILLAN CO. OF CANADA, Ltd.
TORONTO

THE UNITED STATES AS A WORLD POWER

BY

ARCHIBALD CARY COOLIDGE
HARVARD UNIVERSITY

WHITTEMORE LIBRARY
FRAMINGHAM STATE COLLEGE
FRAMINGHAM, MASSACHUSETTS

New York
THE MACMILLAN COMPANY
1908

Republished 1971
Scholarly Press, Inc., 22929 Industrial Drive East
St. Clair Shores, Michigan 48080

COPYRIGHT, 1908,

BY THE MACMILLAN COMPANY.

Library of Congress Catalog Card Number 72-144955
Standard Book Number 403-00907-3

E
713
.C76
1971

PREFACE

No one can be more conscious than the author of this volume how far it is from carrying out the too ambitious promise of its title. Its subject — the United States as a World Power — could well be treated in many different ways. One writer might recount the growth of the country from its earliest infancy to its present stature; to another its economic position in the world to-day might be of surpassing interest; a third might care only for the spiritual influence of the United States, the spread of American ideals of liberty, government and civilization, and the changes those same ideals are now undergoing. The scope of the present work is more modest. It is a study of the part which the United States plays in the great drama of world politics — a part which cannot help being important and which, although impossible to prophesy about in detail, yet is affected by circumstances of geography and of national character, of history and of tradition, of economic and of social conditions susceptible of investigation.

This book was originally prepared in the form of lectures which were delivered at the Sorbonne in the winter of 1906–07 as the Harvard lectures on the Hyde foundation. Since then it has been entirely recast, but it doubtless still retains traces of having been first addressed to a foreign audience, the more so as I have striven to preserve a neutral rather then a specifically American attitude. I have not felt called upon to offer a solution to all the

v

3

viPREFACE

problems to which I have referred or to volunteer my opinion on every disputed question. For my last chapter I wish to make special acknowledgment to my friend Louis Aubert of Paris, whose interesting recent work, *Américains et Japonais*, I have found most helpful, besides being reminded by it of many pleasant discussions we have had together.

A volume covering so broad a field and one so full of controversial matter as the United States as a World Power, is exposed at every point to charges of superficiality and partisanship. No book of the kind could satisfy every one or perhaps any one in all its details. I can only ask that mine may be judged as a whole rather than praised or blamed on the strength of detached passages. As most of the facts cited are well known or easy to look up, copious reference to authorities has seemed needless.

A. C. C.

HARVARD UNIVERSITY,
May, 1908.

CONTENTS

THE UNITED STATES AS A WORLD POWER

INTRODUCTION

TWENTY years ago the expression "world power" was unknown in most languages; to-day it is a political commonplace, bandied about in wide discussion. But the term is lacking in exactness. Men differ as to its meaning, as to the countries to which it can properly be applied, and as to the moment when it first becomes applicable to them. Sometimes it seems to be appropriately used of a country in one connection, but not in another; and in a certain sense it may be applied to nearly all independent states, for all may be called upon to maintain their particular rights and interests in any quarter of the globe, and all may take part in framing regulations for the general welfare of mankind. And yet, uncertain as the limits of the phrase may be, it conveys a pretty definite conception, — a conception that is of recent origin, although there is nothing new in the political sentiments to which it owes its birth.

The idea that one people should control the known world is ancient enough, its most salient expression being found in imperial Rome and equally imperial China; and it is not extinct even now. We may to-day condemn all mere lust of domination, and hope that, as civilization progresses, the stronger peoples will more and more regard the weaker ones as having rights as sacred as their own; but complete equality has never existed, and can never exist, between states of greatly unequal strength. In practice the larger must tend to arrange many matters without consulting every wish of their numerous smaller brethren. The community of nations cannot content itself with anarchy like that of the Polish republic, and submit to the *liberum veto* of its most insignificant member. As there have been in the past, so there will always be, certain leading states which, when they are agreed, will find some way of imposing their decisions upon the rest, and by their mutual jealousies will tend to establish a balance of power among themselves.

Without stopping to trace the working of these principles in earlier days, we note that, by the close of the fifteenth century, certain states had assumed a position which entitles them to the modern designation of "great European powers." The Holy Roman Empire, still first in dignity; France, after she had recovered from the Hundred Years' War and had broken the might of her great feudal nobles; England, in the firm hand of Henry VII; the newly formed kingdom of Spain, which had finally ended Moorish rule in the peninsula, — all these held a position unlike that of their neighbors. The difference between them and such powers as Denmark, the Swiss Confederation, and Venice was one of rank as well as of strength. Politically they were on another plane: they were not merely the leaders, they were the spokesmen, the directors, of the whole community.

As time went on, changes took place in their membership. In the course of the sixteenth century, when the Empire became so dislocated that it was hardly a power at all, its place was taken by Austria, a strangely conglomerate formation, which protected the eastern frontier of Christendom against the Turks. Spain was for a while a real world power, overshadowing all the others, dominant in Europe, supreme in America, and dreaded even in remote Japan.

The seventeenth century witnessed the decline of Spain, the primacy of France, and the temporary rise of Sweden and the Netherlands; but the greatness of these last rested on too small a material foundation to support it after the countries themselves had outlived their heroic period. The eighteenth century saw them subside into relative insignificance, and in their stead two newcomers step to the forefront of European affairs. The huge semi-Asiatic empire of Russia was now, by the genius of Peter the Great, transformed into the outward semblance of a European state; and the little military kingdom of Prussia, the representative of Northern Germany, won for itself a position which its resources hardly warranted, but which, thanks to the extraordinary ability of its rulers and the sense of discipline of its people, it succeeded in maintaining.

After the violent episode of the French Revolution and the Napoleonic wars, the European continent settled down to what seemed to be a stable organization with five great powers, — Russia, England, Austria, Prussia, and France, for the skill of Talleyrand at Vienna prevented France from being even temporarily excluded after her disasters. The Ottoman Empire was still, in spite of Metternich, held to be not quite European; and the weaker countries were consulted but little on general questions. It was not the formal meetings of all the representatives of the nations assembled that decided the affairs of Europe at the Congress of Vienna in 1814: it was a small committee of the leading states. What they, after much wrangling, agreed upon among themselves, the others had to accept.

This arrangement lasted for two generations, although the relative positions of the several states changed not a little. In the seventies, the German Empire, with a mighty development, inherited the international place formerly held by the Prussian kingdom, and a new member was added to the oligarchy by the formation of United Italy.

Since then there have been six great European powers instead of five. This does not mean that they are equal in size and strength: there is, for instance, less difference between Italy, which is recognized as a great power, and Spain or the Ottoman Empire, which technically is not, than between Italy and Germany or Russia; but the line, however artificial, has been clearly drawn by political usage.

In the last quarter of the nineteenth century a new situation, with a far wider horizon, gradually attracted the attention of writers and statesmen. Great Britain, France, Spain, Portugal, and Holland had long owned extensive territories in many climes; but the last three countries had ceased to be of the first rank. Although their distant holdings undoubtedly added to their importance in the world, they could not make up for their weakness at home. As for France, she had formerly had the beginnings of a magnificent empire; but she had sacrificed it in the pursuit of purely European aims, now recognized as of less consequence than what she gave up for them. Even England, who during the eighteenth century so successfully subordinated her continental interests to her colonial ones, had a moment of uncertainty after the loss of most of her American possessions, and for a time the theory prevailed in the mother country that her colonies must eventually fall away from her as ripe fruit falls from a tree (this was the simile usually employed). Nevertheless, the gigantic British Empire continued to grow steadily, but as a result of natural causes rather than of fixed purpose.

Suddenly, almost without warning, the nations entered upon a wild scramble for land wherever it was not strongly held or protected by competing interests. The conquests of Alexander the Great or of the caliphs did not equal in territorial magnitude the changes which the last twenty years have witnessed. The circumstances, the pretexts, the excuses, have differed in the case of each state which has taken part in the movement of expansion; but the fundamental reasons have been the same. Each country has honestly felt a certain reluctance, and has been convinced with truth that its hand has been forced by others; but each has also realized that, unless it were content to let itself be forestalled by its rivals, there was need of haste. Hence the frantic hurry with which many of the annexations have been made. Hence, too, the indiscriminate seizure of regions which were of no immediate value, but which might be of profit some day, — a practice that Lord Rosebery has aptly called "pegging out claims for the future."

In England, the imperial idea of Greater Britain, of which Beaconsfield was one of the first practical exponents, displaced the *laissez-faire* theories of the school of Cobden, and the empire was extended almost from year to year. France, who had with timid steps begun again in Algeria and Cochin China the building up of a new colonial dominion, now, in spite of popular indifference, not to say opposition, rapidly added to her store in Indo-China and in various parts of Africa until, thanks to the energy of Jules Ferry and a few others, her colonies surpassed in extent those which she had lost in earlier days. Germany, becoming aware that, despite her military power and her industrial development, she held but a small spot on the surface of the globe, eagerly began to clutch at new lands wherever there seemed to be a chance of seizing them, although Bismarck, representing the ideas of an older generation, was never more than lukewarm in the cause. Italy decided that she also had need of colonies, and made a beginning on the African coast. The King of the Belgians acquired for his subjects a lien on the Congo Free State. Portugal, baulked in part by the rival ambition of England, tried, too late, to turn many vague claims into real possessions.

Though this fever of rapid expansion affected nearly all the states of Western Europe, it was not confined to them. During the greater part of the nineteenth century, Russia had been pushing southward into the regions of the Caucasus and Central Asia; now, while preparing for further progress in the same directions, she turned her chief attention to the extreme east. Long before, she had reached the Pacific, and had even crossed it far to the north; but she had never had more than a slight hold on these distant and desolate shores. After the middle of the nineteenth century, however, although she disposed of her American possessions, she so added to her domain in eastern Asia as to establish her power there on a new foundation; and a generation later, by the building up of her fleet, the gradual increase of immigration to Siberia, and the construction of the Trans-Siberian railway, she had revolutionized her position in the Far East. She who, at the time of the Crimean War, could muster but a few hundred soldiers in this whole part of the world, now became a menacing power in the Pacific, one that was for a while feared more than any other.

At the same time, to the astonishment of all, including herself, America suddenly accepted the role of a power holding distant colonies. Already her extraordinary economic progress was bringing her more and more to the front; but, though the annexation of Hawaii could be foreseen, no one was prepared for that of Porto Rico and the Philippines, or for the real, if unexpressed, protectorate over Cuba and Panama. Still greater surprise was excited by Japan, who in her war with China in 1894 first gave evidence of her new ambitions, as well as of her ability to realize them, and in her conflict with Russia ten years later furnished even more decisive proof of their remarkable increase. What will be their limits is indeed one of the most important questions of international politics at the present day.

It was in course of the discussions provoked by this succession of startling events that political writers, in formulating the principles of the new state of affairs, began to employ an expression which has now passed into common use, — "world powers"; that is to say, powers which are directly interested in all parts of the world and whose voices must be listened to everywhere. The term is, as we have said, not scientifically exact; for each of the so-called world powers has spheres in which its interests are vitally important, and others in which they are comparatively small, if not inferior to those of less powerful states. Thus Russia can hardly claim to be consulted much about South American questions; and the United States takes no part as yet in a matter so strictly European as the settlement of the affairs of the Ottoman Empire. Nevertheless, both Russia and the United States are certainly world powers in the ordinary acceptance of the term. China, on the other hand, is not, although she is third in size among the states of the world, and has perhaps the largest, as well as the hardest-working, population. However great her potentialities may be, her actual military strength and political influence are not yet such as to entitle her to a place among the arbiters of mankind. This is truer still of Brazil and of the Argentine Republic, which, though they seem assured of more consideration some day, at present count for little in international affairs. Even Austria and Italy do not come under the new category: they are both great European powers in every sense of the term, and as such hold a proud position; but in spite of their armies and their navies, their glories and their high civilization, they have little political influence outside of their own continent. In the case of Japan, the question may seem more doubtful; and if we should give a negative answer to-day, we might have to revise it to-morrow. Her prestige is very great. She has just emerged triumphant from a contest with an adversary

of immense strength, during which she has astonished the
world by her extraordinary progress and her wonderful
display of national efficiency; she has allied herself with
the British Empire under conditions which make it seem
as if her aid had been sought for the protection of England's
Indian frontier; and she is regarded by many as threatening
not only the colonial possessions of the United States in the
Pacific, but even the whole western shores of the American
continents. Be this as it may, since Japan takes no part
in the affairs of Europe, western Asia, Africa, or most of
America, she can hardly be called a world power, though
she is without question one of the eight great powers of
the world.

Turning now to those states whose claim to the title is
beyond question, we find that they are five in number, and
all ruled by peoples of European blood, but in two of
them the dominant whites at home are outnumbered by the
colored inhabitants of the colonies. Of the five, Russia is
the only one which had already attained to something like
its present dimensions by the beginning of the nineteenth
century.

In order to show how these states compare with one
another in certain fundamental respects, such as area and
population, it may be well to give here a few round numbers,
and, without going into an analysis of these figures or a
study of their values, to distinguish between the white
population and the colored. Unscientific and misleading as
this process may be, it is in many ways indispensable for our
purpose; for without venturing into the vexed questions of
the relative superiority or inferiority of different races and
their capabilities of development, we must recognize that at
the present day, at least, all races are not of equal political
value. A single Annamite or Sudanese may be worth more
to France in every respect than a particular Parisian or
Marseillais; but ten million Frenchmen in France mean

something very different from ten million French subjects in Asia or Africa. Again, we should also bear in mind the difference between tropical and non-tropical territories. The white races have not succeeded in getting acclimatized in the tropics, and, except in a few favored spots, there is no immediate prospect of their doing so. Though white men in the prime of life can dwell almost anywhere as officials, soldiers, merchants, or employers of labor, white colonization on a large scale is, in general, possible in the temperate zone only. Finally, we must not forget that all the great empires of to-day contain large tracts of bad land, either wilderness or desert. Northern Canada and northern Siberia, central Australia and central Asia, the arid West in the United States and southwest Africa, are not without value, — they have their comparatively fertile districts, and are in places rich in minerals, — but all contain vast stretches which add little, except on the map, to the importance of their owners. With these considerations in view, let us look at the statistics.

Of the five world powers, the British Empire stands easily first in area, and still more so in population, for in numbers it exceeds any two of its rivals. It extends over nearly eleven and a half million square miles, situated in every part of the globe, and has some four hundred million inhabitants.[1] Of these, however, less than sixty million are whites, of whom some forty-three and a half million live in the home country, most of the rest in Canada, Australia, and South Africa. The ruling white race is thus to the subject colored race in the dangerous ratio of hardly more than one to six; but the whites are in the main homogeneous, although the Irish, the French in Canada, and the Dutch in South Africa form somewhat discordant

---

[1] Not including Egypt and the Anglo-Egyptian Sudan, together about eleven hundred and fifty thousand square miles, with twelve million inhabitants.

elements. The colored population, on the other hand, is
made up of an endless variety of races and nationalities, —
black, yellow, and all shades of brown, — far apart from
one another in almost every respect. The great majority of them live in the tropics. As the mother country
is by no means self-supporting in the matter of food, it is
easy to understand why Englishmen feel that, although
they do not need a large army, the possession of the most
powerful navy in the world, one that will assure the safety
of their communications, is for them a matter of life and
death.

Russia comes next in size, with a territory of a little less
than eight and a half million square miles.[1] In contrast
to the widely scattered British empire, the Russian is
absolutely compact, with no outlying possessions, almost
no islands of importance, and much general sameness in
climate and conditions. Of its one hundred and fifty
million inhabitants, about one hundred and twenty-five
million are of Aryan or Semitic stock, — a larger white
population than that of any other country; but although
the whites are five times as numerous as the Asiatics, one
race here melts into the other to an extent unknown elsewhere. The European element, besides being backward
as a whole, contains several discontented nationalities,
which, resisting absorption into the general mass, are in many
ways a source of weakness rather than of strength. Even
the purely Russian element is divided into three distinct
branches. Russia's natural increase by the surplus of
births over deaths is more than two million a year. Her
undeveloped resources at home are indeed immense; but
she is still poor, and by recent events she has lost temporarily in political influence. She has no territory in the
tropics.

Third among world powers comes Greater France, with

[1] Including Khiva and Bokhara, but not northern Manchuria.

an area of perhaps four and a half million square miles, and some ninety-five million inhabitants. Her territory, like that of Great Britain, is dispersed over the world; but more than half of it is in a solid, if irregularly shaped, block in northern Africa, and her share of the Sahara alone accounts for about two million square miles. The white population of France is not quite forty million, of which three-quarters of a million are in North Africa; the rest are in Europe, and barely increasing in numbers. The colored element, which is to the white as almost six to four, comprises over twenty million each of blacks and Mongolians, living in the tropics; the rest are Berbers, Arabs, Malagasy, Hindus, South Sea Islanders, etc. Most of the colonial possessions of France are recent acquisitions, as yet little developed, but offering a wide field to the capital and enterprise of the mother country. Of them all, only North Africa and New Caledonia are suited to European settlement. The population of France herself, however varied in other ways, is more nationally homogeneous than that of any of her world rivals.

The United States [1] is slightly below France in territory and population, with an area of three million, seven hundred thousand square miles, and ninety-three million inhabitants. On the other hand, it has a considerably larger white element than France, — about seventy-five million. The birthrate is not, as a rule, very high; but the annual immigration has now risen to over a million and a quarter. The colored population, of some eighteen and a half million, is made up of ten million negroes and mulattoes, nearly eight million Filipinos, and the rest Indians, Japanese, Chinese, Hawaiians, etc. Like Russia, the United States forms a compact mass; but it now has outlying dependencies, — Alaska far to the north, and a number of tropical islands. How much most of these possessions add

[1] Not including Cuba and Panama.

to the real strength of the country is, however, a question about which there has been much dispute.

Greater Germany, with only a little over a million and a quarter square miles (scarcely more than a tenth of the number in the British Empire), stands far below her rivals in area; but her white population of more than sixty millions, out of a total of seventy-five, is superior to that of Great Britain or France. These sixty million, which include several unwilling elements, are concentrated on a small tract of not very fertile territory; for the German colonial possessions, nearly five times the size of the home country, are for the most part situated in the tropics, and hence, with the doubtful exception of Southwest Africa, can never support a large number of white settlers. In Germany the annual surplus of births over deaths is more than eight hundred thousand; and the emigration, which was large a few years ago, is now, with the increasing industrial prosperity, under fifty thousand. It is not, then, to be wondered at, if the Germans are not satisfied with their present limits.[1]

Figures like the above are, of course, nothing but a slight framework for any serious comparison. In order to get a more precise idea of the relative resources of the five world powers, we should have to examine many other facts about each, — such as the extent of soil capable of cultivation and its fertility, the wealth in forest and minerals, the climate, the water power, the means of communication, the acquired wealth, the industrial development, and many similar things. Nor would this be all; for we cannot leave

[1] For purposes of comparison, we may note that the present Japanese Empire, not including southern Manchuria, extends over two hundred and fifty thousand square miles (of which only a few thousand are situated in the tropics), with sixty-three million inhabitants. Of these, forty-eight million are Japanese, three million are Chinese in Formosa and the Liaotung district, and ten to twelve million are discontented dependents in Korea.

out of account the moral side, — the degree of civilization of the people of different nations, their industry, their habits of thrift, their skill, intelligence, etc. Any attempt at such a comparison would lead us a long way, and it is not necessary for a study of American international relations. On the other hand, it may not be amiss to note in passing the obvious truth that, although in the modern world certain great states tend more and more to have a dominant position as compared with that of their smaller brethren, they are not necessarily superior to them in civilization or more admirable in any way. From an ethical as well as from an æsthetic point of view, there is still much to be said in favor of small communities.

One effect of the present international evolution has been to modify certain long-accepted formulas. Among these is the idea of a continent as a group of states, each of which has, besides historical traditions of its own, particular ties and interests common to them all, but not shared by the rest of mankind. This has in the past been more or less true of Europe, and as a sentimental bond it deserves respect. In actual politics, however, it is becoming a mere figure of speech. Are we to regard Imperial Britain as a European power, when the greater part of her external interests and difficulties are connected with her situation on other continents? Are not the vast majority of Englishmen more in touch in every way with Australians, Canadians, Americans, than they are with Portuguese, Italians, or Austrians of one sort or another? What strictly European interests does England represent, she who is now joined in close alliance with the Asiatic empire of Japan? Or is Russia European? Although the majority of her inhabitants live on the western side of the open range of hills we call the Urals, much the larger portion of her territory is on the other, and in Europe itself she has many Asiatic elements. In character and population, there is indeed hardly more real separation between European Russia and Siberia than there is between the eastern and western parts of the United States. Of late Russia's foreign policy has been chiefly concerned with Asiatic questions, and it is likely so to continue. As for France, although her national life is, and will remain, centred in the European continent, her many colonies are scattered over the globe. Already some of them are represented in her chambers, and as time goes on they will become, more and more, parts of one organic dominion. A Frenchman born in Algeria regards himself as a European, and with good right; but he is no more so than is the white Australian or the Canadian, or, except in the matter of allegiance, than the American. Under these circumstances, when people abroad talk about a union of the European powers against "the Asiatic peril" or "the American commercial invasion," they are appealing to a community of interests which does not exist.

Between states of small territory and limited horizon a union especially for commercial purposes may be natural. It is quite conceivable, too, that one of the world powers may, from political as well as from economic motives, strive to group about itself a number of satellites, after the famous historical example of Prussia in the Zollverein. Many people in Germany would be glad to bring about a league of this sort in Central Europe, and the United States is accused of a corresponding design in its policy of Pan-Americanism. Such combinations are fair enough, and may be profitable to all concerned in them, but they are not likely to include more than one power of the first rank; for the great powers, with their enormous fields for independent development, are in a position to work out their own destinies, and to take care of themselves without fettering their liberty of action.

A recent writer has declared that, whereas the nineteenth

century has been the age of nationalism, the twentieth will be that of national imperialism.[1] Though this rather sweeping prophecy takes too little account of the tendencies in another direction, especially those of a socialistic nature, and though it looks too far ahead, it is near the truth when applied to the international politics of the present, which have not been seriously affected by the progress of modern ultra-democracy. Indeed, in certain questions, — as, for instance, in the dispute over the admission of Asiatics into the United States, — the feeling of the laboring classes, so far from being the influence in favor of peace which it is often declared to be, is one of the chief difficulties in the situation.

If, then, the political destinies of the globe are to be determined more and more by a few great nations, it is desirable that we should know as much as possible about them, and should try to understand the circumstances which determine their relations with one another. The United States may be a world in itself, but it is also a part of a larger world. There is no doubt that its power for good and for evil is very great. How that power is to be used is of consequence to all humanity.

[1] Reinsch, *World Politics.*

CHAPTER I

FORMATION AND GROWTH

AS the world is constituted at the present day, no state that lacks a broad territorial foundation can hope to enjoy permanently a position of the first rank. In the past this has not been true to the same degree: Athens in antiquity, Venice in the Middle Ages, the Dutch Republic in the seventeenth century, not only made themselves immortal by their contributions to civilization, but were also able to cope with gigantic adversaries, — Persia, the Ottoman Empire, Spain. In modern times, however, when the latest improvements of mechanical industry and military science may be equally the property of all who can pay for them, and when railways and telegraphs enable even the most unwieldy organizations to bring their full strength to bear, mere mass counts in a way it never did before. The size of Russia foiled Napoleon as it had foiled Charles XII, and it deprived the recent Japanese victories of much of the effect which they would otherwise have had. The Japanese, indeed, like the Germans, realize keenly the disadvantage of dwelling in a territory too limited in extent to offer a sufficient outlet to their surplus population or to admit of the full development of their economic energies. Fearing, therefore, that they may be unable to maintain their present rank among nations, they have, to the disquiet of their neighbors, been stimulated to a policy of active expansion. Because of their size, certain states now secondary may look forward with confidence to a more exalted position in the future. Thus, it is safe to predict that, within a few generations, Brazil and Argentina will, unless they break up in the meantime, be of more consequence in international politics than Italy. Furthermore, though all civilized countries, in these days of keen industrial competition and high protective tariffs, aim to be as nearly self-supporting as may be, especially in the great necessary staples, such independence is possible only to the owners of broad lands with much variety of climate and productions. The peoples with fewer resources at their command may, to be sure, do something to counterbalance their disadvantages by a higher display of energy and intelligence; but society is tending toward a general level of enlightenment in which there can be no monopoly of ideas or of methods. More than ever before, political preëminence among nations now rests on quantity as well as on quality.

Among the world powers, the United States is fourth in size as well as in population. If we compare it with the one next above it, Greater France, we note that, although no one section is the equal of France proper, the territory as a whole is of higher value; for about half of the French colonial possessions are in the Sahara, and most of the rest are in the tropics and therefore unfitted to support a considerable white population. The United States has, to be sure, its share of bad lands in Alaska and the arid West, and it has, too, its tropical holdings; but it possesses in the temperate zone several times as much land as France. It is inferior in this respect to Russia; but it has a greater variety of climate and a larger extent of really good soil. Moreover, it is, from its situation, practically invulnerable; though, unlike Russia, it has important dependencies of which it might

c

be deprived by an adversary that controlled the sea. Still, these are insignificant enough as compared with the mass of the home country, whose very size makes it secure against invasion. The United States could not be brought to its knees by one fierce blow at the heart, as England might conceivably be; and it is also less exposed to attack than is either France or Germany. Economically, too, it is the most self-supporting of all modern powers. Even if it can furnish itself with but a small part of the tropical produce which it needs, it is not dependent on any one of its chief rivals, who at present all pay it an irksome tribute for their supply of cotton, one of the most necessary staples for modern manufacture.

Though to a world power a diversity of climates and conditions is a source of strength, a state that is to hold together must have unity of some kind in its essential parts, whether of race, of sentiment, or of interests; and the more it has, the better. Here the influences of geography are to be reckoned with, though they are not infrequently overborne by what seems like mere historical accident. The strongest frontiers are not impassable. Nations in their wanderings stray beyond their natural boundaries, and unfriendly peoples have been brought into lasting union by some chance royal marriage. Well-protected, sharply defined peninsulas like Italy and India have been the scene of repeated invasion. They have been divided between hostile states, and ruled by distant foreigners; while Austria-Hungary, a mere heterogeneous creation, has been a great power for nearly four hundred years. If we want typical instances of the working and of the failure of geographical influences, we find them in the history of the Spanish peninsula: the separation of Spain from France appears natural and inevitable; the growth of Spain and Portugal into two states inhabited by different nationalities is nothing but a freak of fortune. Since mankind may thus develop in opposition to mere geographical influences, it is dangerous to lay much weight on them; yet, though they may be neutralized, if not altogether overcome, it cannot be denied that they are forces of great magnitude. Soil, climate, and situation have always affected national character. Good natural frontiers against the outer world and easy means of communication within are aids in building up the unity of a nation, and go far to insure the maintenance of this unity when once achieved.

The physical geography of North America has been described as "large, simple, and easily comprehensible." [1] There is no such variety and confusion as in the configuration of Europe, with its extraordinarily fantastic outlines, its scattered ranges of mountains, its many divergent river valleys, and its obviously separate regions, like Scandinavia, Spain, Italy, and the Balkan Peninsula; but, on the other hand, America has proportionately much less available coast-line. The interior, though not free from obstacles which in earlier times interfered with the ease of communication, contains no such formidable barriers as the Andes in South America, the Himalayas and the Thien Shan in Asia, and the Sahara in Africa. Like eastern Europe and northern Asia, North America appears as the setting for a few large states rather than for a mosaic of small ones.

The United States (omitting its dependencies) occupies the middle of the continent, and like Europe, it is situated wholly in the temperate zone. No part is too cold for the raising of grain, — to find the American equivalent of northern Scandinavia or northern Russia, one must turn to Alaska and Canada, — and no part, except certain districts in low-lying sections of the South or in the deserts of the Southwest, is too hot for the white man, even when

[1] Shaler.

of North-European descent, to work in the fields; nor is any too cold for the black, though the latter takes naturally to out-door labor in the warmer regions only. The climate, as compared with that of Europe, is more continental, with greater extremes of heat and cold. The isothermal lines are nearer together, hence we find different zones of cultivation closer to one another. Almost all the products of the Old World have flourished in the New; and many of the chief staples of American cultivation to-day, like most of the animals, are of foreign origin, unknown at the coming of white men. The most notable exception to this rule is Indian corn, or maize.

Turning to the configuration of the country, we mark its simple compact mass, — even more simple and compact than that of the Russian Empire, which can better be compared with the United States and Canada together than with the United States alone. On the east and the west the United States has the best of all natural boundaries, the ocean, — or, rather, it had, for since the republic has acquired outlying possessions, the Pacific coast no longer constitutes a first line of defence. Still, these new possessions seem so much like outposts which could be sacrificed without serious loss that Americans have hardly yet come to think of them as imperilling the excellence of their frontiers. The southern boundary of the country, determined in the main by the Rio Grande and the Gila depression, is not unsatisfactory as such lines go; for it consists of clearly marked natural formations in a region for the most part thinly inhabited. It is not ideal, however, and even to-day has along much of its length a mixed population on both sides. The northern frontier is the result of historical accident, of a succession of compromises attained only after many protracted disputes. Through the eastern wilderness and along the Great Lakes the division is still tolerable, although the harbors of New England are, at least in winter, the obvious ports for most of Eastern Canada; but farther west the boundary is one of the most unnatural in the whole world. For thousands of miles it clings to geographical parallels, heedless of the contour of the ground. The country on both sides of it is the same; the rivers and mountains run north and south; and the inhabitants are one people, not only in language and character, but in vital interests. In spite of every artificial diversion of their trade and of their political sympathies, they are steadily drawn together by permanent forces, which will grow in strength as the region on both sides becomes more thickly settled.

Within the United States itself, the great physical lines of division are few and simple. They run north and south, cutting the parallels of latitude and the zones of climate at right angles instead of coinciding with them. This fact has been of far-reaching political importance; for it has worked against sectionalism, and has produced cross currents of interests. Had the chain of the Alleghanies intervened between the free states and the slave states, we may doubt whether the Union would have been preserved, or even have been formed.

Twice in the last two hundred years, but in opposite ways in the two epochs, it has seemed likely that the territory which now constitutes the American republic would be divided among several owners. During much of the eighteenth century, it was fair to suppose that the North America of the future would remain in the hands of three nationalities, each of them holding an immense section, — the English having the smallest part, the Atlantic coast; the French, the interior plains, with the Mississippi, and in the north the valley of the St. Lawrence; the Spanish, the extreme south and the southwest. The lines of separation between the three would in the main have run from north to south, corresponding with physical barriers. Fate decided otherwise, and gave nine-tenths of the whole

continent to the English-speaking peoples, between whom
the chief lines of demarcation have run from east to west,
leaping over natural obstacles.   But no sooner was the
Union assured of its extension from ocean to ocean, across
mountains and rivers and deserts, than it was threatened
with a division into a northern and a southern half, separated
from one another by the arbitrary Mason and Dixon's line.
The long-standing political divergences between these two
sections culminated in a violent attempt at secession. Since
that failed, the unity of the republic has been secure.

The physical geography of the North American continent
explains why the much more numerous English colonists
penetrated into the interior so slowly as compared with
the French settlers farther north.   After the short episode
of Dutch rule in New York, the English possessed the
whole Appalachian coast from New Brunswick to the
Spanish colony of Florida.   At the time of their arrival,
this strip was covered with thick woods, trackless to the
white man.   Numerous rivers, it is true, gave access to the
interior, but none except the Hudson were navigable to any
great distance for ships of considerable size.   In the north
the mountains approached nearer the coast; farther south
they receded, leaving a coastal plain of much wealth and
fertility.   To-day, penetrated in every direction by railways, and inhabited by a dense mining population, the
Alleghanies cannot be regarded as a barrier; two centuries
ago they were a formidable one, more formidable in reality,
though less obvious on the map, than the Urals, the supposed dividing line between Asia and Europe.   The colonists did not succeed in crossing them for several generations.   On the other hand, the Frenchmen, pushing up
the St. Lawrence, whose tide-water extends to Montreal,
had only to continue along the river to reach the Great
Lakes, whence they soon found themselves in the valley of
the Mississippi, and after that, naturally floated down-

stream and explored the whole length of the "Father of Waters." If the population of the French colonies had been large, — France herself had at that time many more inhabitants than England, — a great French dominion might well have been built up which would have confined the Anglo-Saxon race permanently to the eastern coast. The English were slow in establishing themselves in the western hemisphere. A century after the discoveries of Columbus and the building up of an immense Spanish colonial empire, they had not yet gained any permanent foothold. When they did come, it was in a haphazard fashion. The Pilgrim Fathers, aiming for New Jersey, landed farther north, missing the mouth of the Hudson, the best situation on the coast, which fell into the hands of the Dutch. Fortunately for the English, the line of whose settlement was thus cut in two at the most important point, the Dutch never obtained a really strong hold on the territory. When it was conquered by the Duke of York two generations later, some half of the population were already English; and the gradual Anglicization of the rest was a matter of no great difficulty.

One after another, the British colonies in the New World were planted, and grew up in an independent irregular fashion. Circumstances favored them, for the spirit of enterprise that characterized the Elizabethan age, combined with the desire to plunder the Spaniards, had drawn attention in this direction. The economic changes in England had made life so difficult there that the hope of better fortune prompted adventurous spirits to cross the ocean. Another stimulus to emigration was furnished by the religious disputes and intolerance of the time. While France, with the greater logic and the lesser political wisdom characteristic of her people, jealously preserved her colonies from the contamination of heresy, England regarded with comparative indifference the theological vagaries of her stray children in distant lands. Dissenters, Separatists, Catholics, Quakers, could here enjoy a liberty that was refused at home; and many profited by the opportunity.

With the foundation of Georgia in the eighteenth century, the list of the thirteen original colonies was complete. They had, for the most part, grown up independently of one another, and, varying much in size and strength and torn by mutual jealousies which were often exasperated by hopelessly conflicting boundary claims, they could not, for several generations, be brought to feel a common interest or to take united action. They were spread over the three divisions of the Appalachian coast country which we now call New England, the Middle States, and the Old South.

New England, the smallest and poorest of the three in natural resources, had by accident received the greatest immigration. At the time of the Revolution, Boston was larger than New York. The preponderance of this section in which the population was homogeneous and of a strong Anglo-Saxon type has indeed had a profound influence on the destiny of the country; for the New England element has, on the whole, been the dominant one in the formation of the American character. However relatively insignificant this small section may be in the future, in the past it has played a role which can hardly be overestimated, — one which might almost be compared with that of Greece in European history.

The Middle colonies were then, as now, more cosmopolitan than those to the north or to the south of them; but, though the earlier foreign elements, the Dutch and the Swedes, were reinforced in the eighteenth century by the coming of many Germans, it was the English type which predominated, and even before the Revolution the future importance of New York, with its unequalled situation, could be foretold.

The Southern colonies were the largest in area, but, with the exception of Virginia, the smallest in population.

Already the existence of slavery on an extensive scale had developed social and economic conditions of a special nature. For some time, as we may see by the debates of the Constitutional Convention, it was generally believed that the southern half of the country would, on account of its size, its supposedly better climate, and its greater resources, develop faster than the northern, — a belief which, on the invention of the cotton-gin in 1793, was held more confidently than ever. The non-fulfilment of these hopes, which was attributed by Southerners to unfair tariff legislation, was indeed one of the causes that ultimately led to the attempt at secession. In none of the colonies were what we should now call democratic ideas really prevalent. In the North the political power was in the hands of an intelligent middle class, who made up most of the population; in the South the whole economic situation tended to produce a planters' aristocracy, the so-called "slave barons" of a later day.

In process of time, as was inevitable, the attempt on the part of the English colonists to push beyond the mountains came in conflict with the efforts of the French to establish an unbroken line of posts between their Canadian and their Mississippi possessions; and the result was a fierce struggle between the two peoples for supremacy on the continent. There had already been more than one contest between them, in the course of which France had lost what are to-day the Canadian maritime provinces. She still held, however, a much larger territory than her rival, and one with greater possibilities of future development; but owing to the small number of her settlers, her hold on it was far weaker. When, therefore, the English colonists began to spread to the westward, they found nothing to oppose them but a thin chain of French military posts without adequate support. It has been said that France lost her Indian and American empires on the battlefields of Germany; and it is undoubtedly true that, in defence of continental interests, real or fancied, she wasted in Europe energies which would have been better employed in defending her American possessions. It was also her irreparable misfortune that, at this critical moment, when the fate of empires hung in the balance, she was ruled by the indolent and worthless Louis XV, whereas the energies of Britain were stimulated by the fiery spirit of the elder Pitt. Voltaire's famous description of Canada as "a few acres of snow" shows that what we might call the anti-imperialist section of French public opinion was incapable of appreciating the gravity of the issues involved.

On the disputed soil itself, the struggle was from the outset hopelessly one-sided. In spite of the greater unity of design and action on the part of the French authorities in Canada, and of the more military character of the population under their control, in spite too of the superior skill of most of their officers, the English and their American colonists won, as they could not fail to do in the end; for not only were their available resources far greater, owing to the enormous numerical superiority of the English population in the New World, but, in consequence of England's command of the sea, they could obtain reinforcements in ways impossible to their adversaries. In this war, which decided the fate of the North American continent, the French gained most of the glory, but the English got all the profits.

Twenty years later France obtained her revenge, though an incomplete one, in the war of the American Revolution, which deprived England of her most valued possessions and gave birth to the United States. To the young nation which thus came into the world, the question of the extent of its territories was second in importance only to independence itself. Had the new republic remained confined to the limits of the thirteen colonies, it would beyond doubt have had a very different history. Not improbably, if Great Britain had insisted at Versailles on retaining the Ohio Valley, the American commissioners and government, unsupported by France, would have been obliged to yield on this point, and the westward movement of the American people, which has carried them to the shores of the Pacific, might have been checked at the outset. But England, anxious for peace, was not disposed to haggle over terms with her disobedient children. While refusing, naturally enough, the demand of the Americans that Canada should be handed over to them, she yielded with surprising facility on the question of the Ohio Valley, most of which was indeed no longer actually in her hands. The conquest of this region by George Rogers Clark is rightly deemed one of the decisive events in American history, but it is no less true that the definite acquisition of it in 1783 was a stroke of extraordinary good fortune. Yet even this good fortune cannot prevent Americans from regretting that they did not at the same time obtain Canada, as they conceivably might have done; for in that case they would have avoided many of the difficulties which have arisen between the United States and Great Britain since that day, as well as certain grave possibilities in regard to the future. If the success of Clark's enterprise is one of the events for which Americans have every reason to be grateful, the failure of the expedition of Arnold and Montgomery against Quebec is one of the disasters which they have most cause to regret.

The years immediately following the achievement of independence are generally regarded as the most inglorious in American history. The form of confederation adopted by the new states soon proved itself quite insufficient for the purposes of government; but not till after many bitter experiences of its evils, would the states consent to sacrifice their more short-sighted views and selfish interests to the public welfare. Nevertheless, this inglorious period witnessed the promulgation of one of the most important legislative acts in the whole history of the country, — the Northwest Ordinance of 1787, which not only at that time proclaimed the principles by which American expansion was to be regulated as long as it was confined to the continent, but which even to-day, when the United States has stretched beyond the seas, is still recognized as determining its policy, though it may not always be immediately applicable. By the Northwest Ordinance the wide vacant territory west of the mountains was declared a national domain, a reserve tract out of which, as the population increased, new states should be created with rights in every way equal to those of the old ones. Even before such states should come into existence, the settlers in this region were to be granted the right of possession of property, of habeas corpus, of trial by jury, and the other essentials of Anglo-Saxon liberty.

The principle of the Northwest Ordinance was a new one in the history of democratic national expansion. Up to this time, colonies — unless, like the Greek ones, they separated themselves at the start — had been regarded as mere appendages or outposts of the mother country. They might have privileges and liberties of their own, but these privileges were personal : the territory did not form an equal part of the parent state, except in countries with an autocratic form of government, where all lands were at the disposal of the sovereign. Thus, though the emigrant to Eastern Siberia might feel that his position was exactly the same as that of his brother in Moscow, since both were subjects of a despotic ruler, the Englishman in the colonies was not the equal of the one at home, for he could vote for no member of Parliament. No one of the English settlements had enjoyed complete self-government from the beginning; and the American colonies had not contested the right of the mother country to legislate for them. They had merely resisted, as a violation of their inalienable rights as Englishmen, her attempt to impose taxes upon them without their consent; and this resistance had led to the war for independence. Now that they had triumphed and had possessions of their own about which they must legislate, they wisely determined to treat the new sections as the equals of the old, and to impose upon them only such temporary restrictions as were necessary during the period of first development, when they were too weak to walk without guidance. Not only is the Northwest Ordinance thus of fundamental importance in the history of the United States, but it is a landmark in the story of government.

At the census taken in 1790, the population of the newly constituted federal republic numbered a little less than four million inhabitants, unevenly distributed over an area of about nine hundred thousand square miles. Of these the greater number still lived close to the coast, much of the interior being uninhabited save by Indians and traders. The western movement had, however, begun. Kentucky, Vermont, and Tennessee were all admitted as states before the end of the century, and Ohio at the beginning of the new one. And the growth of the country continued in two ways: not only was its area extended from time to time by the addition of broad tracts of land, until it was several times as large as the thirteen original colonies, but while these new lands were being opened up and developed with astonishing rapidity, the population of the older states was increasing by the surplus of births over deaths and by foreign immigration. Thus the great surface expansion of the country did not lead, as some feared that it might, to a dispersal of the resources and a general weakening of the fabric. On the contrary, at the opening of the twentieth century every state in the Union, even mutilated Virginia, had more than doubled the population that it had at the beginning of the nineteenth, and New York alone contained a larger number of inhabitants than the whole republic did one hundred years before. Up to the time of the war with Spain, the lands acquired by the United States had been almost unoccupied ones; but, with the exception of Alaska, they were so well fitted for white colonization that settlers soon began to pour into them in numbers sufficient to submerge the earlier elements. There was consequently little difficulty in applying to them the principles of the Northwest Ordinance, and, as time went on, in erecting new states on the same basis as the old. In Alaska this policy has not yet proved practicable, and may never do so; but this huge desolate waste offers no new problem of government, for its sparse Indian tribes may be treated as other Indians have been. Not indeed till the annexations beginning in 1898, which have brought under the wing of the United States regions already inhabited by very considerable alien populations, did the republic have to face the question whether American ideals and institutions were suitable to territories of this kind.

According to the census of 1800, there were in the United States 5,308,483 persons, of whom about a million were blacks. The gain made in the preceding ten years had been extraordinary, especially as there had been no new accession of territory. Three years later, the area of the republic was doubled by the purchase of Louisiana, one of the most astonishing strokes of good fortune — for it was not the result of any special foresight — that ever befell a nation. Although the American government realized how serious in its consequences would be the cession of this great expanse on its western frontier to a strong power like France, it had not instructed its commissioners to try to purchase more than the island of New Orleans with an insignificant bit of land about it. The proposition for the sale of the whole came from Napoleon himself. His decision was startlingly sudden, was opposed by many of his counsellors, and was a complete surprise to the United States. The commissioners who signed the terms of the purchase acted without instructions; and President Jefferson, who ratified it, believed that he was committing an unconstitutional act, which was justified only by its immense advantage to the country. Many Frenchmen, naturally enough, have ever since deplored the surrender of the last chance of building up a great French-speaking community in the western world. It is doubtful, however, whether France could have kept this distant defenceless region against the inevitable attack of the English; she certainly could not have done so if the Americans had felt driven to ally themselves with Great Britain. France made her fatal mistake, not in 1803, but forty years earlier, when she ceded Louisiana to Spain. Had she kept it then and tried to fill it with settlers, she might, by the beginning of the nineteenth century, have had French colonists enough to maintain permanently the national character of the region; but even this is by no means certain. As it was, the fifty thousand inhabitants, French, Spanish, and black, who did not represent one per cent of the population of the country into which they were now absorbed, could not possibly retain their identity in the long run.

Whether the action of France was wise or not, the gain to the United States was incalculable. At one stroke its territory was increased twofold by the addition of a region which was a hundred years later to be the home of more than sixteen million inhabitants; and at the same time the way was opened for further expansion westward toward the Pacific. Without Louisiana, the Americans could not have reached Oregon, which must before long have fallen into British hands; and yet, as has often been pointed out, this first expansion in their history, which gave them the control of the Mississippi Valley with its untold possibilities, met with the same bitter opposition that we find in all the later and sometimes less justifiable instances.

The purchase of Florida from Spain in the year 1819 was the natural termination of a long series of disputes about boundaries and other matters between the vigorous grasping young republic and a decrepit neighbor. On account of the situation of Florida, the American people coveted it from the first, and their desire was greatly stimulated by their purchase of Louisiana; for after that event the peninsula was in their eyes a dangerous foreign excrescence which broke the continuity of their coast and also threatened one of their most important lines of communication. The weakness of Spain's hold, and the fact that Florida served as a refuge for runaway slaves, hostile Indians, and adventurers of all kinds, continually invited American interference, which more than once took place. Finally, therefore, in 1819, when the greater part of the Spanish colonies were already engaged in a successful revolt which might easily extend to Florida, the government at Madrid decided that the time had come to put an end to a continual source of dispute between the two countries, and to get something for the colony before it was too late. From the point of view of the Americans, the purchase was in every way advantageous; for the seventy thousand square miles thus acquired, which to-day have a population of more than half a million, were of value in themselves, and from their position were almost a necessity to the United States. On the other hand, it is hard for any impartial writer to maintain that the treatment of Spain by the United States for many years before the sale can be justified either by international law or by morality.

The census of 1820 showed that, if the area of the Union

was more than twice what it had been when the century opened, the population, which now numbered 9,638,453, had increased at a nearly equal rate. During the next generation the American republic added to its dominions on four separate occasions, and dreamed of other ventures. This movement of expansion, which was popular with ardent spirits in all sections, was twofold, one side of it being principally for the benefit of the Northern States, the other for that of the Southern, and it was stimulated by their rivalry. In both spheres it was successful, but not to the same extent; for it was pressed with unequal zeal, and it was opposed by adversaries of very different force.

The Northern States, in their dispute about the Oregon frontier, had less at stake than had the South in the affairs of Mexico, and had to deal with a great power, England. Under these circumstances the joint occupation of the territory from 1818 to 1846 ended, after much bickering coupled with threats of war, in a compromise. This settlement was roundly condemned in the United States as a weak-kneed surrender not only of American possessions but even of the sacred Monroe Doctrine itself. On the other hand, it has been regarded by Canadians as one more instance in which Great Britain sacrificed her colony in the interest of peace with the United States. When we remember that the complete claims of neither party rested on a very sound foundation, and that the line of compromise actually agreed on was the obvious one, — namely, the continuation of that which already existed for a long distance, — we may feel satisfied that the settlement was just and honorable to both parties. It gave the United States a tract of about two hundred and ninety thousand square miles, which in 1900 was inhabited by about a million two hundred thousand persons.

In the South the situation was very different. The

D

slave states felt that the acquisition of new territory, by the aid of which they could keep pace with the growing North, was for them a matter of political life and death. Realizing that by the Missouri Compromise they were shut off from all hope of penetrating above Mason and Dixon's line, they saw that they could add to their domain only at the expense of Spain and Mexico. However little we may defend the morality of the conduct of the Americans toward the Mexican republic at this period, we can perfectly understand the tremendous temptation which a huge, valuable, and almost unoccupied region offered to a vigorous neighbor afflicted with land-hunger. History and human nature show us that such conditions lead to but one result, — the spoliation of the weaker by the stronger. We have to comfort ourselves as best we may by the reflection that, in the hands of its new possessors, this region has been so developed as to become of much more value to mankind than it would have been had it remained the property of its former, legitimate owners.

The insurrection of Texas in 1836 was a rising of American colonists, aided by volunteers from across the border, against a distant alien government weakened by continual revolutions. One main object of the revolt was the establishment of slavery, which was instituted as soon as the movement succeeded. When we consider all the circumstances, and remember the dominant influence of the South at this period, we are rather surprised that Texas was not taken into the Union at once. This step was, however, prevented for a time by Northern opposition, the treaty of annexation failing in the Senate in 1844, and the measure being carried through in the following year only by a joint resolution of the two houses. From the point of view of the struggle against slavery, it is fortunate that the new state was not, as had been planned, divided into four states with eight senators, — an arrangement which might be desirable to-day if it were not too late. The territory thus acquired, about three hundred and ninety thousand square miles with one hundred and fifty thousand inhabitants, had in 1900 a population of some three millions. Mexico, as was natural, bitterly resented the loss of one of her most valuable provinces, and the strained relations between the two republics were made worse by boundary disputes and by the unconcealed desire of the Americans for California. Their high-handed action on the Texas frontier led to a war which was one-sided from the beginning. Although the hostilities were on a small scale, the story of the military operations was almost as creditable to the American name as that of the previous diplomatic dealings had been discreditable. By the treaty of Guadalupe Hidalgo in 1848, the United States, in return for a payment of fifteen million dollars as a sort of conscience money, acquired a tract of about five hundred and twenty thousand square miles; and five years later, by the Gadsden Purchase, the boundary was again changed for the benefit of the stronger power. The treaty of peace was almost immediately followed by the discovery of gold in California, and by the rush of immigrants to that region, which in consequence made rapid progress; whereas New Mexico and Arizona have gone ahead so slowly since the cession that they have not yet been admitted as states. In the territory thus taken by the Anglo-Saxon from the Latin-American republic, there are to-day some two million inhabitants, of whom, except in certain thinly settled districts, only a small percentage are Mexicans.

In the half century beginning with the Louisiana Purchase and ending with the Gadsden Purchase, the United States tripled its size, and more than quadrupled its population, which in 1850 exceeded twenty-three million whites, of whom some ten per cent were of foreign birth, chiefly Irish, British, and German.

Such a rate of progress cannot, of course, continue indefinitely, though the most noticeable change thus far has been in the quality rather than in the quantity of the development. Since 1850 the number of inhabitants has quadrupled again; but over eight million of them (more than the total population a hundred years ago) are the black, brown, and yellow brothers brought into the fold by the Spanish War; and twice as many are immigrants who have come from different parts of Europe. Even so the gross increase in millions has been less than that of the Russian Empire by the surplus of births over deaths during the same period. The territorial expansion of the United States in this time has been greater than that of Russia, but less than that of England, France, or Germany. It has covered an area larger than that of the thirteen original colonies, but it has not included one square mile to which the American people have as yet felt justified in granting the full self-government which the older regions enjoy.

The annexations of the first half of the nineteenth century meant the taking over of land capable of being converted into new states of the same kind as the old, a process that will soon be completed. Contrary to expectation, the addition of fresh members to the Union has not weakened the ties that bind it together. Many patriots of an earlier generation prophesied that, if the country extended its boundaries, it must soon break up into several independent communities, and, in particular, that the original states and their younger sisters would not remain long together. Such fears now only provoke a smile. Modern means of communication have revolutionized our conceptions of time and space. As the vacant lands have filled up with settlers, and as railways and telegraphs have multiplied, the different sections, instead of drawing farther apart, have come into an ever closer community of interests, as well as of ideas and traditions. In the case of California, it is true, there was for a while a feeling that the new region differed materially from the rest of the country, and hence might wish to obtain its autonomy; but all danger of a separation of this kind vanished after the completion of the Union Pacific railway. New York and San Francisco are practically nearer to each other than Boston and Philadelphia were at the time of the Revolution, and the distance between them is short as compared with that between St. Petersburg and Vladivostok.

The local antagonism which existed from the early days of the republic and grew steadily stronger until it led to civil war, was not between the new states and the old, or the seacoast and the interior, but between the North and the South. At the root of the trouble was the institution of slavery in the South, where, favored by peculiar natural conditions, it led to a peculiar economic and social development, which sought its protection in the creed of states' rights. The war put an end to slavery forever. Though the scars of the conflict are not entirely forgotten, there is no danger of its recurrence; for the primal cause has been removed, and the constitutional question in dispute has been settled by force of arms. When the generation with personal memories of the struggle has passed away, even Southerners will more and more look upon it as an historical event of which they are proud on account of the heroism they displayed, but which has no bearing on their future interests.

In the years immediately following the war, public opinion occupied itself but little with foreign affairs; for the nation was engaged in recovering from the effects of the struggle. At such a moment, territorial expansion did not appeal either to statesmen or to the people, the general feeling on the subject being very different from what it had been just before 1860. Still, scarcely was the war over when America acquired by purchase half a million more square miles, — a step that met with some criticism, but produced little real opposition. Not that the vast expanse of Russian America, which was offered for sale at an insignificant price, was regarded as having much value in itself. Russia was glad to get rid of it because it was unprofitable from a pecuniary point of view, and could not be defended in the event of a war with England, an emergency which at that time seemed quite probable; and the Americans bought it partly in accordance with a general principle of freeing the continent of European dominion, and partly in order to prevent Great Britain from acquiring the region either by force or by purchase; for if Russia were anxious to sell, she would naturally turn to England next. Some believed, too, that the value of the fisheries and mines was sufficient to justify the expenditure of the very moderate sum of seven million, two hundred thousand dollars. This last calculation has been more than confirmed by events; for, apart from its political advantages, the Alaska Purchase has turned out a very good bargain in itself, the annual value of its products being greater to-day than the whole sum paid for the territory. In making an acquisition which it could not reach and defend by land, the United States seemed, to be sure, to be entering upon a new policy; but it was argued that the new territory was on the same continent, and that by the annexation of Canada, which most Americans believed would take place sooner or later and many expected within a short time, Alaska would be united to the rest of the republic.

In spite of the ease with which this matter went through, the feeling in America for over a generation remained hostile to further expansion. The treaties for the purchase of the Danish West Indies and the acquisition of

San Domingo failed in the Senate, and that for the annexation of Hawaii in 1893 was withdrawn from consideration
by President Cleveland as soon as he came into office.
For thirty years there was little sign that the United States
would soon go beyond its bounds. It is true that the
population increased to some seventy-five millions, and
that there was a great industrial development; and it is
also true that, although there were still many vacant places
in the country, there was no longer an internal "frontier"
of colonization beyond which broad lands lay waiting for
the settler. These facts made for a new era of expansion, but at the time few persons realized the drift of the
current. There was indeed a general belief that the
United States was destined to dominate the western world
and to annex Canada, if not Mexico. No one, however,
dreamed of aggressive action. To use a recent term, we
may say that public opinion was anti-imperialistic.

Suddenly, and without warning, the whole situation
changed, and the country found itself engaged in a
foreign war, and presently, without preparation or design, launched on a career of conquest and expansion.
But before inquiring into the causes and effects of this
startling departure, let us look at the composition of the
American people itself, and the nature of the political ideas
which have guided it up to the present time.

CHAPTER II

NATIONALITY AND IMMIGRATION

THE American Constitution begins with the words, "We, the People of the United States"; and "We, the People" have, in practice as well as in theory, been the sovereign power in the country to an extent rarely equalled in the history of the world. At times the "We" have been negligent or deceived, and their desires have often been thwarted; but in the end, if once they have definitely made up their minds, their will has always overridden every obstruction and become the supreme law of the land. The sovereign American people are the master whose wishes are to be carried out by the servants whom he has appointed. To judge of the conduct of the servants in foreign as well as in domestic affairs, we have to begin by knowing something about the master.

There is another reason why the student of political affairs should devote attention to the character and composition of the people of the United States: the nation is still "in the making." The character of the Americans — "Yankees," as they are called abroad rather than at home — is, indeed, well known, and is as definite as that of Englishmen or Spaniards; but, though they are stamping this character on newcomers to the country with extraordinary success, they are in danger, according to some persons, of being submerged by the ever increasing floods of these strangers. When, therefore, we look closely at the term "the People of the United States," we find that it is not always an exact expression. In 1787, for instance, it could hardly have been said to include the blacks: the negro slaves of the South did not "ordain and establish this Constitution . . . in Order to form a more Perfect Union," and to "secure the blessings of Liberty" to themselves and their posterity. True, much has happened since then; but we may hesitate to term the mass of the negro population part of the sovereign people at the present moment. And this sovereign people itself, — is it what it used to be? What are the prospects that it will maintain its essential unity in the future? With the ever growing influx of new elements and the declining birthrate of the native population, is there no danger that the Americans may some day be a group of separate nationalities instead of one nation?

In spite of the cosmopolitan tendencies of modern socialism, there can be no doubt that the spirit of nationality in one form or another is still a tremendous political force. The last hundred years are full of examples of its action in building up and in destroying. By welding together into national communities states long separated, and by throwing off foreign dominion, it has forged modern Germany, Italy, Roumania, Greece, Servia, and Bulgaria. It has nerved the resistance of Poles, Finns, Armenians, and others against the attempts of alien peoples to absorb them. Under its influence, Norway has separated herself from Sweden, Austria is in peril of going to pieces, and even Great Britain is weakened by Irish disaffection. But the same spirit of nationality that awakens the longing for independence also leads to the persecution of recalcitrant minorities. Race conflicts to-day are as intense in their fierceness as the religious ones of earlier times, and are even harder to adjust by fair compromise. When favored by fortune, the oppressed easily become the oppressors. Governments and nations fear, and not without reason, that what is at first harmless pride in race and language on the part of some minority may easily take the form of political sedition dangerous to the existence of the state. If the American republic is ever threatened with the formation of distinct national communities within its borders, its unity for the future will cease to be secure.

One difficulty in dealing with all such topics as this is the looseness in meaning of the terms we have to use. When we speak of a nation, we usually have in mind an independent people with a common language; but the Swiss, the Belgians, the Austrians, are nations, and each composed of several nationalities with equally acknowledged rights. Nor need a nation be all of the same race, — according to the Fifteenth Amendment to the Constitution, the people of the United States are not. Nor is it always politically independent: the Poles are a nation, though they are under several governments; and the term is sometimes applied to the Jews, who have neither a common speech nor a common dwelling-place. Nevertheless, as the history of the last century has shown, the tendency nowadays is for nations and nationalities to correspond as nearly as may be, and for the idea of nationality to be based on language alone, regardless of descent or of the preferences of those concerned, — a tendency which the French have experienced to their cost in the case of Alsace, which was taken away from them on the ground that its inhabitants were Germans, whether they wanted to be or not, and hence properly belonged to Germany. The movement known as Pan-Germanism is a logical outcome of the same theory. The earlier nationalistic movements proclaimed the right of peoples to determine their own destinies; the later extensions have tended to look on nationality as a sort of higher law which is as much justified in overriding the opposition of minorities as were the Northern States of the Union in putting down the rebellion of the Southern. Such a doctrine may easily be pushed to great lengths: sweet reasonableness, not to say common fairness, is seldom a characteristic of ardent champions of nationality, who, as a rule, calmly overlook the most obvious inconsistencies, and while warmly advocating a policy for the assimilation of all alien elements at home, cry out oppression if the same treatment is given to those of their ilk in foreign lands. The German who favors severe measures in order to denationalize the Poles in Posen is sure to be full of indignation at the way in which the German language is discriminated against in Hungary and in the Baltic provinces; and many an American who has condemned the iniquity of trying to Russianize the Finns or the Armenians believes as a matter of course that the English language should be imposed as soon as possible on the inhabitants of Porto Rico.

In spite of the very liberal policy followed until recently by the United States toward those who sought its shores as a refuge and a home, there has always been a certain amount of opposition among native Americans to the free admission of too many newcomers. Two generations ago, in the time of the Know-Nothing party, this opposition was stimulated by religious motives, by the dislike of American Protestants for Irish Roman Catholics; in the days when German immigration was at its height, there were fears that some whole section of the country might become permanently German in character; and to-day, when elements from eastern and southern Europe are predominant among the new arrivals, many persons dread the disappearance of the old American type in a flood of aliens belonging to what most so-called Anglo-Saxons regard as less highly developed, if not actually inferior, races. Race questions of all kinds are full of pitfalls for the unwary; and when we come to such a subject as the influence on national character of an infusion of foreign blood, we are in a domain in which there is a minimum amount of ascertained fact and the fullest play for fancy. In such a case, prophecy is nothing but guesswork. It does seem clear, however, that if the Americans are to impregnate all their citizens with their ideals and traditions, and thus to maintain the unity of the nation, it is of vital importance that newcomers should sooner or later adopt the national tongue instead of maintaining a speech of their own. Otherwise, how can they ever be completely absorbed into the general mass? That any language besides English has a chance of establishing itself permanently in the country, few Americans believe. Some foreigners have been inclined to regard the question as an open one.

If we turn to the tables of population as given by the census of 1900, there seems at first sight to be cause for alarm. Of the seventy-six million inhabitants of the United States proper, we find that at that date (leaving out of account for the moment the colored races, which must be taken up separately) forty-one million were of native parentage, ten million of foreign birth, and more than fifteen million of foreign parentage, — a total of more than twenty-five million aliens as compared with only forty-one million whites of native birth. When we remember, too, that the annual immigration has of late been over a million, and that the birthrate among the foreign population is higher than among the native, is there not some reason for anxiety? Will not the United States of the future be like Austria or Russia to-day, a country inhabited by many different and often discordant nationalities?

Natural as such fears are, a little study will convince us that thus far there is no cause for apprehension of this kind ; we may rest assured that the American of the future will speak English as his native tongue, except, perhaps, when he is born in Porto Rico or some other outlying possession. When the situation in the United States is compared in detail with that in Russia or Austria, the difference is evident. In the two empires, although there is much mingling of population, each nationality has, as a rule, its particular district in which it outnumbers all others, — its own home, consecrated by history and traditions. Within the American Union, on the contrary, although the inhabitants of foreign origin outnumber the older natives in several states, in no single state does one foreign element predominate to such an extent that it threatens to become supreme, and in no part of the country are foreigners of one language and nationality massed in such groups as to be formidable to the national unity of the whole. The Germans in New York and in the Middle West, the Scandinavians in the North-Central States, the French Canadians in northern New England, are each so counterbalanced by other elements that they are incapable of denationalizing the people about them. The different foreign contingents do not even seek to coalesce against the older sort of Americans; it is between themselves rather than between the earlier and the later comers that national jealousies are usually found.

From the point of view of language, too, the significance of the census figures is greatly diminished by the fact that the English, the Scotch, the Irish, and the English Canadians, who together form more than one-third of the foreign-born, speak English as their native tongue, and hence are an influence in favor of unity rather than of diversity. Moreover, if we examine in detail the composition of the fifteen million Americans of foreign parentage, we discover that one-third of them were only of half-foreign parentage, one parent being a native. They may thus safely be counted as Americans in every sense of the word, and so may most of the other two-thirds. Up to the present time, the United States has, indeed, shown remarkable power of assimilation. Even when the foreign immigrant has come to the country too old to learn English himself, his child is almost certain to do so.

According to the census of 1900, among the children of foreign parentage who were over ten years of age, the proportion of those ignorant of English was in only three states or territories more than eighteen per cent of the whole, — a striking testimony to the enormous influence of the American public school in preserving the national unity. Millions of children of Poles, Bohemians, Italians, Russian Jews, and of other aliens of many sorts come together in this common meeting-place, and in acquiring first and foremost a knowledge of the language of the country in which they are to live, get to feel that they are all equally Americans. The patriotism that is thus taught them may sometimes be of a crude, chauvinistic type, but it is of incalculable service in fusing them into one homogeneous mass of future American citizens.

Another influence which until now has helped to draw the immigrant into the common interests of American life has been the keenness of political strife. The local politician never loses a chance to get votes. If he knows that in his district there is a colony of Italians or of Russian Jews who care nothing about American questions, but whose votes he may be able to obtain for his purposes, he is not likely to leave them long to themselves; he may be trusted to hunt them out, and to persuade them to be naturalized and join the local party organization. His object in such cases is, of course, purely selfish, and the means of persuasion he employs are often far from admirable; but in the long run it is certainly better for a democratic community that every element of the population should be interested in its government than that any should feel that they are foreigners without voice in the general welfare.

The three parts of the Union in which, in 1900, more than eighteen per cent of the children of foreign parentage had no knowledge of English were Texas, Arizona, and New Mexico. It is worthy of remark that as this region represents a conquest at the expense of another civilized state, its Spanish-speaking population is of older date than its English. Without attributing too much importance to the resistance of the earlier language in this particular case, we may note the circumstance; for it helps to emphasize the immense advantage which the United States has enjoyed in other sections from the fact that the foreign element among its citizens is due not, as in Russia, to conquest, or even to peaceful union, but to voluntary immigration. The Russian goes as an alien to the other peoples in the empire, and endeavors to impose upon them his language and his way of thought; but, however justified his efforts may be from the point of view of the general good of the state, to the subject peoples his attempt to Russianize them, to deprive them of the nationality which they held for generations before he appeared in their land, is an act of oppression, which they fiercely resent. In the United States, it is the foreigner who comes of his own free will to live among strangers and to profit by the advantages which such residence offers; he has not, therefore, the same right to complain if they insist upon a certain conformity to their own type. The Pole, the Finn, the Armenian, feels very differently about having to learn Russian in his schools at home and about attending English schools in America. In the first instance, useful as the language may be in itself, he regards the requirement to learn it as an unjustifiable imposition if it is designed to supplant his own; in the second, he looks on the obligation as a privilege by which he is glad to profit.

The mental attitude of the immigrant toward the people of his new country is of vital consequence in determining whether he is going to identify himself with them. If he feels that he belongs to a superior race, that he represents a higher level of civilization than they, he is not likely to strive to become one of them any more than is necessary for his material profit; he will keep his home life and all his more idealistic interests as unchanged as possible. On the other hand, if he has come as a wanderer to a promised land, to one where he will not only have greater opportunities than he has enjoyed at home, but where he can learn from those about him much that will better his condition, the chances are that he will not live apart or cling too jealously to his former inheritance.

The United States, being a prosperous, progressive community, has had the good fortune to find in most of those who seek its shores people eager to learn its lessons and to share in its life. The immigrant may cherish his pride of nationality and love of his former country; but usually he has no feeling of superiority to make him disinclined to become one of the nation about him. On the contrary, he arrives full of enthusiasms and dreams, some of which, it is true, are sadly dissipated later, but most of which are realized. Being an American means for him a rise in the social scale, as well as an increase in the comforts of life; and he is not ungrateful.

For a striking instance of the power of influence of this kind, we have but to turn to the history of the German settlements on the Volga. More than a century and a quarter ago several thousand German colonists were planted by the Empress Catherine II in this region, where they were provided with a liberal allowance of land and various privileges. It was thought not only that they would prosper themselves, but that, by the example of their higher civilization and superior thrift, they might affect for the better the Russian peasantry about them. The experiment has, however, been a partial failure; for although, thanks to their privileges and to their sterling qualities, the colonists have prospered, they have remained a class apart, keeping their own language and customs, and neither influencing their neighbors nor being influenced by them. Though perfectly loyal subjects, they have never regarded themselves as Russians; and they have resisted to the best of their ability the measures of the government to teach them the language of the empire. In recent years, as their special privileges have been curtailed, a number of them have emigrated to the United States, where a curious change is taking place; for these same German colonists who have withstood for so long the influences of their Russian environment are yielding rapidly to their American one. They are beginning to acquire English, and in a generation or two will undoubtedly disappear in the mass of American citizens, a result due not so much to better conditions of life than those which they enjoyed in Russia as to their different attitude toward the people about them. We may note, too, that the German immigrants in southern Brazil have kept their mother tongue and their individuality to a greater extent than have their fellow-countrymen in the United States, a circumstance which may in this case be attributed, at least in part, to their feeling of superiority to their neighbors. Whether such superiority is real or fancied matters little; the essential thing is not the grade of civilization, but the sentiment of aloofness.

In pure theory, the conceptions of religion and those of nationality have nothing to do with each other; but in practice, as all history shows, they are very often confused, and the idea of "our God" and a "chosen people" appeals strongly to the human mind. Doubtless there have been many violent race conflicts in which the rival elements have been of the same creed — as to-day in Austria-Hungary; but the worst are those in which each nationality is the champion of a particular church, and hence feels that it is fighting for its faith as well as for its individuality. In such cases the clergy, instead of being apostles of peace, whose mission is to allay passions, are promoters of discord. Differences in religious belief also prevent

E

mixed marriages, the most effectual means of fusing two peoples into one. The fact that the lines of cleavage have not coincided has done more than anything else to preserve the peace between the nationalities and between the faiths in Switzerland. Among both the German and the French Swiss, Catholics and Protestants are so evenly divided that religious and national questions, instead of inflaming each other, act as mutual restraints; but in western Russia, where religion and nationality are nearly inseparable, — Pole and Catholic, German and Protestant, Russian and Orthodox, meaning one and the same thing, — the task of combining these elements into one nation, or even of maintaining the peace between them is, indeed, formidable.

Here, again, the United States has been singularly fortunate. Although at the beginning of the nineteenth century the Catholics formed but a small minority of the population, which was looked on somewhat askance by the rest, they had full religious liberty. The first Catholic immigrants to come in considerable numbers were the Irish, who, though they bore no love to England, spoke the English language, and thus never felt themselves to be foreigners in their new home. In spite of some natural friction with the American Protestant element, they soon became an integral part of the community. When later Catholics of foreign speech — Italians, Poles, Bohemians, French Canadians — began to arrive in force, they found to welcome them a Catholic church, large, flourishing, and so thoroughly patriotic in its feeling that, far from helping the newcomers to safeguard their own nationalities, it has served to Americanize them in language as well as in ideas. Another most fortunate circumstance is that the Catholic church in the United States is not sectional. Its adherents are scattered over the country, varying in strength in the different parts,[1] but

[1] Massachusetts, the home of the Puritan, is now a Roman Catholic state.

so thoroughly mixed up with others that they nowhere form a compact block, as they do in French Canada and in many parts of Europe. There seems to be little chance anywhere of such clear-cut divisions into Catholic and Protestant districts as we find in Germany and Switzerland.

Owing to various causes, some of which are easy, others very hard, to determine, the divers nationalities among the immigrants to America are not assimilated with equal rapidity. Some of them — the Scotch, the Irish, the English, and even more the English Canadians — are, for practical purposes, assimilated from the beginning; for, although there is a certain clannishness among them, it does not seriously affect their value as citizens. The Irish differ more from the earlier American type than do the English; but they are more desirous of becoming citizens at once, and they play a prominent part in local politics, which have been much affected by their activity. Whatever may be the psychological influence of these elements in the make-up of the future American character, they constitute, from the point of view of language, a reinforcement to the earlier inhabitants and a powerful aid in the maintenance of national unity.

In the last twenty years, Jewish emigrants from Russia have been coming into the United States in overwhelming numbers. Although they have spread over the country, they tend to congregate in the great cities, and particularly in and about New York, where there are now some seven hundred and fifty thousand of them. Very few, on their arrival, know any English; and they differ much in mentality from the average American citizen. On the other hand, they have no national idiom, but only a jargon to which they are seldom attached, and no people are more eager to learn English as soon as possible, or readier to adopt it as their medium of expression not only in public but in their homes, — a circumstance which often leads to a really tragic difference between parents and children, for, with the speech, the latter are apt to abandon the habits, the opinions, and even the faith of their fathers.

In spite of this ready adaptability on the part of the Jew, there is in the United States an anti-Semitic feeling, new in its present intensity, and, as in France, quite at variance with the traditions of two generations ago. It is strongest among the upper classes. In most American cities few or no outspoken Jews will be found in fashionable society; and even in the universities in which they are at all numerous, they are left much to themselves by the other students. The subject is rather carefully avoided by the newspapers; for the American Jews are already a power to be feared, and quick to take offence.

In the United States, as elsewhere, the French are noted for their tenacity in maintaining their national individuality. If they had been more numerous at the time of the Louisiana Purchase, it is quite possible that a considerable section of the South might long have retained a French character. As it was, they were soon outnumbered by the American settlers; and as time has gone on, their significance has dwindled more and more. French society held its own in New Orleans till the days of the Civil War, but in the ruin of the planters which accompanied the conflict it received a blow from which it never recovered, and though French memories in Louisiana to-day are interesting and picturesque, they are not politically important. France herself has contributed few immigrants to the American population during the nineteenth century; and those she has sent have not been agriculturalists, but have followed certain special occupations, and thus have scattered all over the country instead of concentrating in any one region.

The quota of French Canadians has been of much more importance. Attracted by the high wages of the New England mills, the "habitants" have come down from

Canada in very considerable numbers, until, according to the census of 1900, there were three hundred and ninety-five thousand of them in the country and four hundred and thirty-six thousand children born in the United States, of whom the great majority are to be found in the northern New England States, and chiefly in a few manufacturing towns. As they keep much to themselves, they form an element which is but slowly affected by its surroundings. A few writers, who have not sufficiently investigated the question, have talked of the probability of their Frenchifying northern New England. There is no reason to expect anything of this kind, for, although the process of assimilation is more gradual in their case than in that of most others, it is just as surely at work. After they have settled in the United States, they are, for instance, less under the influence of the church, which has been one of the strongest forces in preserving their nationality in Canada; and they show this independence even when they have their own priests, and not, as sometimes happens, Irish ones. They are also beginning to learn English, and to take an interest in politics. Although in certain important centres they form a large proportion of the population, and have occupied some abandoned farms, they have not yet spread over the country districts; and in Boston, the chief city of New England, their number is insignificant. Of late years the immigration of the French Canadians has declined, and it does not seem likely to begin again on the old scale. Their places in the mills are being taken to a certain extent by Portuguese, Armenians, and others.

The Scandinavians, in spite of the fact that they cling to their own language with tenacity and often live rather secluded lives, are viewed with general favor; for they have the reputation of being steady and industrious, and, unlike most of the other immigrants to-day, they go chiefly to the country rather than to the towns. In the northern parts of the land, they encounter conditions of climate and life resembling those to which they were accustomed at home; and in the richer soil with its abundant crops they find opportunities to prosper such as they never knew before. They constitute a very important element, but not one large enough to threaten seriously the English-speaking character of the region. They are most numerous in Minnesota, where (including their children born in the United States) they number over half a million, or less than a third of the total population of the state. In 1900 the two hundred and thirty-six thousand foreign-born Scandinavians in Minnesota were divided into sixteen thousand Danes, one hundred and five thousand Norwegians, and one hundred and fifteen thousand Swedes; but the three nationalities, in spite of their nearness of kin, do not always live on cordial terms with one another.

The Italians, Poles, Bohemians, Slovaks, Hungarians, etc., who in recent years have sought the United States in ever increasing swarms, usually settle either in the cities or in the manufacturing and mining districts, and contribute little to the agricultural population. All of these elements are to-day more backward and ignorant, more alien to the native American in ways of thought and in habits of life, than were their predecessors of twenty years ago, a fact which, taken in connection with their large numbers, has caused some disquiet. But we must not forget that the ordinary statistics of immigration do not convey a perfectly correct impression: besides taking no account of arrivals by land (and thus leaving out the Canadians), they include immigrants who have been in America before, but have returned home for a time, a practice especially common among the Italians. Then, too, if we are to get at the true annual addition to the foreign-born population, — an addition greater in itself than ever before, but not a much larger percentage of the whole than it was two generations back, — we must subtract all those who, for one cause or another, return to their own country. All this, of course, serves only to attenuate, not to change, the fact that a veritable flood of aliens arrives every year from southern and eastern Europe. Their presence, however, though it may aggravate certain social dangers, cannot yet be regarded as a political peril; for no one nationality among them can hope to acquire a permanent foothold as such, nor has any shown desire to do so. Moreover, the fact that the newcomers flock to the cities rather than to the country, if perhaps economically unfortunate, tends, nevertheless, to bring them more quickly under the influence of their surroundings, and, through the powerful influence of the public schools, to promote the spread of English among the children. In some of the congested mining and manufacturing districts the process of converting them into intelligent American citizens is much slower.

The Germans form the largest and the most important element from the European continent. In 1900 they included 2,669,164 foreign-born, and 5,155,283 children of German parentage, though of this number 1,580,874 had but one German parent. Can we marvel that patriotic Germans lament the loss of this enormous number of fellow-countrymen who, had they gone to Australia, or Brazil, or Argentine, might have built up a future great German state? Most German writers have had to console themselves with the unsubstantial satisfaction of pointing out how beneficial these lost sheep have been to the New World, and with the hope that they will retain their national affections as long as possible; but here and there a more imaginative spirit, excited perhaps by the brilliant dreams of Pan-Germanism, has managed to believe that they may hold to their national individuality and add to the number of German-speaking peoples in the world. A first glance at the figures may, indeed, seem to justify confidence of this kind; but a closer examination leads all whose judgment has not been warped by their patriotism to admit that such a prospect is hopeless of realization.

Curiously enough, if there was ever a danger that a portion of America would become permanently German, the peril existed in the earlier, rather than in the later, period of the national history. During the seventeenth and eighteenth centuries there was a large German immigration into Pennsylvania: it has been estimated that at the time of the Revolution the so-called Pennsylvania Dutch formed one-half the population of the colony. These people led a life much to themselves, and, if they had received reinforcements at a later date, might perhaps have become the nucleus of a considerable German community. Such, however, was not the case. In the course of three-quarters of a century after the war for American independence, the Pennsylvania Dutch, though still retaining many of their older characteristics, had become in the main Anglicized; and when the new current of German immigration set in with force, it did not turn to this particular region, nor did it, indeed, concentrate itself in any one territory.

The result of this dispersion is that, numerous as are the Americans of German origin, they are nowhere preponderant, the highest proportion in any single state — 710,000 in Wisconsin, out of a total population of 2,069,000 — being little more than one-third of the whole population. The greatest number of Germans to be found in any state is 1,217,000 in New York; but even here they formed, in 1900, barely more than one-sixth of the total population of 7,268,894. Moreover, immigration from Germany has fallen off enormously in the last few years. Between 1880 and 1890 it numbered nearly one million and a half (1,452,970); from 1890 to 1900 it was not much more than one-third as large (543,922); for the year 1906 it was about thirty-seven thousand, or less than the total number of Germans from Austria, Russia, etc. Such small accessions as the German-Americans at present receive are not enough to make up for the continual loss which they suffer by death and by absorption. Furthermore, even if economic causes in Germany should produce a fresh immigration on the old scale (which is hardly likely), the time is past when it could make a serious impression.

One reason for this is the well-known truth, admitted by German writers themselves, that no elements of the foreign population, except the Russian Jews, are more eager than the Germans to learn the English language or readier to denationalize themselves and become patriotic Americans. This has long been the case; and coupled with the sterling character of most of the German immigrants, it explains why they have been regarded with particular favor. No mistake could be greater than to think of most of the children of German parents in the United States as foreigners. Not only do the great majority of them speak English rather than German by preference, but many avoid the language of their fathers, and some are even ashamed of it. Certainly they all deem themselves thoroughly American. For that matter, so do a large proportion of the German-Americans born in Germany. Those who have come to their new home at an advanced age cling to their native customs and language, keep up their societies, cherish old memories, and always feel a little strange in their new environment; but the young folks are little affected by such sentiments. So strong, indeed, is the loyalty of the German-Americans that, according to the opinion of competent observers, although they would regard a war between their adopted country and the Fatherland as a terrible calamity, they would nevertheless, in such an event, be true to the former. Another evidence of their denationalization is seen in the fact that in the United States to-day German schools and newspapers are declining in numbers, and German-American literature has taken no deep root. The situation may, indeed, best be summed up in the words of a recent German writer, "Das Deutsch-Amerikanerthum hat nur eine Gegenwart aber keine Zukunft," — German-Americanism has only a present, but no future.[1]

Until recently the traditional policy of the Americans has been to welcome newcomers to their shores. They have proclaimed the right of expatriation as part of the inalienable privilege of the freeman; and with happy confidence in themselves, their land, and their institutions, they have felt sure that the foreigner would be only too glad to identify himself with them as soon as possible. Experience has shown that on the whole they have been right. For generations the United States has been able to remain the land of liberty, with wide-open doors for the poor and the oppressed, who have been taken freely into the family, and in return have not been wanting in gratitude, but have made good use of the hospitality accorded to them.

Of late years a certain reaction has set in. Alarmed at the coming of so many aliens, of whom a smaller and smaller proportion belong to the English-speaking peoples, the Americans are becoming imbued with that advanced form of nationalism characteristic of the present day, which demands uniformity of language on the part of all the inhabitants of the state. Although they have not, like the Germans and the Russians, applied severe pressure to the national minorities, there has been a growing tendency to teach "patriotism," — for instance, in the cult of the flag, — and to insist on a prompt knowledge of English. People feel less safe than they did a generation ago in leaving matters to the quiet working of time. In certain western states where German was formerly the medium of instruction in some of the public schools, it has been

[1] Polenz, *Das Land der Zukunft*, p. 381.

displaced by English. In other states a knowledge of English is requisite for the suffrage; and by the federal law of 1906 the ability to speak English is henceforth necessary for naturalization. This last step is an important departure from the earlier policy of the republic; for it means that a larger contingent of immigrants will keep their foreign allegiance, a circumstance not only undesirable in itself, but likely to complicate the relations of the United States with other governments. Although there is much to be said in favor of the new provision, it cannot be denied that, whether wise or not, it belongs to the class of nationalistic legislation which Americans are prone to condemn in other countries.[1]

Not merely in regard to the foreigners actually settled in the United States have precautions been taken, but immigration itself has recently been made more difficult than it used to be. Mormons, contract laborers, paupers, anarchists, diseased persons, are excluded with increasing rigor; and in view of the ever greater tide of arrivals from southern and eastern Europe, the demand grows louder that some sort of barrier be erected to check this invasion. There is much division of opinion on the subject. The capitalists, wishing, as employers of labor, to obtain it on as cheap terms as possible, are entirely opposed to restrictions; and they are supported by the older idealist sentiment that the land of liberty should be, as it has been, free to all, a refuge for the oppressed and the unfortunate. On the other hand, the labor-unions, in spite of the sympathy of the foreigners among them for their fellow-countrymen, dread the competition to which unlimited immigration exposes them. Their fears are shared by disinterested thinkers who, anxious

[1] The same statute curtails an old but growing evil, the practice by which foreigners have obtained American citizenship for no other purpose than that they might enjoy its protection in their own land, — an abuse which has made many troubles for American diplomats in the past.

only for the welfare of the country as a whole, are seriously alarmed at the enormous quantity of new elements which American society is required to digest, and believe that it is time to call a halt. Several measures looking in this direction have been voted in the last few years, but the law of 1907 did not mark any great progress, for the provisions requiring an educational test of the immigrant and a higher property qualification were struck out of the bill. Still, fresh legislation on the subject is not improbable, especially if there is to be a period of financial depression, with a glut in the labor market.

It is obvious that the American people of the future will have more variety in their ancestry than their fathers had, and this variety may, and probably will, produce serious changes in the national characteristics; but what these changes will be, no man can predict. There will be local differences, too, in spite of the increasing ease of communication due to modern invention; and such local variations may be accentuated by a preponderance of one or another national strain in the blood. They will hardly be greater, however, than those of the Prussian and the Bavarian, of the Norman and the Provençal, of the Piedmontese and the Neapolitan to-day, with their long ages of local life and separate development behind them, and yet none of these differences seriously threatens the unity of Germany, France, or Italy. In the same way, the United States of the future bids fair to be an English-speaking community, of mixed origin, but fused by common traditions, interests, aspirations, and language into one essentially homogeneous people. Unfortunately this assurance leaves out of account a question of great magnitude. In all our considerations thus far we have been thinking only of the white race, and the conclusions reached apply to it alone. The problem of the colored races on the American continent is quite another matter.

CHAPTER III

A LL the world powers own land which they have won by the sword, and which they hold in subjection by sheer force. They all have to pay the penalty in one form or another. In a few fortunate instances — as in that of the territories which the Americans took from Mexico — the lands acquired have been practically vacant; the earlier population has been so scant that it has soon given way to the later comers. Ordinarily, however, instead of disappearing, it has increased in numbers; and, thanks often to the regeneration which better government has produced, it is now becoming insistent on what it believes to be its rights. Under a despotism, when all subjects are so far below the ruler that a little more or less is not of much importance, conquerors and conquered may be on about the same level, — their monarch is equally lord of them all but in these days of sovereign peoples, the subject ones are feeling more sharply the humiliation of their position. They, too, have had an awakening, and are beginning to clamor for liberty and equality. With such pretensions, a king by divine right need have no sympathy; but a government based on democratic principles and the rights of man cannot logically reject them, except on the ground that the claimants are unworthy, — that is to say, that they belong to inferior, or at least backward, races.

The treatment of alien races gives rise to complex

questions, some of them of infinite difficulty. The simplest
ones relate to the peoples lowest in the social scale. It is
comparatively easy to rule over mere savages, especially
if they are, like the natives of tropical Africa, far enough
away; for in such cases firmness, honesty, patience, and
common sense, qualities in which the English as colonial
administrators have been preëminent, are the chief requi-
sites. It is another matter to handle people with a
higher grade of intelligence and with a history and civilization of their own, such as the Hindus, the Egyptians, or the
Arabs of Algeria and Tunis; for the more that is done to
educate them and to improve their condition, the more
impatient they become at being kept in a state of political inferiority.

Every nation holding colonies will have to face such
problems sooner or later. In this respect the Germans have
least to trouble them; for their outlying possessions are not
numerous, and the few they have are inhabited by peoples
who are in such a low state of civilization that it will be long
before they can claim self-government of any kind. Many
Germans, to be sure, think of the Poles within their own
boundaries as an inferior breed; but this inferiority would
vanish at once if only the Poles would consent to be Ger-
manized. Greater France contains more subjects than citizens, and the British Empire has some six inhabitants of
the subject races to one of the ruling people. Both empires include — one in north, the other in south, Africa —
possessions of the kind most difficult to manage; namely,
those where the native population is increasing rapidly,
but where there are also not merely a few officials and
merchants, but a large body of immigrant colonists. The
same thing is true of Japan in Korea. It is in such cases,
when conquerors and conquered meet in every walk of
life, that it is hardest to establish good relations between
them. The arrogance of the privileged poor white or the

coolie is more galling than the domination of the official; and the task of the home government in reconciling the support which it is obliged to give its colonists with its duty toward the natives under its rule is arduous in the extreme. France and Great Britain, however, enjoy, like Germany, the immense blessing of having no race questions in their home countries, no populations of different color: whatever may happen at a distance, house and home at least are secure from the horrors of race war. In this respect Russia is less favorably situated, for her various peoples all live in one unbroken block of territory, though most of them are within fairly definite separate areas. But they shade into one another to such an extent that it would be hard to say just where the inferior peoples begin. From top to bottom there is no such gap as there is between the American and the negro.

Of all countries, the United States is afflicted with the most complicated race problems. The Filipinos and the Hawaiians are indeed far way, and America could get along pretty well without them; but inside her own borders are populations whose presence brings with it difficulties that tax all the wisdom of her statesmen and make every demand on the self-control, not to say the generosity, of her citizens. Of these populations, only an insignificant fraction represents the original dispossessed inhabitants: the vast majority have inherited an even worse grievance, for they are the descendants of imported slaves. The proper treatment of these people is a matter of momentous importance for the future of the republic. All we have time for here is to note a few facts essential to an understanding of the present situation.

Taken together, the various non-European elements in the dominions of the United States number about eighteen million persons, belonging to five separate branches of the human family, usually known as the Indian, the Negro, the

Mongolian, the Polynesian, and the Malay. These five races differ from one another profoundly, in some cases perhaps more profoundly than they do from the white man; and the questions which arise in dealing with them are not at all the same. Nevertheless, there are certain characteristics, not so much of the races themselves as of their relations with the whites, which are common to them all.

To begin with, we have to reckon with the ingrained belief of the white man in his own superiority. This sentiment is probably stronger among people of north-European, than among those of south-European, blood; and it is supposed, rightly or wrongly, to be especially developed among the English-speaking peoples. It is something that goes deeper than ordinary national pride; it seems, indeed, a matter of physical instinct almost as much as of reason. The successes of Japan may have given a rude blow to the complacent assumption of the peoples of Europe and America that they were called upon to rule the world; but this has not altered a whit the determination of the Californian or the Australian to keep his land, at any cost, "a white man's country." The man of European blood will gladly have servants of any sort; he will welcome the Asiatic (though seldom the African) as an honored guest in his university, and even in his home; he will like him and admire him; but he resents his coming into competition with him on even terms, and he would reject with indignation the suggestion that a man of another race might marry a member of his family. How many of the countless Englishmen and Americans who sympathized enthusiastically with the Japanese in the late war would prefer Japanese to Russians as husbands for their daughters or sisters? And yet the Japanese have entered so whole-heartedly into European civilization, and have proved themselves such adepts at it, that we can imagine their being regarded as virtually one of the white peoples.

In the matter of interbreeding between the white and the colored races we find curious inconsistencies. The white male has seldom shown much aversion to consorting with women of any color, and to having children by them. In India, in Japan, in the Philippines, — everywhere it has been the same story; and, when we reflect on the origin of the millions of mulattoes in the South, there is something almost comical in the heat of the feeling of Southerners about the danger of "miscegenation." There have, also, been legal unions with Asiatic and even with African women, but they have been rare; and the white has always recoiled with horror from the idea of his womenkind having sexual intercourse with men of another color. In the eyes of the English colony in India, of the French in Indo-China, of the American in the Philippines, a fellow-countryman who weds a native woman, even one of exalted rank, loses caste, but a white woman who marries a native man is at once beyond the pale. Such sentiments are, of course, not equally extreme in regard to all races; but the instinctive aversion is always there.

Even if we were to admit that all such antipathies are based on prejudice and should vanish with increasing enlightenment and human brotherhood, there is still a reason why we should hesitate before approving of mixed marriages: it is by no means sure that the offspring of parents racially far apart are likely to be satisfactory. Among English-speaking peoples especially there is a strong conviction to the contrary; and this conviction cannot be dismissed contemptuously as mere prejudice, for there is sound evidence in support of it. At all events, the popular saying that children of mixed blood have the vices of both sides and the virtues of neither corresponds with a widespread belief. Granting that many an individual mulatto or Eurasian may be in every respect of a fine type of humanity, does it necessarily follow that a large population of this

F

sort would be a good addition to mankind? Or, even if we think that the mulatto is superior to the unadulterated negro, do we want the white race to be thrown into the melting-pot in order to produce this blend? But we need not take up the question of superiority at all: mere differences may be sufficient, as in the case of certain animals. Dogs, for instance, can often be profitably crossed if they belong to species not too far apart; but if kinds that are too alien to one another are bred together, the product is a worthless mongrel. May not something of the same sort hold true of human beings? The fact that the chief European nations of the present day have been formed by the mingling of several elements not greatly dissimilar does not prove it to be desirable that the American people of the future should be a compound of whites, negroes, and Chinese.

The inhabitants of southern Europe seem to mix, not only more freely but perhaps with better result, with some of the darker races than do people farther north. For this there may be physiological reasons. But in all such questions we are on very debatable ground, and our theories and beliefs cannot yet claim acceptance as ascertained scientific truth. One thing, however, is certain, — public opinion in the United States is overwhelmingly opposed to intermarriage with either Asiatics or Africans. This aversion, which goes so far as to produce strict prohibitory legislation in some states, is a fact of the utmost magnitude; for as long as it exists there can never be amalgamation on a large scale between the different races in the country. We should entertain no illusions on this point. The colored elements may live in perfect agreement with the whites; they may be thoroughly patriotic in sentiment, and may feel that they are as American as anybody; but they will still remain something different, with traditions and mentality not quite the same, — something insoluble in the body politic. Com-

plete fusion is not even an ideal to be aimed at: all that we
can hope to obtain is harmony and a community of ideals.

In considering the position of the different non-European
peoples in the territories of the United States, we may begin
by disassociating those in the insular possessions from those
on the continent. The problems connected with the former
are in many respects the same as those which have to be
dealt with by other powers owning dependencies, and may
best be taken up in connection with the colonial policy of
the country. But the latter class, the representatives of
the colored races in the Union itself, by their presence impose on the Americans difficulties peculiarly their own.

At the present day, the question of the American Indians
is chiefly a sentimental one, and no longer of serious political
importance. In 1905 there were 284,079 of them on reservations aggregating about ninety thousand square miles;
a few thousand more are dispersed throughout the country. Although no one will pretend that the history of
the treatment they have received has been creditable to the
Americans either in colonial times or since, there has undoubtedly been a great deal of exaggeration on the subject.
The idea that a dense native population has been swept
away by the sword and the fire-water of the white man is
not historically correct. When the New World was discovered, various peoples, scattered about in unequal
numbers over vast regions, were in possession of the two
American continents. Those occupying the territory of
what is now the United States were for the most part
warlike seminomadic tribes, who supported themselves by
hunting, or by a little rough cultivation of the soil, carried
on by the women. Although we cannot estimate accurately
what the total Indian population was when the whites first
arrived, there is no reason to believe that it was much
greater than it is now. The tribes were numerous but
small. Even the powerful confederation of the Iroquois,

who terrorized a tract of the size of France, was never able
to bring ten thousand warriors into the field.

As in Siberia and in Australia, the native population was
doomed from the first; for, however picturesque and attractive the noble savage may be, he is a savage, whom it takes
long generations to convert from his nomadic habits to the
humdrum work of civilized life. A race of lazy warriors
cannot be transformed in a day into industrious farmers.
Such a change might, indeed, have taken place in course of
time, as it has in Mexico, if white immigrants had not
come in such numbers as to upset everything. The colonist
can never be made to see the justice of leaving great
stretches of good land lying idle in the hands of an indolent red man when he himself is prepared to develop
them, — for his own benefit, to be sure, but also for that of
society. Under such circumstances he easily gets to feel
that "the only good Indian is a dead Indian."

The government at Washington has, in the main, tried
to do its best for the wards of the nation; but the clam-
orous demands of the frontiersmen, the pressing claims of
greedy white adventurers with political influence, the difficulty of preserving order and, still more, of preventing
the illicit sale of liquor in thinly settled districts, and
finally, owing to a deficient civil service, the appointment
of unworthy local agents, — all these things have proved
too much for the American people and their representatives,
in spite of honest intentions. The tale of the relations between the white man and the red in America forms one of
the many unsatisfactory chapters in the history of dealings
between the stronger and the weaker races of the world;
but this chapter is neither so disgraceful nor so important
as has been made out.

To-day the red men form less than a half of one per cent
of the population of the Union; and, though the birthrate among them is about equal to the deathrate, they are

apparently doomed to extinction. Already many so-called Indians have either white or black blood in their veins, and sooner or later they will all doubtless be absorbed by the surrounding population, which they are not numerous enough to affect materially. The virtues of the Indian have been such as to appeal to the imagination, and romantic fiction has helped to make him popular. Any one who has seen an athletic team from one of the Indian schools in the United States playing against white students of a university will bear witness to the fact that the red men have the sympathy of the crowd. They are also assured of the friendly feelings of their white antagonists, antagonists who would never consent to play against a team composed of blacks.

The foreign relations of the United States have been little affected by the presence of the Indian. The employment of savages by the mother country in the war against her colonists roused bitter feeling, and was one of the grievances set forth in the Declaration of Independence; yet it may be doubted whether the patriots would have had any scruples themselves if they had been able to find valuable native allies. Again, some years later, the fact that the Spaniards were unable to control the Indians in Florida served as both reason and pretext for American interference.

Far more difficult than the Indian question is the negro question in America. It presents one of the most serious problems which any nation in the world is called upon to solve; but it is useless to try to shirk it. The facts must be faced as they are, whether pleasant or not.

To begin with, the negro question is not going to solve itself. In the United States to-day are about nine million colored people, either blacks or mulattoes. These may be separated by fierce jealousies, and one may look down on the other; but in the eyes of the whites both are negroes. Moreover, far from being ready to disappear, they are steadily increasing in numbers; and there seems to be no reason why this increase should not continue, at least for some time. In fact, census figures show that in the so-called "black belt" the disproportion between the two races is becoming constantly greater; the presence of so many negroes militates against white immigration, and where the blacks have a considerable preponderance of numbers the whites tend to move away, and more blacks come in.

Owing to the social system produced by slavery, the colored population before the war was continually receiving fresh infusions of white blood; but this is no longer true, except in very slight measure. Marriage between the two races is sternly forbidden by the laws of many states, and even illegitimate connections are now frowned upon by public opinion in the South in a way unknown in old days; hence the negro bids fair to revert in time to a more purely black type than that now prevailing. Amalgamation is quite out of the question.

In the second place certain political truths must be recognized. Experience since the Civil War has proved that the Southern whites will go to almost any lengths rather than submit to "black domination." That the South, with its inherited slave-holding traditions, is an absolute unit on this point may not be surprising. What is surprising is that, within the lifetime of thousands of men who fought for the freedom of the slaves, the victorious North has accepted the Southern view to such a degree that the dominant Republican party has submitted, with very little murmuring, to a series of laws on the part of the Southern States designed to evade, if they do not actually violate, the amendments to the Constitution guaranteeing equality to the negro. This extraordinary change of attitude is due in part to the abuses committed in the period of negro domination, of the so-called "carpet-bag rule";

but the real causes lie deeper. The substitution in the
North, during the last twenty years, of whites for blacks
in such occupations as those of waiters and barbers seems
to point to an increased, rather than a diminished, natural
aversion. Now that the negro can no longer provoke the
sympathy which he excited in the days of *Uncle Tom's
Cabin*, he finds fewer champions. Moreover, the political
philosophy of the day, with its theories of race inferiority,
does not make for equal treatment. Only by force of arms
can the South be obliged to grant him the promised rights;
and there is no disposition in the North to resort to any
such pressure. On the contrary, many people in that
section sympathize with the attitude of the Southerners,
and pity them for having such a terrible burden on their
hands.

In the South, at the present time, the relations between
the two races are, to say the least, very unsatisfactory,—
worse, perhaps, than they were twenty years ago. Among
the negroes, there exists a sullen resentment at the loss of
their political rights, as well as at the increasing tendency to
segregate them in the public conveyances and, in general, to
impress upon them unmistakably that they belong to a lower
order of mankind. Among the whites, the fear of negro
rule has grown into a perfect frenzy of wrath against whatever appears like an assertion on the part of the colored
population of political or of social equality. Even their
education is regarded with a suspicion that reminds one
of the days of slavery; and the situation with regard to
lynching is terrible. When the whites in country districts
get to feel that their women, unless accompanied, are not
safe against assault a few hundred yards from their own
homes, their exasperation makes them capable of any act
of savagery. An epidemic of social crime on the one hand
has engendered an epidemic of wild lawless punishment on
the other, leaving both sides more embittered than ever.

To add to the difficulties, the two compete with each other in daily life to an extent unknown before.

Under the system of slavery there was no actual rivalry between the black man and the white: each had his own sphere of action, somewhat as the different classes of society in mediæval Europe had theirs. But the feelings of an ancient aristocracy forced to meet a newly emancipated lower class on even terms are mild compared with those of white workmen at the prospect that their standard of wages may be kept down to the lowest point by the competition of a former servile population of another color. It is small wonder that the labor-unions do not admit negroes to their ranks, but look on them as the ignorant tool of the capitalist and a peril to the white workingman. It is to be feared that the recent industrial development of the South may embitter, rather than allay, the existing hostility.

In regard to the progress made by the negroes since they have had the gift of freedom, there have been hot disputes. Such statistics as we have are, on the whole, encouraging, whereas the violent criticisms that we hear rest on allegations not always easy to prove. These questions need not be discussed; but it is worth remarking that the negro, unlike the Russian peasant, was not provided with land on which to support himself in his new liberty. True, the mujik with his land has not prospered in a way to give cause for envy; but he has had disadvantages of his own to contend with.

The probable result of the present tendencies in the South will be an increasing segregation of the two races. Except in the cities, they may come to inhabit almost separate territories, an outcome which might easily prove disastrous from an economic point of view. Some persons fear, too, that the negroes of the black belt, if left to themselves, may relapse into something very like barbarism.

The negro question has more than once affected the for-

eign policy of the United States: the desire to get new
lands for slavery was the main reason for the annexation
of Texas, for the Mexican War, and for the attempts to
acquire Cuba a few years later; and the hatred of the South
for the emancipated slave prevented the recognition of Haiti
up to the time of the Civil War. At the present day, the
relations of the republic to the West India Islands, and in
a lesser degree to Latin America and even to the Philippines,
are complicated by the race problem at home.

Abounding in troubles as the whole situation is, it has at
least one good feature, — it is free from conflict of religions
or of civilizations. The blacks and the whites in the United
States do not represent two different types of culture. The
negro, though an alien element, possesses no civilization of his
own: such as he has, he has got from the white man. The
blacks brought into the colonies for generations came from
different tribes, speaking independent languages; and in
no case were enough of them imported from any given
region at one time for them to maintain their native tongue
in their new home. The American negroes speak English,
and nothing but English. They have been influenced by no
foreign culture except that of their former masters, nor have
they shown themselves capable of originating one of their
own. Their standards may be lower than those of their
white neighbors; but they differ in degree, not in kind.
Their intellectual influence is a passive one; and, as yet,
they present a social problem, not a political danger.

Colored soldiers have been used with good results, against
the Indians and in Cuba. In the Philippines they did not
prove so satisfactory; for, although they fought well
enough, it was difficult to keep them in proper discipline
in out-of-the-way posts, and their pursuit of the native
women provoked much anger among the men, giving rise
to fresh insurrection in districts which had been pacified. Their employment at all was bitterly resented by

the Filipinos, who regard themselves as belonging to a race superior to the African.[1] Nevertheless, the latter undoubtedly constitute an important military resource, and as an economic one they seem to be indispensable to the Southern States; for it is their labor which produces almost the whole of the immense cotton crop. Whatever, therefore, may be thought about internal perils, the presence of the black man in the territory of the republic cannot be said to diminish its external power.

Compared with nine million negroes, the couple of hundred thousand Japanese, Chinese, Koreans, and Hindus in the United States appear insignificant enough; indeed, their numbers do not together equal even that of the North American Indians. Unlike the Indians, however, they are not the remnants of peoples that are disappearing. On the contrary, they form the vanguard of an army of hundreds of millions, who, far from retreating before the white man, thrive and multiply in competition with him. It is not they, but he, who retires from the field.

We can easily understand why, in these days of easy communication, Chinese and Japanese should flock into a thinly populated land where the climate is perfectly suited to them, where there are vast resources not yet developed, and where wages are so high that, living as they do, they can hope to save in a few years a sum of money that will be a fortune at home. In the long discussion over their admittance, the two peoples have been the object of much unfair criticism. They have been inconsistently charged with taking money out of the country by the very people who make the loudest objections when they propose to stay permanently; they have been attacked on the ground of immorality, — a subject on which a good deal might be

---

[1] The Filipinos were infuriated at the suggestion, made in the United States, that their islands should be colonized by the surplus of the American colored population.

said with little result; and divers other complaints have been brought against them. Leaving all such accusations out of account, however, and condemning no one, we still have to admit the existence of certain social facts which American statesmen, however free from anti-foreign prejudice, must take into consideration.

In the first place if, as is generally thought, a racial intermixture of the newcomers with the white population is undesirable, it follows that they can never be entirely assimilated. Now the whole American theory of welcoming settlers from foreign lands has rested on the confident belief, which has thus far been justified by events, that sooner or later they will become Americans in every respect and be merged with the rest. When this is impossible, should immigrants, no matter what may be their virtues, be allowed to establish themselves in large numbers in the country? In view of the terrible difficulties presented by the negro problem, is the United States going to saddle itself light-heartedly with the possibility of a Mongolian or a Hindu one? This does not mean that we liken Orientals to negroes, or that the complications which their presence might give rise to would be the same in all respects. None the less, if the coming of Asiatics bids fair to burden the United States with another insoluble race question, is it not better to nip the danger in the bud by limiting admission from the start?

This danger has still another aspect. All the evidence we have on the subject goes to prove that white men, as a working class, cannot maintain themselves in the long run against the competition of Chinese, Japanese, Hindus, and perhaps others. The reasons are not far to seek. It is not that Asiatics will content themselves with any lower wages than they can get, for experience has shown they are prompt enough to obtain whatever they can; but as they are willing to work for longer hours, and have a lower standard of requisite comfort and a higher standard of sobriety than white men, they can afford to underbid them. We may grant that in time their conditions tend to approximate those of their neighbors, and that, if there were but a handful of them, the solution might well be left to time; but the few thousand Asiatics on the American continent have behind them the countless millions of their teeming native lands. If they come in any considerable numbers, the white capitalist, the white shopkeeper on a large scale, and certain kinds of white skilled laborers may be able to maintain themselves in the midst of an Asiatic population, though even this would be doubtful in the long run; but the white workman cannot. He must go to the wall, or he must leave.

The question, then, may present itself in this way: Is the future population of the Pacific coast to be white or is it to be Oriental? If the Americans are constrained to face matters in this direct form, there can be little doubt that they will take measures to prevent what may come to be regarded as a deadly peril. Such measures might, of course, be tributes to the virtues, rather than to the vices, of the Asiatic, — the desire to exclude him might, like the determination of the negroes to keep white men out of Haiti, be construed as an admission of his superiority. Be it so. A protective tariff may be called a confession of weakness, but that does not prevent nations from adopting it. No mere taunts will keep the American people from taking whatever steps they believe to be necessary to protect the standard of living of their workingmen, of which they are not a little proud; and they will go to any extreme before they will allow their Pacific coast to become the domain of the yellow race or of any but the white. Such action need not be a reflection upon the Chinese and the Japanese. It simply means that, if white men and Mongolians cannot live side by side in the same land, the Americans, being white themselves, will reserve their territory for the people of their own blood.

In like manner, the Russians, who are traditionally supposed to be tolerant in their dealings with Asiatics, have been alarmed of late, and with good reason, by the prospect that their East Siberian possessions may be overrun by Chinese, a catastrophe which they will certainly do their utmost to prevent. We may, indeed, assert with confidence that there is not a state in Europe in which the annual arrival of, let us say, fifty thousand Chinese would not provoke such active opposition that means would soon be found to check the movement.

As might be expected, there is much division of opinion in America in regard to Chinese and Japanese immigration. The western coast is particularly exposed to it, and is correspondingly hostile, and determined to repress it at any cost. The East, being less exposed than the West, is not so much in favor of restriction; and even the South, in spite of its intense feeling on race topics, which makes it sympathize with California, sometimes thinks longingly of what its fields might be made to produce by the importation of yellow laborers, so superior in steadiness to the black. Capitalists, too, desiring to get their workmen in large numbers and at as cheap rates as possible, would be glad to tap the inexhaustible supply in Asia. And the old-fashioned school of uncompromising liberalism still believes that the land of liberty should be open to all, and that such intelligent peoples as the Orientals could be brought before long to the level of the whites in every respect. On the other hand, the labor-unions are unanimous in their opposition; and they are supported by a general feeling that the United States must remain "a white man's country."

Unlike the problems in regard to the Indian and the negro, which are internal matters and not the concern of any foreign nation, the question of the Asiatic is one which the United States is not at liberty to settle off-hand according to its own impulses.   In the case of the Hindus, Great Britain may be unable to remonstrate, for while she allows her own colonies to shut out her Asiatic subjects, she cannot complain if other states exclude them; but behind the Chinese and the Japanese stand two great empires, neither of which is indifferent to the treatment meted out to its citizens, and both of which have more than one way of retaliating if they conceive themselves to be injured.

CHAPTER IV

IDEALS AND SHIBBOLETHS

ON March 4, 1897, Mr. William McKinley was inaugurated President of the United States. This date, hardly more than ten years ago, now seems strangely distant to Americans in view of the changes which they have witnessed since that time. Then they were quite unconscious that great events were impending. Though every one knew that the country was gaining in strength year by year, even the few who believed that it might soon be called upon to make use of this strength had little conception of what the broader results of such action might be. Foreign relations appeared to be following the normal course which they had taken for a generation. The United States was at peace with the world, and seemed likely to remain so. True, the continuance of the Cuban revolt was attracting more and more attention and sympathy, which might easily crystallize into a resolve to interfere; but thus far the interest of the public in the matter was not equal to that of the newspapers.

The American people as a whole were wrapped up in their home affairs, and in particular in the discussion of the proper remedies for the "hard times" through which the country had just been passing. The presidential election had turned on internal questions, the national platforms of both parties containing mere perfunctory declarations on the subject of foreign policy. The new President, who had first become generally known as the father of a high-tariff bill, was primarily interested in the development of American industries; he had just been nominated and elected as the champion of a sound currency and of business interests, his opponent representing the spirit of dissatisfaction with existing economic conditions. Mr. McKinley was an honest, conscientious statesman, of earnest purpose and high sense of duty, a self-made man,—in many ways a typical American of the time. He had never taken a prominent part in foreign questions; indeed, like most of his fellow-countrymen, he knew and cared little about them. It is said that when on the day of his inauguration he was told by a retired general that the most important event in his presidency would be a war with Spain, he was astonished at the prediction.

The Venezuela flurry was by this time happily over, and to the satisfaction of the American people, who were pleased with the stand which they had taken in the affair; for their action, if somewhat emphatic, had been in their opinion conservative, as they had only reasserted and maintained a principle of self-defence which had long been dear to them. They were the more pleased at having got the best of the dispute for the reason that they had run very serious risks, more serious, in truth, than they had realized at the moment. But for this episode, the Democratic administration of President Cleveland had been eminently peaceful. Whatever stray writers might predict about the future expansion of the country, there seemed no valid reason to expect any sudden change in its programme of tranquil activity.

In the one hundred and twenty years of their independent existence the American people had had time for a full development of their national individuality. While sharing many of the virtues and faults, ideals and illusions of others, they possessed characteristics of their own which were sufficiently marked. They had their own position in the world, their accepted views of themselves and of others, and especially their cherished traditions, which usually guided and always influenced them in their management of their home affairs as well as in their dealings with foreign nations. In order to appreciate the changes of the last few years, we need to keep well in mind the heritage of temperament and of doctrines with which the people of the United States faced the new problems so soon to be presented to them.

From the beginning of time, all nations have shown a tendency to divide mankind into two categories, Greeks and Barbarians, — that is, ourselves and everybody else; and the idea that "we" are the chosen people is still far from being extinct. The Americans, like others, have cherished this pleasing belief, and they have also entertained to the full the ordinary national illusions, — for instance, that they have grown great by their virtues and by the disposition of a kindly Providence, whereas the progress of other nations has been marked by unscrupulous rapacity; that their support gives an extraordinary moral weight to any cause they espouse, and that no fair-minded person can doubt the honesty of their intentions, but that they must keep a sharp watch on the nefarious designs of their neighbors; that in their simplicity they are in constant danger of being overreached by wily adversaries; that their chief faults, as they modestly admit, are self-depreciation, admiration of foreign things, and too much good nature, — in short, that their hearts are better than their heads.

In accordance with this common theory, the people of the United States were sure of their own good intentions. Their attitude toward the rest of humanity was friendly, for they were pretty well satisfied with the world in general and with themselves in particular, a content-

G

ment not to be wondered at, and to be ascribed chiefly to the same cause that has helped to make optimism one of the salient traits in the national character, — the consciousness of success. In 1897 they had already long been imbued with the feeling, not since diminished, that the history of their country had been one of tremendous achievement. In a little over a century it had grown to be, without question, one of the greatest—in their opinion the greatest — in the world. In spite of the recent pinch of hard times, it was rich and prosperous; and its progress from year to year was eminently gratifying. The Americans were convinced that this progress was not all due to the favors which nature had lavished upon them, but that to an equal exent it was the result of their own endeavors. They were proud not only of the size of their population and of the wealth of their resources, but even more of their own energy and activity, of their achievements in industry and invention. They were proud of the freedom which had made their land a haven of refuge for oppressed millions from the Old World; proud of their popular government, which had stood the test of time and the strain of a tremendous civil war; proud of the courage, endurance, and self-sacrifice shown by both parties during that war; and, finally, proud of the way in which the wounds of the war had been healed, leaving the nation stronger and more united than ever. They believed their country to be the best, the freest, the richest, the happiest, in the world, and they gave due recognition to their own merits which had made it so.

With the assurance of vigorous youth, they were disposed to attach little weight to the experience of others. The fact that others had done things in a particular way was no reason, in their eyes, why they should do them in the same way; and the failure of a European nation in a given task was no proof that Americans might not be more successful. With this self-confidence we find an idealism which sometimes surprises foreign observers. According to a common impression abroad, the people of the United States are a race of prosaic money-makers, who care for nothing but getting rich, unless it be for marrying their daughters to foreigners with titles. In reality, though European critics seldom perceive it, the Americans are not lacking in generous imagination, even if it does not crop out much in everyday life. Their ideals, as compared with European ones, may sometimes appear material rather than æsthetic, but they are none the less noble, and they are very real.

The general feeling of self-satisfaction prevailing in the country at this period did not, of course, prevent clear-sighted men from recognizing that there were many shadows in the picture: the negro problem was becoming ever more difficult; the increasing antagonism between labor and capital, coupled with the growth of huge unions and trusts and with corruption in local politics, alarmed honest and patriotic citizens ; the recent financial depression had made bad feeling between different classes, and even between different sections, of the Union; the lamentable decay of the merchant marine, once the just pride of the nation, proved that Americans were not equally successful in all kinds of economic enterprise; and finally in the higher domains of literature, art, and pure science, the United States was not contributing a very notable quota to the wealth of the world. All this the broad-minded patriot had to admit and deplore; but for the average man American optimism came to the rescue. With a fine self-confidence, public opinion, when forced to admit the charges brought against anything American, consoled itself with the belief that things would soon be better. There was a comfortable conviction that, if the Americans had failed in any respect, it was only because they had been too busy elsewhere to turn their attention in that particular direction; that, when once they had established their material conditions on a thoroughly firm foundation, they could attend to such matters as tinkering the weak places in the machine of government, or developing the æsthetic capabilities of the race. The saying ran: "When Chicago gets hold of culture, culture will have to hum." Many a traveller has been struck by the fact that in a new American town the patriotic citizen will oftener talk about the future than about the present; that, however boastful he may be of what his own place has already achieved, he will declare that it is nothing to what it is going to be some day. Every inland mart means to be a new Chicago; every port hopes to surpass New York.

Crude as the expression of such sentiments may be, the frame of mind which they represent not only helps to make life pleasanter, but also constitutes an element of very real national strength. A robust faith of this sort enables a nation, as well as a man, to bear misfortune serenely, and to persist in the face of apparently overwhelming difficulties until success is wrung from an unwilling fate. A decadent philosophy may be more picturesque in itself; but when decadent individuals or peoples come into collision with self-reliant ones, they are at a disadvantage from the start. The peril of the American lies in the opposite direction. Like the Russian, he is too prone to think that, whatever his previous negligence may have been, in the last resort he will manage to "pull through somehow"; and consequently he has the same impatience of careful precautions, — impatience that may cost dear.

The quality of boastfulness which so many foreigners have noticed as characteristic of the free citizens of the United States had declined since the Civil War. This self-assertion, besides being a sign of the exuberance of green youth, and betraying in its very extravagance an uncom-

fortable doubt that it might not bring conviction to the
listener, had also been a reply to the condescension, kindly
or unkindly, which the American met with in European
society. With the growth of the country, there had come
from outside a more general acknowledgment of its position, especially since the great events of the war, and the
boastfulness of its citizens had diminished correspondingly.

In spite of the fact that millions of people of European
birth lived in the New World and that increasing numbers
of American tourists visited the old one every year, in spite,
also, of the presence of students who had attended German
universities, of painters who had lived in France, of educated
men and women who delighted in European literature and
art, the attitude of the immense majority of people in the
United States toward things European was at this time one
of good-natured indifference, not to say superiority. Educated Americans, it is true, knew, know, and ought to know
more about Europe than Europeans about America; but
the general public took little interest in the affairs of European countries, and not much more in the external relations of their own. A proof of this indifference may be
found in the little care with which the American diplomatic representatives abroad were selected. With the exception of the all-important office of minister to England, in
which it was so evidently desirable to have a distinguished
man that such a one was usually appointed, the American
diplomatic posts were too often filled with more attention
to political influence than to the suitability of the candidates. As for the consular service, it is strange that a
nation of business men should have been content to recruit
it in the same haphazard fashion. It was not until 1906,
after many scandals in the history of American consulates,
that the system at last began to be put on a sound basis.
News and comment from across the ocean usually came
through English channels, and Americans knew little and

cared less about the opinions which foreigners might entertain of them.

One unpleasant result of this indifference was the recklessness which prevailed not only in the American papers, but in the utterances of public men, in regard to foreign nations. If a Congressman believed that his remarks would please his constituents, it mattered little to him that they might make bad blood in Austria or Russia, and thus complicate the work of the state department. Even American diplomacy did not enjoy abroad a reputation for good manners. At the same time, though it cannot be denied that American methods of treating international politics were, often, largely for "home consumption," it is possible to push this theory too far. Foreigners, Englishmen in particular, have now and then made the mistake of thinking that the declarations of American statesmen were not meant seriously, when, as events showed, they were made in all earnestness.

Another trait in the national character which more than once made difficulties for those in charge of the destiny of the republic, was an impatience of the bonds imposed by written agreements that were no longer deemed in keeping with existing conditions. When a compact ceased to be advantageous, there was a tendency to regard it as a dead letter; and irresponsible members of Congress could always be found to give expression to this sentiment. In the notable instance of the Clayton-Bulwer treaty, the United States chafed so violently that England was in the end virtually forced to consent to its abrogation; and, again, the conduct of the government at Washington in dealing with the subject of Chinese immigration was hardly in accordance with its pledged treaty word. It is true that an impatience of mere paper bonds, of "musty parchments," is a general characteristic of modern democracy, — witness, for example, the recent repudiation of the concordat with the papacy by the French republic, — but it must be admitted that there is a strain of lawlessness in the American, a result of individualism and of the independence of his development. Although he recognizes the necessity of law, he does not look upon it as sacred, or even as indispensable on all occasions. His practical bent and his lack of understanding of the full value of social solidarity incline him to pay more attention to the necessities of the moment than to abstract general principles. At the same time, the American people have shown as high a sense of honor as any other, and they usually take their moral obligations with all seriousness; indeed, no modern people has shown itself more willing to make painful sacrifices in order to carry out its principles.

Nations, like individuals, are often inconsistent, thereby laying themselves open to the charge of dishonesty on the part of uncharitable neighbors. This is particularly true of the Anglo-Saxon peoples, whose minds are not so uncompromisingly logical as those of the French or the Russians; it explains, for instance, why the English have so often been accused of hypocrisy. When the Englishman or the American finds that his premises lead him to conclusions that he dislikes, he is pretty sure to kick over the traces and, regardless of the premises, to accept other conclusions that suit him better. He never allows previous logical subtleties to tempt him into a position which his common sense condemns; but guided by a sound instinct, he acts as he thinks best in each instance, careless of the fact that, by any course of general reasoning, he will appear inconsistent. For a striking example of the difference between Latin and Anglo-Saxon political conceptions, we have but to compare two well-known sayings, — the "Périssent les colonies plutôt qu'un principe" of the French Revolution, and Cleveland's famous remark, "It is a condition which confronts us, not a theory." It is highly characteristic that even Jefferson, perhaps the most theoretical of all American statesmen, accepted without hesitation the responsibility of the purchase of Louisiana, although he believed that he had no constitutional right to take such action.

This impatience of precedent has in no wise prevented the Americans from having traditions of their own, to which they have believed themselves to be strongly attached. In the main their foreign policy, up to the time of the Spanish War, had not been haphazard, whatever party was at the helm. The international relations of the country had, indeed, seldom been complicated; for it had kept out of general European affairs, and most of Europe had had no part in those of the United States. For these reasons, the Americans had not often been obliged to take into consideration more than one foreign power at a time in any question in which they were involved; and since they achieved their independence they had had but one European war, — that with Great Britain in 1812. They had not, of course, been exempt from their share of miscellaneous disputes; but most of their quarrels, being on such tangible matters as discussions of boundary, had not called for far-seeing statecraft, and none of them, except that with Mexico, had ended in actual hostilities. With time, the boast "We are a peaceful people" had become a fixed article of the national creed. The truth of this statement was, however, open to some doubt. If it meant that the Union had had few wars in the past and had made little preparation for any in the future, it was beyond dispute; but if it signified that the Americans, individually or collectively, were of a peaceful temperament, it was far from being exact, for no people were quicker to resent a provocation or more determined to return blow for blow. Their comparative immunity from the necessity of taking up arms had been due to their situation rather than to any innate gentleness of disposition; and yet, with a record of forty-seven disputes referred to arbitration, — more than half of all the cases thus submitted, — the United States could well claim that it had shown a real desire for peace and justice. In proof of their peaceful disposition, Americans pointed to the smallness of their military forces; but it would, perhaps, have been more correct to ascribe this to their inherited English dislike of a standing army as a "foe to liberty," and, still more, to the careless confidence which trusted that, when necessity should arise, the means would be found to meet it. We need not wonder that their regular army had dwindled since the Civil War till it numbered less than thirty thousand enlisted men, with no reserve but a very imperfect militia organization: a country which has no fear of being invaded is apt to feel that it will always have time enough to find soldiers. What is more surprising is that the wealthy coast cities should have been left for so long without any modern system of defence, and that the navy, of whose past achievements all Americans were justly proud, should have been permitted to decline until, about 1885, it was hardly worthy of a third-rate power. Certainly no fair-minded observer could at that date have accused the United States of "meditating aggression" against any one.

On the other hand, it was a gross mistake to think, as did many people in Europe, that the American republic would be kept from any course of action by fear of the greater military preparedness of rival powers. The people who, with thousands of miles of undefended coast-line and a still infant navy, were ready to risk a war with the British Empire on a question of principle about a matter of such slight intrinsic value as the exact location of a corner of the boundary of Venezuela, were not likely to shrink from any conflict, if their passions were aroused. The danger was just the opposite: it lay rather in the confidence of the American people that they could "lick creation," — a belief which tended to make public opinion recklessly irresponsible. Moreover, the larger part of the country could hardly, under any circumstances, be exposed to foreign attack. New York and San Francisco might be at the mercy of a hostile fleet; but the citizen of Kansas City or Denver knew that he had nothing to fear, and hence was under small temptation to make concessions to an overweening foe. He might, to be sure, suffer economic loss sometime in the future, but he could easily overlook such a possibility in the excitement of the moment; and at any rate, he need never see an enemy unless he went out of his way to find him.

A rather curious contention, savoring of earlier years, was frequently expressed in the phrase "We are a plain people," — a notion based on the fact that in the United States there was no king or court or titled aristocracy, and not at all on any greater simplicity of living prevailing among Americans. True, the mass of the population lived plainly enough, — they do everywhere, — but the leisure class was already characterized by just as much luxury as in any country in the world; and persons of moderate means enjoyed perhaps greater comfort than anywhere else. Life was as complicated, pleasure as riotous, display as profuse, as in other lands; and yet the American people not only expected a republican simplicity in the demeanor of their officials, but, by the same token, generally underpaid them, with the undemocratic result that some of the posts, especially in the diplomatic service, could with difficulty be accepted by any but men of independent wealth. There was, too, a strange dislike to certain titles, as, for instance, to anything above lieutenant-general in the army, even more to the title of admiral in the navy, and most of all to that of ambassador. While repelling with scorn the suggestion that the United States should not be treated as the equal of any other great nation, many

Americans regarded it as democratic that their representative abroad should be an official of only the second recognized grade; but few of those who thought that the term "ambassador" sounded aristocratic realized that the full appellation which they preferred was "envoy extraordinary and minister plenipotentiary," a title hardly suggestive of simplicity. When the office of ambassador was at last instituted in 1893, the provision that created it was smuggled through Congress as quietly as possible for fear of a public outcry.

In most essentials, American political ideals had not at this time undergone any revolutionary changes since the early days of the republic. The teachings of the fathers had not lost their force. The Declaration of Independence had proclaimed that "all men are created equal" and have "unalienable rights" to "life, liberty, and the pursuit of happiness"; and even if the Declaration had been described as a tissue of glittering generalities, Americans still believed in liberty and equality. But these two terms can doubtless be understood in several ways. In the days before the Civil War, the South managed to reconcile them with the possession of negro slaves, just as the governing aristocracy in Poland, when the mass of the population was in hopeless serfdom, had believed that theirs was the only free country in Europe. Recently the Southern States had by one means or another well-nigh disfranchised the blacks in spite of the Constitution, and the North had not interfered.

However we may feel about the consistency of all this, it would be unjust to accuse the people of the United States of hypocrisy. They had sympathized enthusiastically with the revolutions in France, in Italy, in Greece, in Hungary, in South America; and they had given Kossuth such tremendous ovations when he visited them that he had been misled into expecting armed intervention in behalf of his

cause. They had never let themselves be restrained by
caution, or by politeness, from expressing their generous
sentiments, or from proclaiming the superiority of their
form of government. They had given asylum to countless
political fugitives. They had favored broad laws of neutrality, freedom of navigation in rivers and straits, an open
door in the Far East, and modern and enlightened principles in international dealings in general. True, they had
once had the blot of slavery on their scutcheon, but they
had washed it out with blood; and now the phrase "the
land of liberty" was no mere flourish of patriotic rhetoric,
but the expression of a truth that could not be gainsaid.

Liberty, however, is a thing that men get used to. If
they have always enjoyed it, it becomes, like health or
fresh air, something taken for granted, — a priceless gift,
but too much a part of everyday life to awaken ready
enthusiasm. The Americans had learned by experience,
too, that liberty was not a panacea for political ills. In
addition, they were not so sure as they had once been that
every people was capable of self-government, and that
their own successful institutions were equally suited to
others. They had applauded the independence of Latin
America, but they had not been edified by the history
of most of her republics; for they were too orderly themselves to approve of an uninterrupted series of revolutions,
even if the uprisings took place in the name of liberty.
Still they believed, as a general truth, that government
(except for the Southern negroes) should be by the consent of the governed; and they were proud of not owning
foreign colonies that would have to be held down by brute
force. They felt that they could moralize with comfortable
superiority over the greed of the various European powers
as shown in recent years in the furious scramble for lands
in Asia and Africa.

In their foreign policy, they had followed the same

general principles as other modern nations. In the many
treaties they had concluded, they had aimed not only to
cultivate mutually beneficial relations with other peoples,
but to promote their own trade and to protect their
citizens in every part of the world. Their efforts had
been crowned with gratifying success, and they could pride
themselves on the result. In all this there was nothing
peculiar to them. What was peculiar was their following of certain precepts that have had a decisive influence on the whole course of their foreign relations. The
first of these was to avoid "entangling alliances."

Washington, in his farewell address, — a document which
in the American mind ranks second only to the Declaration
of Independence, — solemnly warned his fellow-countrymen
against foreign alliances. He himself had had experience
with such things. The treaty with France, concluded in
1778, had been of this nature; but, though it had led to
the independence of the colonies and the humiliation of
England, it had not proved entirely satisfactory to either
of the contracting parties. At the conclusion of peace in
1783, their interests had been divergent, and there had been
some slight friction between them. Later a much more
serious difficulty had arisen in the question whether the
United States was bound to assist France when, after the
fall of her monarchy, she found herself again at war with
England. On the face of the text it certainly seemed so;
but the government of President Washington decided that
circumstances were so entirely different from what they had
been at the time the treaty was concluded that its provisions
were no longer applicable to the existing situation. This
decision was doubtless politically wise, and the judgment of
Washington has been ratified by the unanimous approval
of American historians ever since. On the other hand,
members of his own cabinet to whom the question was submitted, including Jefferson, the secretary of state, had given

it as their opinion that the United States was bound by treaty to aid France; and a man as high-minded as Washington could hardly have helped feeling that the repudiation of a formal obligation of this kind, however justified, cast a shadow of suspicion on the honor of his country. The United States got out of its difficulties, but in a way that left an uncomfortable impression; and the lesson of the incident was reflected in the President's farewell address.

The advice given in this famous document has been consistently followed by American statesmen ever since, and with satisfactory results. Again and again the United States has refused to become a party to agreements with European powers, basing its decisions on this very ground of avoiding entangling alliances. Except in the Far East, where joint action of the Christian powers has sometimes been necessary, it has preferred to follow out its own interests separately, even when they have coincided with those of other, and friendly, nations.

This policy has, to be sure, caused occasional irritation abroad, where the Americans have been accused of selfish unwillingness to take part in work for the common good; but from the American point of view it has so far been wise. Whether it can be maintained in our new period of world questions is open to doubt.

Another peculiar principle of American foreign policy has, however, by its originality and its importance, attracted far more attention abroad, and is more vital to-day. When any foreigner begins to talk of the attitude of the United States toward the rest of the world, one of the first things he will be sure to mention is the Monroe Doctrine.

CHAPTER V

THE MONROE DOCTRINE

THE late Mr. John Hay, for nearly seven years secretary of state, and one of the best that his country ever had, once said of his policy that the Monroe Doctrine and the Golden Rule were a sufficient basis of action. "The principles which have guided us," he added, "have been of limpid simplicity." To his mind, at least, there was no contradiction between his two principles, no matter what may be the difference between them. The Golden Rule is, let us say, a precept as commonly, or as uncommonly, observed by one people as by another; the Monroe Doctrine is something specifically American, and cannot claim respect on quite the same grounds. Its origin, its meaning, and its justification have been the subjects of long controversy both at home and abroad. Here we need repeat only so much of the well-known story as serves to bring the essential features clearly before us.

The Monroe Doctrine was promulgated on December 2, 1823. It was based on the idea, then common in the United States, that there was a natural separation between the Old World and the New. As ex-President Jefferson put it, "Our first and fundamental maxim should be never to entangle ourselves in the broils of Europe; our second, never to suffer Europe to meddle with cisatlantic affairs." The immediate cause of the famous declaration was twofold, — a dispute with Russia over the limits of her posses-

sions in the northwest, and alarm at French intervention in
Spain. This last step awakened a fear that the powers of
the Holy Alliance might attempt to aid the Spanish King
to regain control of his revolted American colonies, and
thus perhaps acquire territory for themselves in the New
World. When the British Prime Minister, George Canning,
suggested a joint declaration on the part of England and the
United States that they would oppose any such attempt, his
plan was at first received with favor in Washington; but
finally, under the influence of the secretary of state, John
Quincy Adams, President Monroe decided on an independent
expression of policy.

The two questions at issue were taken up in the same
message, but they were not connected in such a way as
to call for a declaration of general principles which should
apply to both; they were, in fact, separated from each other
by a considerable quantity of intervening matter. The decisive passages run as follows: —

(1) "The American continents, by the free and independent condition which they have assumed and maintain, are
henceforth not to be considered as subjects for future
colonization by any European powers;" and (2) "In the
wars of the European powers in matters relating to themselves we have never taken any part, nor does it comport
with our policy so to do. . . . The political system of the
allied powers is essentially different in this respect from that
of America. This difference proceeds from that which
exists in their respective governments; and to the defence
of our own, which has been achieved by the loss of so much
blood and treasure, and matured by the wisdom of their
most enlightened citizens, and under which we have enjoyed
unexampled felicity, this whole nation is devoted. We
owe it, therefore, to candor and to the amicable relations
existing between the United States and those powers to
declare that we should consider any attempt on their part

to extend their system to any portion of this hemisphere as dangerous to our peace and safety. With the existing colonies or dependencies of any European power we have not interfered and shall not interfere. But with the governments who have declared their independence and maintained it, and whose independence we have, on great consideration and on just principles, acknowledged, we could not view any interposition for the purpose of oppressing them, or controlling in any other manner their destiny, by any European power in any other light than as the manifestation of an unfriendly disposition toward the United States." The principle thus enunciated may be briefly summed up as one of "Hands off," or of "America for the Americans."

From the date of its appearance down to the present day, this doctrine has met with almost universal approval at home. For many reasons it appealed immediately to popular imagination and at the same time commended itself to the judgment of statesmen. In the eyes of the Americans, it was a proclamation of their cherished ideals, of their belief in the right of free peoples to determine their own destinies. By it the United States declared that, while respecting existing institutions of which it did not approve, it would never consent to let similar ones be imposed by force on any of the inhabitants of the New World who had already freed themselves from such trammels. In other words, it announced that it was not only a land of liberty, but likewise the protector of liberty. Surely here was just cause for national pride. In the President's message there was, furthermore, an expression of the feeling that the New World, as something essentially different from the Old, should have its independent development. Already ardent patriots were dreaming of a future epoch in which the glories of the western hemisphere should outshine those of the earlier homes of civilization; they believed that the

H

whole of both American continents should be included in the Promised Land.

While sentimental considerations of this sort roused honest enthusiasm, the practical merits of the new policy were also such as to assure it of favor. Nations have always found it convenient that their nearest neighbors should be inferior to themselves in strength, and have been prone to resent the approach of their equals as a menace. This idea has been a fundamental principle of British policy in regard to India. Similarly, the Americans dreaded the thought that dangerous enemies might hold military positions close to their borders. They also realized that, for commercial as well as for political reasons, it was to their advantage to keep all of the western hemisphere that they could in what would to-day be termed their "sphere of influence." In supporting the stand taken by President Monroe, they at the same time extended a protecting hand over their weaker brethren, and followed the behests of enlightened self-interest.

The last feature of the doctrine that went to make it popular was its appearance of unusual daring. The young American republic, with its scant ten million inhabitants, and almost without an army, appeared to be throwing down the glove to the great military monarchies of Europe. This was enough to stir the blood of patriots. In actual fact, the peril was not serious; for as long as England was on the side of the United States, the Americans, being at a safe distance, had nothing to fear from the continental powers. And the views of the British government on the South American question were well known. Though the news had not reached Washington, Canning had already told Prince Polignac, the French ambassador, that Great Britain would not tolerate any European interference in Spanish-American matters, and Polignac had replied that France had no thought of interfering in them. Nevertheless, the apparent triumph of the new doctrine was complete. All talk of intervention soon died out, a result which the Americans of course assumed to be entirely due to their attitude. Even Canning gave countenance to this belief by declaring proudly, if inaccurately, "I called the New World into existence to redress the balance of the Old."

We may note here a curious similarity between the policy pursued by England in 1823 and that followed in 1902. On both occasions, finding herself isolated and in opposition to the chief military states of continental Europe, she sought her ally at a distance, regardless of any sentimental twaddle about the community of European nations. She acted, in short, like a true world power, unfettered by local prejudice. If the United States had accepted Canning's overtures and joined with Great Britain, as might quite conceivably have happened, the parallel would have been more exact; or we may imagine that Japan, if she had felt strong enough, might have preferred to proclaim on her own responsibility the doctrine of "Asia for the Asiatics." Russia, however, was a very different menace to Japan in 1902 from what she was to the United States in 1823.[1]

When we compare the two passages in which the Monroe Doctrine was proclaimed, we see that, although disconnected and dealing with different matters, they are, after all, expressions of the same idea of hostility to European intervention in American affairs. Of the two, the second passage has enjoyed the greater celebrity, partly because it is a careful argument not, like the first, a mere pronouncement, but chiefly because of its reputed brilliant success in blocking the proposed intervention of the Holy Alliance in the troubles of the New World. It also emerged tri-

[1] And yet Secretary Adams had said to the British minister, October, 1820, "I find proof enough to put down the Russian argument; but how shall I answer the Russian cannon?"

umphant when its principle was violated by Napoleon III
in his attempt to create, with the aid of French troops, a
Mexican empire for Archduke Maximilian of Austria.[1]   No
one can well call it obsolete to-day; for it frequently appears
in discussion, and it would be maintained with vigor if a
case that came under its provision should arise.   None
the less, we may question whether the Monroe Doctrine in
its present form does not rest satisfactorily on the President's
simple statement about European colonization.

In the longer declaration there is much that is now somewhat antiquated.   Wedded as the Americans are to a republican form of government, they have to admit that a
monarchy is not necessarily a despotism; that in most of
the countries of Europe the people are the real sovereigns;
and on the other hand, they have seen examples of a very
queer sort of liberty in some of the republics of Latin America.   Although, in the Venezuelan dispute of 1895–1896,
the old cry about the protection of republican institutions
in the New World was raised, it was difficult for any intelligent American to believe that the inhabitants of the
disputed territory would be worse off or less secure of the
"unalienable rights of life, liberty, and the pursuit of happiness" under the rule of Queen Victoria than under the sway
of a Venezuelan dictator.   The American objection to European interference in the western hemisphere is in reality
no longer based on any "hereditary differences of political
systems."   The United States would oppose just as reso-
lutely an attempt of the French republic to acquire new
lands in South America as it would similar action on the
part of the Russian Empire.   Even if the arguments used
in the two cases might not be the same, the reasons would
at bottom be identical.

[1] Curiously enough, Mr. Seward, in his long discussions with the French
government, never once referred to the Monroe Doctrine as the basis of his
arguments.

The announcement that the "American continents are henceforth not to be considered as subjects for future colonization by any European powers" contains the kernel of the Monroe Doctrine. But the meaning of the word "colonization" has been expanded until it covers not only all acquisition of territory, but also, and to an increasing degree, forcible intervention for nearly any purpose. It is true that the contingency which called forth this clause soon passed away; for by the treaty of 1824 the southern boundary of Russian America was agreed upon to the satisfaction of both parties. President Monroe's message probably had no influence on the settlement of the dispute; indeed, he said nothing on the subject that had not been already said to Russia with more emphasis by his secretary of state. And the only foreign country that paid any particular attention to the President's dictum about colonization was England. Canning did not relish the thought that he had "called the New World into existence" to prevent Great Britain from acquiring more territory in it; nor could he "acknowledge the right of any power to proclaim such a principle, much less to bind other countries to the observance of it." He termed the declaration "very extraordinary," and one which His Majesty's government was "prepared to combat in the most unequivocal manner."

In spite of these brave words, the "very extraordinary" declaration has continued to guide the policy of the United States ever since, and has come out victorious from many encounters. Not that the Americans have always had things their own way; for in their disputes with Great Britain they have had to make concessions which have been attacked as surrenders of principle. Nor can it be denied that the English possessions in the western hemisphere are larger to-day than they were in 1823; what was then a shadowy protectorate in Belize has grown into actual ownership of the colony of British Honduras; and by the Oregon boundary treaty of 1846 lands which the Americans had claimed as theirs were awarded to Great Britain. Still, the fact that the United States has been obliged to compromise with a nation of equal strength does not signify any abandonment of principle on its part. It has even gone to the length of inviting a European sovereign to decide as to the justice of a contention; for instance, in 1871 it made the Emperor of Germany arbitrator in the San Juan da Fuca controversy. If his decision had been in favor of Great Britain, we may suspect that the Americans might have declared that he ought never to have been called in at all; but as it was, they had no cause to complain of his participation, for the islands in dispute were allotted to them.

Although the message of President Monroe attracted some attention abroad at the moment, it was soon forgotten by all but a few; only within very recent years, indeed, has the European public recognized its importance, or even realized that it existed. Meanwhile, in the country of its origin it had become a part of the national creed. The maxims set forth in it were accepted as beyond dispute, and the government, no matter what party was in power, was ready to act in accordance with them. There were, to be sure, some lapses from consistency, the most noticeable being the signing of the Clayton-Bulwer treaty with England, a step that was soon repented of; but an occasional slip of this kind was not enough to weaken the general principle. As new cases for its application have arisen, new conclusions have been drawn from it,[1] until it has been amplified in a way not foreseen by its first expounders.

[1] The declaration of President Polk in 1845 that the United States could not permit any European intervention on the North American continent, on the one hand, pushed the theory farther than it has been carried out in practice, and, on the other, it restricted the original idea by failing to include the southern continent.

In the discussions about Cuba and about the Isthmian Canal, we find it quoted again and again; but the world did not wake up to its full significance till the year 1895, when, to the astonishment of all beholders, the Americans suddenly showed themselves ready to go to war with England over a question which few persons had heard about, and which affected the direct interests of the United States in hardly the slightest degree, — the settlement of the boundary between Venezuela and British Guiana.

Secretary Olney, in his despatch of July 20, 1895, not only urged the claims of Venezuela and demanded arbitration, but also proceeded to restate the Monroe Doctrine and to explain its history and application in full. Some of his remarks were sufficiently startling. After speaking of the differences between the two hemispheres, he declared, "That distance and three thousand miles of intervening ocean make any permanent political union between an European and an American state unnatural and inexpedient, will hardly be denied"; and, he added, "The states of America, South as well as North, by geographical proximity, by natural sympathy, by similarity of Governmental Constitutions, are friends and allies, commercially and politically, of the United States." Nor was this all. "To-day," he continued, "the United States is practically sovereign on this continent, and its fiat is law upon the subjects to which it confines its interposition. . . . There is, then, a doctrine of American public law, well founded in principle and abundantly sanctioned by precedent, which entitles and requires the United States to treat as an injury to itself the forcible assumption by an European power of political control over an American state."

Lord Salisbury, in reply, flatly denied Secretary Olney's contentions, asserting that the Monroe Doctrine was neither international law nor applicable to this particular controversy. Thereupon President Cleveland laid the whole correspondence before Congress. He proposed that the United States should appoint a commission to investigate and decide upon the merits of the boundary question, and should then enforce the decision. "In making these recommendations," he added, "I am fully alive to the full responsibility incurred, and keenly realize all the consequences that may follow."

The effect of this message was instantaneous. Heretofore Mr. Cleveland had shown himself so peaceful and conservative a statesman that no one had foreseen violent action on his part. Now, all at once, a wave of passion swept through the country. The newspapers, with few exceptions, were loud in their denunciation of Great Britain; and both political parties rallied to the support of the President. When the more conservative elements had a chance to express themselves, when stocks and bonds came tumbling down, and when the nation began to realize the undefended condition of its coasts, a reaction did indeed take place; but there can be little doubt that the majority of the American people were fully determined to fight rather than to yield in the question at issue.

In England the first feeling was one of utter bewilderment; for, if the American public had known little about the Venezuelan dispute, the English knew even less, and they had never dreamed of it as a matter of serious consequence. The storm of violent abuse in the American press provoked sharp replies; but the government remained cool. As it had no thought of going to war over an insignificant matter of this sort unless absolutely forced to do so, it proceeded to extricate itself from the situation with as little loss of dignity as possible. To this end, it negotiated with Venezuela for a treaty of arbitration, and thus settled the affair without awaiting a report from the American commission. The English people felt some soreness over the incident; but they soon found an outlet for the pent-up anger which had not been discharged against the Americans by venting it on the German emperor when he sent his famous telegram to President Kruger at the time of the Jameson raid. It is fortunate that the raid did not occur before President Cleveland's message; for it was owing to the good temper shown by the British people, as well as by the government of Lord Salisbury, that the Venezuelan war cloud vanished so quickly.

Although the decision of the arbitrators awarded the larger part of the disputed territory to Great Britain, the outcome of the dispute was a notable triumph for the United States. Even if many Americans would still hesitate to indorse all the views of Secretary Olney, most of them may be said to accept his exposition of the Monroe Doctrine as an official statement of a policy now more popular than ever. Since 1896 they have seldom let slip a chance to reiterate their belief in it. At the close of the first peace congress at The Hague, the American delegates signed the resolutions agreed upon, but with the reservation that "nothing contained in this Convention shall be so construed as to require the United States of America to depart from its traditional policy of not entering upon, interfering with, or entangling itself in the political questions of international administration of any foreign state, nor shall anything contained in the said Convention be so construed as to require the relinquishment, by the United States of America, of its traditional attitude toward purely American questions." The Republican platform of 1900 proclaimed, "We reassert the Monroe Doctrine in its full extent;" and the Democratic, not to be outdone, announced, "The Monroe Doctrine as originally declared and interpreted by succeeding Presidents, is a permanent part of the foreign policy of the United States, and must at all times be maintained." Finally, President Roosevelt has again and again, in speeches and messages, referred to the Monroe Doctrine and expounded its principles.[1]

Another result of the Venezuelan controversy of 1895 was that it brought the Monroe Doctrine much more prominently to the notice of the outside world. The European powers have at last realized that, whether they like the idea or not, they must recognize that this principle is a corner-stone of American foreign policy, and that no one can venture to disregard it except at the peril of immediate trouble with the United States, — a truth further emphasized by the angry suspicion with which American public opinion viewed the sending of British and German warships to Venezuela in 1902. Under these circumstances, European nations have shown a certain readiness to acquiesce in the doctrine, not indeed with enthusiasm, but as a thing which exists and must be reckoned with, and which, in view of the strength of the United States, might as well be accepted with good grace. Most of them have made no definite declaration on the subject; but England, the power which in the past has most frequently come into collision with American political aims, now seems to have made up her mind to make the best of them. In 1903 the Duke of Devonshire declared, "Great Britain accepts the Monroe Doctrine unreservedly," a pronouncement which may be regarded as an official statement of the attitude of the British government to-day. Whether other states follow this example or not is a matter of no great consequence.[2] What is of consequence to them, as well as

[1] Perhaps the best recent exposition of the doctrine is to be found in Captain Mahan's article in the *National Review* of February, 1903.

[2] The declaration of Germany on December 11, 1901, that in her proposed measures against Venezuela she had "no purpose or intention to make even the smallest acquisition of territory on the South American continent or the islands adjacent," has been regarded as an acknowledgment of the principle, but it was nothing but a statement of intentions on a particular occasion and in no way binding for the future.

to the United States, is the question of the exact nature and scope of the doctrine at the present time.

Before attempting to examine this subject from the positive side, let us begin by clearing out of the way certain mistaken ideas. In the first place, the Monroe Doctrine is not an international "impertinence," as Bismarck is said to have called it, and as some foreign writers are still prone to regard it. Such an epithet cannot be seriously applied to the well-considered policy of one of the first nations in the world, — a policy successfully upheld for generations, and one which the country will support at any cost.

Secondly, the Monroe Doctrine is not a part of international law, although many Americans have said that it was, and although President Roosevelt has expressed the hope that it may be some day. Even if it were to be accepted by all nations, it would remain simply an expression of individual policy, respected on account of the might of the nation that asserted it. Though based on sound considerations, it is not in itself a general principle, but belongs to the same class of dogmas as, let us say, the French objection to the seating of a German prince on the throne of Spain, or as the British protectorate of the Persian Gulf and the maintenance of buffer states on the Indian frontier. Legitimate as these tenets may be, no one would call them part of international law.

Thirdly, it is not a doctrine of expansion, but only of self-defence. Although the ultimate result of measures of self-defence may conceivably be aggrandizement, the Monroe Doctrine in itself does not warrant anything of the sort. Since it presupposes the right of people to govern themselves, the Latin-American states have nothing to fear from it, — a point which has been emphasized by Secretary Root in his recent South American journey. Like other growing countries, the United States has, in the course

of its history, sometimes been guilty of aggression, of adding to its territories by force, and it may be destined to
expand still more in the future; but, whether we approve
of aggrandizement or not, we have no right to accuse the
Monroe Doctrine, which, like anything else, may be made
to serve unfair purposes.[1] Even the Golden Rule may be
distorted into a pretext for rapacity.

Fourthly, the Monroe Doctrine is no longer the literal
teaching of President Monroe. Although first expressed in
his famous message, it has in course of time been developed
to meet new conditions, a fact overlooked by Lord Salisbury
when he said that it was inapplicable to "the state of
things in which we live at the present day." [2] The question
whether its application to any particular set of circumstances would have met with the approval of Monroe and
his advisers, is one which belongs to the history of political theories, but has no bearing on actual politics.

While some of the ideas set forth by the fathers of the
doctrine have grown, others, as we have seen, are no longer
an essential part of it, even if the public has not always
recognized the fact. For instance, educated Americans
know not only that the United States is nearer in almost
every way to Europe than to South America, but that
the average American has more in common, not with the
Englishman alone, but with the German, the Frenchman, or
the Russian than with the Mexican, the Peruvian, or the
Brazilian. This has, indeed, always been true; but it was
less realized at a time when it seemed possible to divide
civilized peoples into two categories, — those who were
ruled by irresponsible authority and those who enjoyed
self-government. Such a division is now out of date, and
race feeling, on the contrary, is more active than ever.
When we remember how small and mixed is the white

[1] As for instance by President Polk when he wished to seize Yucatan.
[2] Venezuelan Correspondence.

element in some of the Latin-American countries, and how strong the prejudice against colored blood in the United States, we can appreciate some of the difficulties in the way of union of soul with the sister republics.

After all, we ask, would not a close bond between the United States and Greater Britain, and one between Spain and her former revolted colonies, be more in keeping with the tendencies of the day? Anglo-American friendship and Pan-Americanism can, of course, exist side by side; but they might easily conflict, and the question might arise as to which had the more natural foundation. In this age of world powers, geographical divisions are disappearing even faster than differences of government. If "Europe" is antiquated as a political conception, why is not "America" equally so? If it is, the Monroe Doctrine would appear to rest upon a fiction.

But this is going too far. The geographical situation of the United States, and its "paramount interest" in the affairs of the western hemisphere, impose upon it certain rules of policy toward its immediate neighbors, whether there be an inborn communion of sentiment between them or not. Furthermore, it is wise to cultivate good and profitable relations of every kind with all countries. The reasons for cordiality will vary according to circumstances. For instance, the grounds for friendship between France and Spain are quite dissimilar to those existing between France and Russia. A certain community of institutions, interests, and ideals does exist between the republics of the western hemisphere, though it would be hard to say just how far it extends. Nothing, therefore, could be more legitimate than the attempt to strengthen and multiply these ties. To make them more real, it is wise to dwell frequently upon them.

It must be admitted that there are persons, even in the United States, who think it would be better if certain parts of Latin America were under the control of some European power, instead of being left to the guidance of their own unrestrained wills. If we accept this view, we cannot defend the United States for protecting their independence except on the ground that such protection is necessary for the furtherance of legitimate, if selfish, American interests. In that case, the question as to what would be best for the world and for civilization might be rather delicate. However, it is unfair to say that the Monroe Doctrine is an entirely selfish policy. It may not be so full of altruism as Americans are inclined to think; but it has at least been unselfishly applied so far as the states of Latin America are concerned. No one who has studied the expansion of Europe in the last part of the nineteenth century can escape the conclusion that the partition of lands in Asia and the scramble for Africa might, but for the Monroe Doctrine, have been accompanied, or followed, by a movement of the same sort in Latin America. The conditions in many of her states have been such as to give plenty of pretext for foreign interference; and here, as well as elsewhere, the rivalry of the great powers would only have hastened the seizure of lands weakly held. There may never have been any deep designs of this kind, but expansion has often been haphazard. The danger was none the less there.

In return for the immense service it has thus rendered, the United States has as yet demanded absolutely nothing. Of course in its attempts to promote friendly relations between Anglo-Saxon and Latin America, it has not forgotten material advantages, and it has made the most of friendly sentiments in order to help American commerce to the advantage of all parties. Motives of this sort are fair enough in themselves, and are usual under like circumstances in private, as well as in public, life. The Latin Americans are not forced to buy goods from the United States if they can get them elsewhere with more profit. So far, then, they have good cause to be grateful for the existence of the Monroe Doctrine, and for the way in which it has been applied up to the present day.

As has been well said by Captain Mahan, "The precise value of the Monroe Doctrine is understood very loosely by most Americans, but the effect of the familiar phrase has been to develop a national sensitiveness which is a more frequent cause of war than material interests." The application of the theory may well vary according to the temper of the time or the views of the administration; but it has steadily tended to become broader. Thus the Venezuelan controversy of 1895–1896 may be regarded as having settled the point that, in a boundary dispute between a European power and an American one, the former must be willing to submit to arbitration; but so far the United States has not demanded that the arbitrator should be an American: indeed, at the very time when the Venezuelan discussion had reached its most critical phase, a long-standing difference as to the frontier of French Guiana and Brazil was referred to the Emperor of Russia for decision without raising a protest from Washington.[1]

Nevertheless, American public opinion is increasingly opposed to European intervention of any kind in transatlantic affairs, and may be expected to forbid in the future things which it has tolerated in the past, — a change which may be ascribed to a consciousness of greater strength, as well as to the keen chauvinism of the national sentiment to-day. Although admitting in theory the right of European nations to obtain redress from delinquent American ones, even by force, the United States has in

[1] In spite of the declaration of Mr. Frelinghuysen (January 4, 1883), that "The Department of State will not sanction an arbitration by European states in South American difficulties even with the consent of the parties."

practice become very suspicious of such action, and is hostile to any landing of European troops on American soil. The experience of Egypt, for example, shows how easily a temporary occupation may become a permanent one, even when a promise to evacuate has been made in perfect good faith.

While the United States was occupied with the Civil War, the Spaniards, heedless of its protests, reëstablished their former sovereignty at San Domingo. They did so with the consent of the Dominicans, though they were soon driven out again. With this case in mind, President Grant declared in 1870 that "No European power can acquire by any means, — war, colonization, or annexation, — even when the annexed people demands it, any portion of American territory."

A still further extension of the principle is the idea, now generally accepted, that no transfer of American territory from one European power to another can henceforth be allowed, — a proposition that was set forth in the particular case of Cuba as early as 1808. The United States permits the existence of foreign colonies in its neighborhood, but will resist any changes in their alien ownership; for such changes would be in the nature of the colonization which it forbids. We may feel sure that it would risk all the hazards of war rather than acquiesce in the sale of St. Thomas to Germany. This might seem to be pushing the doctrine pretty far; for it would limit the right of free transaction between two independent nations, one of them a world power. Nevertheless, it would not be unprecedented, and might be justified by the importance of the interests involved. The establishment of such a fortified coaling station within a short distance of the American coast would be something which the United States would no more tolerate, so long as it was capable of effectual resistance, than England and France would agree to the transfer from Spain to Germany of the African fortress of Ceuta.

Other complications in the West Indies are also conceivable. It has been asserted [1] that, if Holland were to become part of the Germanic Confederation, the United States could not consent to the inclusion of the Dutch colonies of the western hemisphere. This view, we may surmise, would almost certainly be taken by the American government and people if a union between Holland and Germany were brought about by some sudden act. In case, however, of the gradual absorption of Holland into the German Empire by some slow process of ever closer alliance, it might be hard to say when or how the Americans could interfere, although they would doubtless wish to do so. They would also, in all probability, object to the cession of Guadeloupe and Martinique as an indemnity, if France were defeated in a war with Germany or Great Britain. If this supposition is correct, they thus practically guarantee to France her possessions in the Caribbean Sea.

It may be noted in passing that since the declaration of President Grant there has been a transfer of American territory from one European power to another, and that it met with no opposition on the part of the United States. When, in 1878, Sweden ceded to France the little island of St. Barthélemi, the Americans took no notice of the proceeding, an indifference which may be explained partly by their lack of interest in foreign affairs so soon after the Civil War, and partly by the insignificance of the island ceded, which did not materially add to the strength of the French in West Indian waters. It is nevertheless strange 'that no attention whatever was paid to the transaction, and that, though it seems to present a certain analogy to a sale of St. Thomas to Germany, it seems to have escaped the notice of writers on the Monroe Doctrine, as well as of American historians generally.

The extreme interpretation of the Monroe Doctrine may

[1] By Captain Mahan, in the *National Review*, February, 1903.

I

be found in the assertion, first made officially by President
Grant, that "The time is not so far distant when, in the
natural course of events, the European political connection
with this continent will cease;" and the same idea has often
been repeated since, notably by Secretary Olney, with his
usual emphasis, in 1895. No wonder that European nations
holding territory in America have been disquieted by it,
even though there is as yet no serious foundation for such
a fear. Monroe himself said explicitly, "With the existing
colonies or dependencies of any European power we have
not interfered, and shall not interfere," — a declaration of
policy which has ever since been scrupulously observed by
the United States, except in the case of Cuba, where circumstances were of a peculiar nature. The Americans may be
counted upon to sympathize with any people in the western
hemisphere who are struggling to emancipate themselves
from the rule of a European mother country; but no European nation need apprehend aggressive action on the part
of the United States so long as its colonies are contented
with their lot.

Thus far we have been considering the Monroe Doctrine
from its positive side, — that of its advantages to America.
Let us now look at the negative, — at the obligations which
it entails. We may, of course, say that it does not entail
any, if we believe that it is a matter of selfish policy, upheld
by physical force only. That it does depend chiefly on force
is obvious, — it would never have been accepted by other
nations on account of its inherent virtue; and yet in up-
holding it, the Americans justify their action by moral
considerations, and admit the existence of duties on their
part. What are, then, some of these duties?

The first question that arises is, Are the Americans bound
to carry out the doctrine they have proclaimed, even when
it is contrary to their interests to do so? Such a limitation
would be out of keeping with the practical nature of the

Anglo-Saxon, which makes him dislike being subject to mere theories. As a matter of fact, in spite of the applause which greeted Monroe's words, American public opinion showed itself lukewarm about the Congress of Panama, a meeting called shortly afterwards with the avowed intention of furthering the new creed. The country preferred to reserve its own liberty of action without hampering itself by outside agreements. In the course of debate on the subject, Henry Clay declared that the President's message was meant to enlighten opinion at home and not to be construed as a promise to any foreign nation. When, on various occasions since that time, the United States has refused to listen to appeals for assistance from one or another of the Latin-American states, it has, of course, always been charged with treason to its principles; but it has felt free to act according to its own judgment. In the case of the French intervention in Mexico, for instance, the government at Washington did not adopt an attitude of resolute opposition until the Civil War at home was nearly over. On the other hand, in 1895 Secretary Olney, supported by President Cleveland, took the ground that the Monroe Doctrine "entitles and requires" the United States to intervene in behalf of Venezuela. If we accept this view, we admit the existence of a serious obligation; but a country whose "fiat is law" is likely to decide for itself whether the situation "requires" action on its part or not. Americans are far too realistic to sacrifice themselves on the altar of their own shibboleths. When they find these becoming antiquated, they will never hesitate to adapt them to circumstances or, if need be, to abandon them altogether.

One obligation imposed by the Monroe Doctrine has recently been coming into unpleasant prominence. If a Latin-American state is guilty of an injury to a European power for which redress can be fairly exacted, and if there is no effective way in which punishment can be applied except by occupation of American soil, what will happen? Although the government at Washington has repeatedly declared that it will not protect any state in wrong-doing, and has not prevented punishment in the past, public opinion is becoming more and more unwilling to permit a European occupation of American territory for any reason whatsoever. This means that the United States must accept the responsibility of satisfying the injured party, a thing which it can very likely do only by taking action against the wrong-doer. But the role of "international policeman" in American affairs is one which the country has no desire to assume; for it would very soon lead to conflict with some of the other republics, who, while they welcome the Monroe Doctrine as a protection against Europe, dread nothing so much as interference on the part of their powerful sister at the north. Moreover, besides acting as guardian of the peace, the United States would have to play the arbiter as to the right and the wrong of any question under dispute; in fact, there is no end to the difficulties in which it might become involved.

These difficulties are now well recognized. President Roosevelt deserves credit for having been one of the first to perceive and to face them. Unluckily, even facing a difficulty does not remove it. The policy of the government at the present time seems to be to make the best of each case as it comes along, to try to persuade all parties to be reasonable, to warn the Latin-American republics that they will not be shielded, and may have to be punished, if they misbehave, but at the same time to keep the Monroe Doctrine prominently before the eyes of Europe. A conspicuous instance of an attempt of this kind to arrange matters equitably between a debtor American state and its European creditors is seen in the agreement with San Domingo. The trouble with this opportunist policy of the administration is that every intervention of a strong power in the affairs of a weak one tends to establish a protectorate of some sort.

The theory of a natural separation between the New World and the Old is an essential part of the reasoning on which the Monroe Doctrine was based. In conformity with this idea, in the same breath in which it protests against European colonization of America it announces with equal emphasis, "In the wars of the European powers in matters relating to themselves we have never taken any part, nor does it comport with our policy to do so." This declaration has been repeated in one form or another many times,[1] and has been adhered to. President Monroe himself had intended to put into his message of December, 1823, an expression of sympathy with the Greek revolution, but was persuaded by his secretary of state, Mr. Adams, not to do so, as it would appear like an interference in European affairs. The same policy has been followed ever since. American public men have sometimes criticised European events with a frankness, not to say a rudeness, which has provoked anger on the other side; but they have had no thought of taking action in affairs which did not concern them. Not that the United States has not felt the duty of protecting its citizens and its commerce when they have been in danger of suffering injury. This is a right common to all states; but such a thing, let us say, as the sending of an ironclad to Smyrna to look after American missionaries would be a very different matter from taking part in a congress to discuss the Eastern question. The United States, while looking after its own interests wherever they have been affected, has sedulously kept out of general European politics.

President Monroe talked only about Europe and America, without taking into consideration other parts of the world. What is the bearing of his doctrine upon Asia? Is the

[1] Notably at the first Hague Conference.

United States confined by traditional policy to the western hemisphere? or, since Asia is not mentioned in the President's message, is that continent open to every kind of American activity?

Europe would have been glad to see the first view prevail, and this was the one indorsed by the Democratic platform in 1900. In truth, it seems absurd to assert that the Atlantic is a natural barrier between peoples, but that the Pacific is not. Nevertheless, the second interpretation has won the day: the Americans have taken an active part in the opening up of Eastern Asia, they have frequently joined with other powers in common action, and they have established themselves in the Philippines. After all, it would have been strange if they, the nearest civilized neighbors to the Far East, had sat by while their European competitors disposed of it to suit themselves, and this, forsooth, because a principle which they had themselves invented for a totally different set of circumstances might be construed as restricting their liberty of action! The Americans are not given to doctrinaire weakness of this sort. When the question came up in a concrete form, they decided that their rule of non-interference in European affairs did not prevent them from acquiring islands in the Pacific, no matter in which hemisphere they were situated. Captain Mahan says: "In my apprehension, Europe construed by the Monroe Doctrine would include Africa with the Levant and India. . . . It would not include Japan, China, nor the Pacific generally." This definition, though somewhat arbitrary and not final, represents fairly well the present geographical limits of the doctrine in the American mind.

There is, however, another side to this Asiatic question which is usually overlooked in the United States. If Asia does not come within the scope of the Monroe Doctrine, why should the Asiatic powers feel bound to observe it? If it has not prevented the Americans from establishing themselves in the eastern hemisphere, how can it exclude the Japanese from the western? Would Japanese possession of Ecuador, let us say, be more serious for the United States than American ownership of the Philippines is for Japan? We can only reply that facts have to be taken as they are. Ten years ago Japan was not in a position to defend the principle of "Asia for the Asiatics"; and to-day she has to accept the existing situation, just as the United States has to with regard to European possessions in the New World. True as this may be, the Americans, in forbidding Asiatic interference in the western hemisphere, cannot fall back on the argument of reciprocity which they apply to Europe.

Yet even toward Europe their policy is not quite what it once was; for it cannot be denied that of late years they have shown a greater disposition than of old to take part in European questions. As a civilized nation the United States has, of course, appeared at various international scientific and philanthropic meetings; it was also represented at the Berlin conference of 1885, which laid the foundations of the Congo Free State, and at Algeciras in 1906, where it helped to regulate the affairs of Morocco, even signing (if with some reservations) the general act of agreement. Furthermore, Secretary Hay protested against the oppression of the Jews in Roumania, and in his official capacity transmitted to Russia a Jewish-American petition about the Kishinev massacre, — acts which, whether we approve of them or not, were scarcely in consonance with the traditions of American foreign policy. None of these things have been of decisive consequence in themselves, but they may be taken as indications of a rather different attitude toward the future, the more so as they are in keeping with the growing tendency among all nations to be interested everywhere. In the event of a repetition of the

Armenian massacres of 1895, the United States, whatever
may be the precepts of the Monroe Doctrine, would probably not remain as passive as it did then; and we can conceive of its taking action to protect the natives in the
Congo Free State.

Now if this is so, if the United States is going to abandon that portion of the Monroe Doctrine which forbids
interference in European affairs, how can it nsist that
Europe shall not meddle in those of America? Logically,
perhaps, it can not; but, on the broad ground of national
welfare, it might maintain that its intere ts were "paramount" in one region without necessarily being non-
existent elsewhere. An attitude of this sort would,
however, be somewhat weak morally, and would give the
European powers a legitimate cause of complaint against
the restrictions now imposed upon them. This is one reason
why the Americans are anxious to keep out of purely
European questions. Whether they will be able to do so
is another matter.

CHAPTER VI

THE SPANISH WAR

EARLY in the year 1901, a foreign ambassador at Washington remarked in the course of conversation that, although he had been in America only a short time, he had seen two different countries,—the United States before the war with Spain, and the United States since the war with Spain. This was a picturesque way of expressing the truth, now generally accepted, that the war of 1898 was a turning-point in the history of the American republic. The reason therefor is usually summed up in the phrase that since that date the United States has been a world power. This assertion is, however, vigorously disputed by two sets of opponents, and on exactly opposite grounds. Some writers labor to prove that the United States is not, or if it is, ought not to be, a world power to-day; others maintain that it has always been one, because ever since its independence it has been interested in affairs in many parts of the world, — which is also true of Holland. Evidently the term has not the same meaning to the two parties. But without entering into discussion, we can confine ourselves to the indisputable fact that the Spanish War brought about in American public feeling a change important enough to mark the beginning of an epoch.

When we come to analyze the causes of this sudden evolution, we must concede that at first sight the magnitude of the result seems out of all proportion to that of the military operations. The war was a short, bloodless one between two nations of very unequal resources. There were but three battles worthy of the name, — two on the water and one on the land. The two sea-fights were brilliantly conducted, and the completeness of the success, coupled with the almost entire absence of loss on the part of the Americans, constituted a pleasing testimony to the efficiency of their new navy; but the difference in strength between the combatants made the victory a foregone conclusion. The one battle on land was marked by creditable fighting on both sides, rather than by any display of generalship, and the forces engaged and the losses incurred were too small for the encounter to deserve the name of a great battle. Though the United States had good reason to be satisfied with the outcome, there was, when all is said, no cause for undue elation; nor had there been any severe strain on the country.

In considering the causes of the war, we should remember, to begin with, that the relations between Spain and the United States had never been really cordial, nor was there any reason why they should have been. The Americans had inherited the anti-Spanish prejudices of their English ancestors, and the traditions of their feuds, and as colonists they had taken part in the wars of the seventeenth and eighteenth centuries. It is true that Spain had fought on their side in their struggle for independence, but under compulsion as the ally of France, and after expressly warning the French against the perils of such a course of action. The Spaniards, in spite of their old hatred of England, could not but see that the successful revolt of the British colonies would prove a dangerous example to their own; accordingly, at the peace negotiations in Paris in 1783, the Spanish government did all that it could to keep the territory of the new republic within as narrow limits as possible. The Americans, on their part, had a separate understanding with Great Britain about the northern boundary of Florida, — an understanding which led to a prolonged boundary dispute with Spain.

This boundary dispute was but the first of a series that lasted for more than a generation. The plain truth was that the Americans coveted the valuable and thinly settled Spanish territories which shut them off from the Gulf of Mexico. On one side, we find a lusty, rapidly growing nation, keenly alive to its own rights and interests and not too mindful of those of others. Opposed to it was a weak people with a decrepit government, unable to occupy effectively much of the land it held, and too feeble to keep order in its possessions or to prevent legitimate cause of complaint on the part of its neighbors. As might have been expected, the conduct of the Americans was rough and high-handed, that of the Spanish shuffling and dilatory. For years these controversies continued until they were ended by the sale, almost under compulsion, of East Florida to the young republic. West Florida had been previously occupied by force.

Almost before these matters were settled, the Americans gave fresh cause of offence by recognizing the independence of the revolted Spanish colonies, — a recognition that would have been granted earlier if the government had not wished to make sure of Florida before offering Spain further provocation. A worse blow soon followed. In the minds of the Americans, the Monroe Doctrine was primarily directed against the Holy Alliance, not against Spain. Though they did not believe that she could reconquer her lost possessions, they did not contest her right to try. None the less, from the Spanish point of view, the adoption of this principle was a grievous injury; for it cut Spain off in her hour of weakness from the hope of outside aid, without which she was unable to recover her territories.

Surely she could not be expected to feel anything but resentment for unfriendly conduct so persistent and so unprovoked. Yet in time old grievances might have been forgotten, had no new ones been added. After her insurgent children had achieved their independence, she no longer held a foot of land on either American continent, so there would have been nothing left to quarrel about if it had not been for Cuba.

A glance at the map is enough to convince any one of the unique importance of this island to the United States. Strategically it commands at one end the entrance to the Gulf of Mexico, — the outlet to the huge Mississippi Valley, — and at the other it fronts on the Caribbean Sea and any future isthmian canal. Its situation may be compared with that of Crete in the Eastern Mediterranean, but Cuba is much the larger and the richer of the two.

The worth of this "Pearl of the Antilles" was so evident that the Americans appreciated it from the first. Even Jefferson, who was a cautious, conservative statesman, disinclined to an adventurous foreign policy, admitted that he had always "looked on Cuba as the most interesting addition which could ever be made to our system of states." After the purchase of Florida, the thought of owning the farther side of the entrance to the Gulf became more attractive still. In any event, the Americans were determined that, if Cuba could not be theirs, it should not pass into the hands of any strong naval power. For a while they were in equal dread that Napoleon might get possession of it, and that the English might forestall him in doing so. In 1808 President Jefferson officially declared that the United States would view with alarm the cession of Cuba to either England or France. The same fears came up again at the time of the French intervention in Spain in 1823; and two years later the government at Washington sent a circular note to its ministers abroad with the declaration that it would oppose the transfer of the island to any other European power. At a later date we find fresh anxiety of the same kind. In 1840 the United States went so far as to offer to guarantee Cuba to the Spaniards against foreign aggression, but refused to join England and France in a triple agreement to this end. Contrary to their usual principles and to the spirit of the Monroe Doctrine, the Americans did not even wish to see the island independent, preferring that it should remain as it was rather than fall into any hands but their own. They regarded it as of immense value to them, and they never had anything but contempt for the military strength of Spain. For many years the real clew to their policy was to be found in the negro question at home.

Unlike most of the Spanish-American colonies on the mainland, Cuba contained a large servile population, whose numbers, after the nominal abolition of the slave-trade, were kept up till about 1860 by clandestine shipments. Independence by the aid of South America, where slavery had disappeared with Spanish rule, meant emancipation of the negroes, and, since at that time the whites were in the minority, probably black domination in the end. Such a prospect was more than enough to excite violent alarm in the South. It is true that even the Southern States had sympathized with the revolt of Latin America; but they had never consented to recognize the republics of Haiti and San Domingo, and had looked askance at the Congress of Panama because those states had been invited to participate in it.[1] To the Southerners a republic of emancipated slaves was not only a thing abhorrent in itself, but in their near vicinity it meant a source of contagion, a menace to the whole structure of their society. The American government therefore set its face against proposed attempts on

[1] Haiti and San Domingo were not recognized by the United States until after the outbreak of the Civil War.

the part of Mexico and Venezuela to continue the war of liberation by extending it to the Spanish islands, and it thus helped preserve them to Spain for another sixty years.

As the nineteenth century advanced, the slaveholders of the South became more eager in their desires. Here, at their door, was a fresh supply of slaves, a commodity whose price was rising steadily, and, what was of still greater consequence, material for two or three new slave states by means of which the dreaded preponderance of the North might be averted. In the West, where the successes of the Mexican War had stimulated a strong sentiment in favor of national expansion, annexation had also many partisans. Between 1845 and 1860, therefore, we find Congress continually debating the Cuban question, and successive administrations forming new plans to get hold of the coveted territory. In 1848 and 1853 attempts were made to buy it from Spain, but these were sharply repulsed at Madrid. In 1854 the American ministers to London, Paris, and Madrid met and issued the "Ostend Manifesto," which proclaimed the right of the United States to take Cuba by force in case a reasonable offer of purchase were refused. They had gone, however, farther than the country was ready to follow, and were disavowed in Washington. By this time, too, opinion in the Northern States was becoming roused to such vigorous opposition that annexation finally ceased to be feasible, and a discreditable chapter in American annals came to an end. It was an important fact during the whole period that the population of Cuba itself remained quiet and apparently contented. There was no rising of sufficient size to offer a decent pretext for outside interference.

Soon the situation was reversed. Just as the Americans, after the Civil War and the emancipation of the Southern slaves, had ceased to want the island, an insurrection broke out there, which a few years earlier would have tempted them to intervene. In 1868 an uprising took place that the home government was unable to subdue, in spite of the large number of troops brought into the field. For ten years the struggle dragged along, without any decisive results, but with continual and unavoidable friction between Spain and the United States. Cuban sympathizers prepared filibustering expeditions on American soil, some of which were checked by the authorities, while others either escaped notice or were connived at in ways that gave rise to much recrimination between Washington and Madrid. The ill treatment of American citizens residing in the island (usually persons of Cuban origin) was a perpetual cause of complaint, and various inconveniences, especially the disturbance of trade, kept up irritation in the United States. Finally the shooting of Americans captured on the filibustering vessel *Virginius* almost brought on war. Yet, after all, peace was preserved, and the Spaniards were allowed to settle their affairs without direct intervention, although this would surely have come if the fighting had continued much longer. By the Convention of Zanjon, Spain made concessions to the insurgents, who thereupon laid down their arms.

Then followed seventeen quiet years. Slavery was abolished, and the island prospered. The Americans were too busy at home to pay much attention to it, and if the Spaniards had succeeded in contenting the natives, would have continued indifferent. Meanwhile a considerable amount of American capital had been invested in Cuba, the holders of which were not in favor of rebellion or of disturbance from any quarter; but their presence made it certain that if disorders should again arise, the government at Washington would have to interest itself, whether it wished to or not. In 1895 a new revolt started, which soon gathered strength enough to defy the efforts to suppress it, and as it went on fruitlessly

month after month and year after year, the feeling grew
ever stronger in the United States that the situation was
intolerable. It was not merely that the Americans had a
natural sympathy for the insurgents as a people striving
to free themselves from tyranny, but they were tired of a
commotion at their very door. The conviction took firm
hold that something must be done for the " abatement
of a nuisance," if on no other account. Then occurred
the mysterious incident of the blowing up of the *Maine*
in Havana harbor, which greatly excited the nation and
hastened, but did not in itself cause, the actual outbreak
of hostilities.

There is a curious resemblance between the conduct of
the United States at this time and that of Russia before the
Turkish war of 1877–1878. In each case we find at the
head of the government a man of peaceful disposition,
who consented slowly and reluctantly to a conflict forced
upon him by the pressure of public opinion and by difficulties which seemed otherwise inextricable. In each country
the popular passions were for many months continually
inflamed by fresh incidents. The risings of the small states
of the Balkans and the Cuban insurrection appealed to
the sympathies of the masses in Russia and America respectively, the sentiments aroused being at bottom the
same, though cloaked under different names. In one instance, the appeal was that of fellow-Christians, of brother
Slavs, to their traditional friend and protector; in the
other, it was that of fellow-Americans straining to
cast off a European yoke and looking hopefully to
the great republic which had always represented the
cause of liberty. The Bulgarian atrocities and the
horrors of reconcentration, both awful enough in themselves, were described and exaggerated by a sensational
and sometimes unscrupulous press, till the feelings of
Russia in 1877 and of the United States in 1898 were

wrought up to such a pitch that the governments deemed that they had no choice but to yield. Both Russians and Americans began war with a declaration that they were acting from unselfish motives, a statement which, as far as the great majority of the people were concerned, may be regarded as true. Later, when the wars ended in victory, and both countries believed that they had a right to compensate themselves for their expenditure of effort and for their losses, they were at once accused of hypocrisy by the outside world, which declared that their motive from the first had been sheer greed. But we note a difference in the outcome. After a far more exhausting struggle, the triumphant Russians got much less in return than did the Americans; not because they deserved or desired less, but because the political situation was such that it was worth the while of other powers to restrain them by force if necessary. We may also note that the position of Cuba after Spanish evacuation was not unlike that of Bulgaria immediately after the treaty of Berlin. Fortunately for themselves, the Americans showed much more tact in dealing with a delicate situation than did the Russians.

In order to demonstrate that the United States was acting from no selfish motives, Congress, in declaring war against Spain, proclaimed that its intention was to free Cuba from Spanish rule, and not to annex the island. This self-denying ordinance was voted in a moment of excitement, and in all sincerity. When the war ended, the country felt that a promise had been made; and the promise was kept, in spite of much temptation to break it, and in spite of the usual specious reasoning to prove that it need not be regarded as binding. History has shown that the most solemn assurances of the sort, even when made in perfect good faith, somehow or other lose their force as time goes on. Other nations may talk loudly of violated pledges,

K

but the one interested can prove to its own satisfaction that it is no longer bound by the word rashly given. We must admit that by the Platt amendment the Americans attached conditions to the independence which they bestowed; but, though we may regret that there was a flaw in their generosity, recent events have proved that the conditions were wise. Whatever may be the fate of Cuba in the future, the treatment she has received at the hands of the United States in the decade since she was made free will remain something to be proud of.

The liberation of Cuba was not the only result of the Spanish War; the effects on the United States were many and important. Considering how little fighting took place, the territorial changes brought about by the conflict were very large. They gave the Americans a stronger strategic position in the Gulf of Mexico and in the Caribbean Sea, coaling stations in the Pacific, and a base of operations in the Far East. But, though they made the United States stronger for offensive purposes, in some ways they weakened it for defensive ones. Up to 1898 Alaska was the only possession which could be seized by a foe with a superior fleet; now Hawaii, the Philippines, and other Pacific islands, as well as Porto Rico, could hardly be defended against an adversary who controlled the sea. None the less, however the gain and the loss may balance, they both represent far-reaching changes in the military position of the country; yet even these are not sufficient to account for the difference in the American attitude before and after the war.

Like so many other things, an attitude has two faces, a subjective and an objective one. The people of the republic, if not actually transformed by their short victorious conflict, were much affected by it, both as they saw themselves and as others saw them. To the greater part of Europe the war itself, and the course which it took, came as an unpleasant surprise. During most of the nine-

teenth century the United States had enjoyed a remarkable popularity abroad. Many Englishmen were well disposed toward it because it was inhabited by their kin; Frenchmen were proud of it because they had assisted in its creation; Russia was a traditional friend; liberals all over Europe sympathized with its democratic institutions; zealous Roman Catholics were pleased with the flourishing condition of their church across the water. Countless European children had delighted in the Indians of Fenimore Cooper, and millions of kindly souls had read and wept over *Uncle Tom's Cabin*. Travelling Americans, though sometimes forth-putting, were open-handed and good-natured. In the later years of the century American students in numbers had frequented the art schools in Paris and the universities in Germany, and had given a good account of themselves. The fame of the country's wealth and prosperity, of the ingenuity and practical abilities of its inhabitants, and especially of their eagerness to make money, was wide-spread. But in the great game of international politics they took little part. European statesmen could usually leave them out of their reckonings. Well-informed persons were aware that the United States was a power of great resources, — how great in a military way had been shown by the Civil War, — and that, as the Mexican, and quite lately the Venezuelan, incident had proved, it was resolved to stand by its traditional policy. But if one let that policy alone and kept clear of the Monroe Doctrine, in which most of Europe had small interest, then in practice the United States need not often be taken into consideration. It belonged, so to speak, to a different world.

All this was changed by the Spanish War. Continental Europe, without defending Spanish misgovernment in Cuba, regarded the action of the Americans as brutal aggression against a smaller nation. How could it be pleased with the cry, so often raised across the sea, that European rule in the western hemisphere ought to be brought to an end? But the Americans did more than expel the Spaniards from Cuba and Porto Rico: they proved that they possessed a most efficient modern fleet, they crossed the Pacific and established themselves in the Far East, they threatened to send ships to attack Spain in her own waters. It was evident that they had assumed a new position among nations; that henceforth they would have to be counted with as one of the chief forces in international affairs. Although, as usually happens for the victorious, a revulsion of sentiment soon took place in their favor, and many persons hastened to testify that they had always been on their side, still the appearance of a new factor of such magnitude interfered with many old calculations. The former easy popularity of the United States was gone, probably never to return. Some idealists mournfully declared that what the Union had gained in political importance it had lost in moral greatness; that it had forfeited its real eminence, and was now only one more huge, aggressive, selfish power. Be this as it may, its situation, for better or for worse, was radically changed in the eyes of the outside world.

The change was equally decisive in the consciousness of the Americans themselves. The war aroused within them a feeling of strength which had until then been latent. It opened their eyes to new horizons, suggested new outlets for their energies, and made them confident that they could deal with problems which had never before attracted their attention. They had always been proud of their country, — aggressively so, foreigners thought, — but they had regarded it as something different from the others, and leading its own life apart. Now, all at once, they were willing to give up their isolation and plunge into the fray. They felt that the day had come when they were called upon to play a part in the broader affairs of mankind even at the cost of sacrificing some of their cherished ideals. They were indeed unable, as well as unwilling, to return to their earlier point of view. Full of joyous self-reliance, they were prepared to meet all the difficulties and to accept all the burdens of their new position.

CHAPTER VII

THE ACQUISITION OF COLONIES

DURING the negotiations which preceded the war with
Spain, as well as in the course of the struggle itself,
the American people, regardless of party, supported the
policy of the government almost with unanimity. This
unanimity vanished when it became necessary to decide
what use should be made of their victory. While the public
as a whole hesitated between respect for its cherished traditions and the allurements of the new prospects, the more
partisan on both sides wrangled fiercely over the question
whether the country should or should not retain its new
acquisitions. The two points of view are usually called the
Imperialist and the Anti-imperialist; but whereas the Anti-
imperialists have adopted their name and gloried in it, the
so-called Imperialists have never quite accepted an epithet
fastened on them by their adversaries. After all, the title
is hardly in keeping with American republican ideals, whatever may be the truth about the policy which it represents.

In the long and bitter disputes as to what should be
done with the new insular possessions, argument centred
on the retention of the Philippines. Anti-imperialists
did, indeed, condemn the annexation of Hawaii. They
declared that the revolution by which the queen had
been overthrown was a usurpation of power by a handful
of foreigners who would never have succeeded but for the

landing of American troops, and that the islands properly belonged to their native inhabitants, — a view which President Cleveland had taken when he withdrew from the consideration of the Senate the treaty submitted by his predecessor. The annexation was carried out during the excitement of the Spanish War, not by treaty, — for fear that the necessary two-thirds majority could not be secured in the Senate, — but by joint resolution of the two houses of Congress. However, no one could deny the unique naval situation of Hawaii in the Pacific; and, much as the Anti-imperialists might condemn the means by which the territory had been acquired, the fact that the natives now formed a small and dwindling minority of the population rendered it difficult to put them once more in control. In the case of Porto Rico, although again the extreme Anti-imperialists were opposed to acquisition, they were deprived of their strongest plea by the evident willingness of the inhabitants to enjoy the benefits of American rule. In regard to the Philippines no such excuse could be put forward. Here there was no pretence of a wish to come under American domination; on the contrary, the islands had first to be conquered from a people that was doing the very thing with which Americans had been taught to sympathize, — striving to obtain its independence.

Amidst the multitude of conflicting statements at this time, we can recognize a few main contentions which reappear again and again. In the first place, the Anti-imperialists asserted that there were plenty of unsolved problems at home to which the nation should devote all its energies instead of squandering them elsewhere, especially as the Americans had no experience in colonial matters. To this, reply was made that every colonial power had duties to discharge at home, but that the management of domestic affairs, far from being interfered with by the care of distant possessions, gained from the knowledge and the sense of responsibility required in dealing with them; that a state could never have too many outlets for the energies of its citizens; that, even if the Americans lacked experience in colonial matters, they could profit by the experience of others, and they were starting unfettered by previous mistakes. They were not inferior in intelligence to other ruling peoples; why, then, should they not succeed even better? The political and commercial arguments employed on both sides turned on such topics as the relative advantages of extension and concentration, — on the question whether trade follows the flag, and kindred debatable themes, — with the result, of course, that neither side was in the least convinced by the other. But the fiercest and most effective attacks of the Anti-imperialists were based on the charge that the new policy was an abandonment, not only of the wise traditions of the fathers of the republic, but of the noble ideals which had made the Union honored throughout the world. Even the Monroe Doctrine was called into service, but elicited the reply that it had no reference to Asia. Besides, it was not a lifeless bond, but one which could be adapted to meet new circumstances.

The advocates of a policy of expansion met the assertion that, according to American ideals, government should be by the consent of the governed, with the declaration that this was true only when the governed were capable of taking care of themselves; that, when they were not, the progress of the governed — which meant also the advancement of civilization — was more important than their consent. This at once raised the question whether the Filipinos were capable of self-government, and if so to what extent, — a point which no mere argument could settle. With a certain inconsistency, the Democratic party, which had, at least tacitly, accepted the Southern view that the negroes could not be allowed to vote where they were numerous, proclaimed, none the less, that the Filipinos were quite capable of ruling themselves. As the Republican party, on the other hand, had abandoned the attempt to impose negro suffrage on the South, its refusal of independence to an "inferior race" in the tropics was less illogical.

The charge that the acquisition of colonial possessions was contrary to the traditional policy of the United States was met in one of two ways, — either by admitting its truth but declaring that the time had now come for a change, or by denying the historical accuracy of the statement. According to the writers who support the latter view, colonization has been the dominant characteristic of the whole growth of the country. Not only has the United States been from the first a rapidly expanding power, adding to its territories in every generation, but it has repeatedly held lands which were virtually colonies, whose inhabitants did not enjoy the rights of self-government. Not to speak of the Indians, — "the wards of the nation," — we must not forget that in Louisiana, Florida, New Mexico, and California, there were French and Spanish populations which were in no way consulted when they were handed over to the United States. In each of these cases the form of government first instituted was a military despotism, albeit one of short duration. After all, one might ask, what is a colony? If we declare that the title cannot be applied to contiguous territory, then it is a mistake to term Siberia and Central Asia colonies of Russia, as has often been done. The settlement of Siberia has taken place in much the same way as the opening up of the American West. What importance has mere separation by a stretch of water? It has never been the custom to call Ireland an English colony, even if it does not touch Great Britain, and was held down by force in the past and at one time systematically colonized. Colonization is nothing

but a form of national growth, which, from being internal,
becomes external when the home territory no longer offers
a sufficient field for expansion. It is no mere coincidence
that, only when the interior frontier disappears from
American history, does the extension of the frontier beyond the continent begin. Both movements are but parts
of the same healthy process of development.

The main trouble with the above argument is that it
leaves out of consideration the essential difference between
the acquisitions of the United States before and after 1898.
Granting that in each case we have a process of expansion,
and that the second not unnaturally came after the first,
this does not alter the fundamental distinction between
the two movements. All the territory acquired by the
Americans before the Spanish War was in regions suitable
for white colonization. Whatever may have been the character of its inhabitants at the time it was obtained, there
was no doubt that before long they would be submerged
by an American population similar to that in the older
parts of the country. Military or even territorial government was thus but a temporary measure for a period of
transition: the newest lands would sooner or later be in
every way on an equal footing with the oldest. The one
exception was Alaska, where, owing to the inhospitable
climate, there was not, and may never be, a sufficient
population to form an independent state. But it must be
remembered that in 1867, when Alaska was purchased,
most Americans believed that Canada would shortly come
into the Union, after which Alaska would cease to be a
detached fragment, and become the natural northwestern
frontier of the country. At any rate, a possession whose
incapacity for complete self-government arises only from
lack of inhabitants does not present any arduous political
problems.

Tropical lands already thickly settled by natives foreign

in speech and civilization come under a different category, for in them we cannot expect a speedy triumph of Anglo-Saxon ideals, or an immigration of Americans sufficient to modify the population. When this population belongs to races which may not for centuries be capable of governing themselves with a fair amount of law and order, the attempt to apply the old system breaks down. The American people have in the past been aware of this distinction, and have more than once shown their repugnance to holding alien dependencies. We have an instance of this in the history of their relations with Liberia. In 1820 a band of negroes sent by the American Colonization Society founded a settlement on the west African coast, the United States taking no official part in the affair except to send government supplies at one time to keep the colonists alive. In 1837 they formed themselves into a commonwealth, and ten years later assumed the title of a sovereign state, which, owing to the feeling against free negroes in the South, was not recognized by the United States until 1862, after the outbreak of the Civil War. One might have expected the Americans to maintain some sort of protectorate over the little black republic, especially as they have had occasion to make representation to powers in its behalf. In this connection, Secretary Frelinghuysen, in 1884, used the phrase "a quasi-parental relationship"; but such a relationship is unknown to international law. Although the Americans would not view with indifference the forcible annexation of Liberia by a European power, they are not likely to push their concern for her farther. For additional examples of the policy of keeping free from outlying territories inhabited by people of another race, we may turn to the refusal of the Senate to ratify the treaties for the annexation of St. Thomas (1867) and San Domingo (1870), and to President Cleveland's withdrawal of the Hawaiian treaty (1893).

From the beginning of the Spanish War, there has been another tale to tell. In July, 1898, Hawaii was annexed, and at the end of the same year the peace of Paris assured to the United States possession of Porto Rico, of the Philippines, and of Guam in the Ladrones. In 1899, as the result of a treaty with Germany and Great Britain, the Americans acquired the island of Tutuila and its dependencies (in the Samoa group) as a naval station. In 1902 they concluded an arrangement for the purchase of the Danish West Indies, but the treaty was not ratified by the Danish senate. In 1903 they got from the newly constituted republic of Panama practical possession of a strip of land on each side of the future Isthmian Canal. In 1906 the collapse of the Cuban government in the face of an insurrection led to the landing of American troops, with consequences still hard to determine.

For better or for worse, the United States has thus become a colonial power in the fullest sense of the word. Its latest acquisitions, near and far, are all situated in the tropics, and are therefore subject to the limitations imposed by tropical conditions. They are small in extent as compared with the holdings of Great Britain, France, Holland, Portugal, or even Germany; but they are thickly settled, and have been so long used to European rule that they have acquired a more or less civilized, if foreign, stamp. Owing to certain peculiar characteristics, the problems they present are not quite the same as those of the colonies of the various European nations; and as the special ideals of their American owners add another element of variety, their relation to the country which holds them is in some ways novel.

Before the American government could regulate the status of the new lands which had so suddenly come under its care, it had first to clear up the uncertainty about their position under the American Constitution, a document

not framed to meet contingencies of the kind. This fundamental question was settled in a rather extraordinary manner by the two "Insular Decisions" of the Supreme Court of the United States. In each case the court gave its verdict by a vote of five to four, and the majority was transferred from one side to the other by the vote of one judge, who followed a course of reasoning which appeared inconsistent to his eight colleagues, not to speak of the general public. According to these decisions, new territories belonging to the United States are from the date of their acquisition *parts* of the country, not mere *possessions;* but only those, which, like Texas and Hawaii, have come in by the action of both branches of Congress, enjoy from the first the full rights of the American Constitution. Territory obtained by a treaty, like that gained from Spain, is subject to legislation of Congress, as if it were a mere possession. Consequently, tariff duties cannot be imposed on importations from Hawaii, but may be, and were for a time, on goods from Porto Rico, and are still on those from the Philippines.

We need not dwell on the details of the form of government instituted in most of the American colonies. Tutuila and Guam are mere coaling stations, suitable for naval purposes, and they have so few inhabitants that they are easy to rule. The Hawaiian Islands, too, are of interest chiefly on account of their commercial and strategic value. In their social structure they are unlike the territories obtained by the Spanish War; for, although Americans form but a small minority of the total population, their influence has been dominant for many years. Whatever civilization the natives have acquired is of Anglo-Saxon origin, and English is the language of the government and the schools, as well as of the public life.

The administration of Hawaii does not differ materially

from that of an ordinary American territory. The governor and the judges are appointed from Washington, and, owing to the political immaturity of the natives, who have at times controlled the legislature, the veto power has been frequently applied. At bottom, the chief difference between the régime in Hawaii and the system of which there have been so many examples in the United States itself, lies in the fact that, on the mainland, territorial government has been regarded as transitory, as destined before long to be replaced by full statehood, which has not been presupposed for Hawaii.

In Porto Rico the aboriginal Indians died off many generations ago, and their places have been taken by the descendants of Spanish settlers and of imported negro slaves. As Spanish immigration continued throughout the nineteenth century, the white inhabitants to-day — at least on paper — outnumber the colored, most of whom are mulattoes. According to the census of 1899, out of a total population of 953,243, 589,426 were whites; but these figures, we must remember, like similar ones in other countries where there is a difference of race, must be accepted with much allowance. The census takers have often no way of determining the color of the persons they put down on their lists, except by the statements of those interested; and in view of the social prestige of the white race, we may feel sure that every doubtful case, besides many that are not doubtful, will be decided in its favor. This practice repeated on a large scale must vitiate the statistics. It remains true, however, that Porto Rico is not only a thickly inhabited territory, but one in which the majority of the inhabitants regard themselves as being of white, that is to say, of Spanish, blood, and so heirs to Latin civilization. Although this is enough to force us to the conclusion that they will not be satisfied with the position of an inferior race, incapable of self-government, unluckily it does not prove at present that they really are capable of it.

The annexation of Porto Rico, being a natural consequence of the Spanish War, met with little opposition from any quarter. At the time of the signing of the armistice, the Americans had already overrun a large part of the island, and in a few days more would have become masters of the rest. Nowhere had they met with hostility from the inhabitants; on the contrary, they had been welcomed by them in a way which made a painful impression upon Spain, for it had been supposed in the mother country that, because the Porto Ricans were submissive, they were loyal. In truth, they were excited by the hope of liberty — an alluring term of whose meaning they had but vague conceptions — and by the prospect of financial prosperity, to result from their connection with the United States. The Americans, on their side, were determined to expel the Spaniards from the western hemisphere. They had taken Porto Rico, and, not being bound by any promise of disinterestedness, as they were in regard to Cuba, they saw no reason why they should not keep it. The island was too small to set up a government for itself, and since Porto Rico is an obvious stopping-place between Europe and Panama, its strategic value was great in view of an isthmian canal. In this instance, the American Anti-imperialists themselves made no serious protest; they were busy enough elsewhere.

After a first stage of military rule, which was beneficial during the period of transition, when the resident Spaniards had occasionally to be protected against the revenge of their former subjects, the present system of government in Porto Rico was established. But the inhabitants, though granted such liberties as they had never known before, were bitterly disappointed: they had fondly imagined that their island would at once be made

a full-fledged state in the American Union. This arrangement did not commend itself to public opinion in the
United States, where it was felt that a territory with a
mixed population of whom but seventeen per cent could
read or write, and with no experience in self-administra-
tion, must pass through a process of education before it
could manage its own destinies. The Americans were
sincerely anxious to treat their new fellow-citizens as
liberally as possible; and they did act with kindness as
well as with discretion. Even the temporary imposition
of a tariff duty of fifteen per cent on Porto Rican goods
brought into the Union, a step roundly condemned at
the time as an act of oppression, was only an assertion of
principle on the part of Congress. The duty (which was
soon abolished) did not, while it existed, perceptibly interfere with trade; and the sum of money collected by it
was presented to Porto Rico, and has since been of welcome service for internal improvements.

The form of government established for the island,
though a novelty as an American institution, is not in itself
original. It is much like that of several of the English
crown colonies, where we find the same sort of provision
for an assembly consisting of two chambers, the lower
chosen by the people, the upper composed of the chief
officials and of native members who, as well as the governor and the judges, are appointed by the home authorities. In local affairs the Porto Ricans elect their own
officers, but there is a low property and educational
qualification for the suffrage.

Under this system, thanks to wise administration and to
the good sense shown by the people themselves, the land
has been able to profit by its natural resources, and by
the advantages of its connection with the United States.
Prosperity did not come at once, to be sure, for at first the
sudden severance of its old relation with Spain produced

an economic disturbance, and in 1899 a terrible hurricane, the most disastrous in the history of the island, destroyed about nine-tenths of the coffee bushes. When we remember that the coffee crop was the chief source of export in Spanish days, and that it takes coffee bushes seven or eight years to reach maturity, we can appreciate the extent of the disaster. It is, indeed, not likely that Porto Rican coffee will ever be as profitable again. On the Spanish market it was favored by protective duties which it no longer enjoys; in the United States it has to compete with the long-established supply from Brazil. The American people are great coffee drinkers; and as the bean is not raised in their own country, coffee is one of the few imports that pay no duty. It is therefore hardly to be expected that the country as a whole will submit, for the sole benefit of Porto Rico, to a tax on an article of almost universal consumption. The place of coffee in the island has been taken by other productions, especially sugar and tobacco, the export of which has increased enormously, the total value of trade in 1906 being almost three times as large as it was five years earlier. Most of this growth has been due to commerce with the United States. Foreign capital has been chary in coming in; for the measures taken to prevent the island from being exploited by powerful financial organizations, though perhaps necessary, have tended to keep away possible investors. Public works of various kinds have been undertaken, and the number of children in the schools is increasing steadily. All told, the record of American rule has been satisfactory and creditable.

The political future offers some uncertainty. Thus far, the Porto Ricans appear to have made good use of the rights that have been granted to them, though they plunge into politics with a zeal out of proportion to the issues involved, which are too often personal. It stands to

L

reason, however, that they will not remain satisfied with their present privileges, which may indeed seem sufficient to outsiders, but which, so long as they are not the equal of those of other American citizens, bear with them a certain stamp of inferiority. Now, in these days there are fewer and fewer peoples who are willing to regard themselves as inferior, or as incompetent to take charge of their own destinies. The demand of Porto Rico for more liberties will be hard to deny; for the plea of a territory whose population is larger than that of more than a third of the states already in the Union, appeals to the American sense of fairness as well as to the old liberal tradition. On the other hand, many Americans do not believe that the Porto Ricans, who are still very young in political experience, will soon be qualified for the difficult work of governing themselves properly. Once a state, Porto Rico cannot be kept in leading-strings; and there is no provision in the Constitution for taking away the privilege of statehood, however much it may be abused. It is not strange that the Americans hesitate before committing themselves beyond recall. The Porto Ricans, on their part, may well lament the course of recent events in Cuba: the people of the two countries are so similar that there is no obvious reason why one island should be more capable of self-government than the other. If the Cubans are not competent to manage their own affairs, why should their kinsmen be more so?

Another question of no small difficulty is what degree of assimilation the United States is entitled to expect, or can rightly demand, of its new territory. Here the matter of the language is perhaps crucial. As the people all speak the same tongue, and that a great European one, Spanish, which has a glorious literary heritage, they will be slow to abandon it for English, in spite of all the efforts of the schools. Would it be any more just to attempt to enforce such a change than it was for the Russians to try like measures in Finland, a proceeding which called forth lively indignation in America? Porto Rico may become a state in course of time, for American traditions in favor of equality are still very strong; but we cannot foresee any near future when it will cease to be a somewhat alien element in the body politic. Happily it is not large enough to be a source of positive danger, or even of serious trouble. For the same reason, it has attracted but little attention to itself, and cannot, in the importance of the problems it presents, be compared with Cuba or the Philippine Islands, a fact for which Americans have every reason to be thankful.

CHAPTER VIII

THE PHILIPPINE QUESTION

PREMEDITATION and deep design are qualities which nations are prompt to attribute to one another, and slow to acknowledge in themselves. Each is conscious of its own hesitations, fears, changes of mind, but it judges the intentions of others by results only. This is especially true when the results take the form of territorial gains. The rest of the world will never believe them to be accidental: it will always find proof to its own satisfaction that they are the fruit of long-matured plans.

In Europe this charge has often been made about the acquisition of the Philippine Islands by the United States; yet seldom has an event of the kind been less due to foresight or premeditation. We may admit that among those who dreamed dreams about the Pacific, there were perhaps a few who hoped that the weak, ill-governed insular possessions of Spain might fall into American hands some day, and naval officers have had visions of coaling stations in all sorts of places, but it is safe to say that, when orders were sent to Admiral Dewey to proceed to Manila, President McKinley and his cabinet had no thought of getting possession of the three thousand odd islands which have since come into American hands.[1] The feeling of the

[1] "At the beginning of the war there was perhaps not a soul in the whole Republic who so much as thought of the possibility of his nation becoming a sovereign power in the Orient." — Reinsch: *World Politics*, p. 64. This is a bit emphatic.

148

people about the Philippines at the time has been well described by a satirical writer who said, "They didn't know whether they were islands or canned goods."

One good reason why the American fleet was sent to Manila at the outbreak of the Spanish War was that there was nothing else very obvious for it to do. It could not remain in Hongkong or another neutral port; it could not make an inglorious retreat to the Pacific coast without exciting anger at home; and the only course left was to seek the enemy at his own headquarters. A proof of the absence of ulterior design on the part of the government may be found in the fact that no provision had been made for taking advantage of Dewey's victory.

When, after destroying Montojo's fleet off Cavite, the American admiral telegraphed that he could capture Manila at any time but needed troops to hold it, the authorities at Washington felt that they had no choice but to follow up his success. It has been said that he might have been ordered to sail away at once and return home for supplies and repairs. Many people, including all Anti-imperialists, have regretted ever since that this was not done, and have declared that a fatal mistake was committed at this juncture. But such a step would have required great courage on the part of the President and his advisers, even if they had been convinced, as they were not, that it was the proper one. At a moment when the American people were wild with delight over the brilliant triumph of their young navy, popular disappointment would have been intense if the victorious fleet had thereupon turned round and skulked home. Sober-minded critics would, moreover, have condemned the whole expedition as a useless raid without any bearing on the course of the war. When Admiral Dewey asked for troops, the natural thing to do was to send them. To the question of how many were needed, he replied five thousand, — an optimistic estimate which was not accepted by the general appointed to command the expedition, who insisted that he must have twenty thousand, and got them. But as there were none available then and there, and as no means of transport had been provided beforehand, months elapsed before they reached the scene of action.

Meanwhile, many things had happened. By the time the American army was ready to take the offensive, not only were the insurgents in Luzon masters of the whole open country, and besieging Manila from the land, but the Spaniards had been beaten in Cuba, and were anxious for peace. Owing, however, to the fact that early in the war cable communication with the Philippines had been severed, the American troops attacked and, after a pretence of resistance, captured Manila before news reached them that an armistice had already been signed in Washington putting an end to hostilities, and handing over the city to their keeping. Some dispute arose in consequence as to the tenure of the Americans, — whether they held the place by right of conquest or under the terms of the agreement. After all, it mattered little. What did matter was that this fresh exploit, prearranged as we now know it to have been, excited a popular clamor in the United States for the retention of the town, which appeared more precious as a trophy than as a pledge.

In the Washington armistice there was a vaguely worded clause by which the American government intended to reserve the question of the disposal of the Philippines to its own later decision. Not only the administration but the public were undecided enough on the whole subject. When the peace commissioners set out for Paris, they were divided in opinion among themselves, and had no definite instructions from President McKinley, who had not yet been able to make up his mind as to what was the best course to pursue. He appears very truly on this occasion not as the leader, but as the representative, of the American people

in their hesitations, groping rather blindly and thinking
out loud.

Several courses of action seemed possible. The first
was to retire from the islands, perhaps keeping one of them,
or a mere port, as a coaling station, and leaving the Spaniards and the Filipinos to settle affairs between themselves
as best they might; but after the alliance between Dewey
and Aguinaldo this would have been called a betrayal.

Another way was to force Spain to evacuate the whole
group and to hand it over to the insurgents; but many
people in America doubted the capacity of the Filipinos
for self-government. They also feared foreign greed.
Whenever a nation hesitates whether or not to appropriate
something, this old cry is raised. Some rival is pointed
out as impatiently waiting to profit by the opportunity,
and this real or imaginary danger furnishes an effective
argument in favor of annexation. In the Philippines the
dreaded rival was Germany; for the presence of a strong
German fleet in Manila Bay had awakened much suspicion,
not to say wrath, in the United States, where it was believed that the Germans were on the watch to pick up
any territory they could get, and would upon the withdrawal of American authority promptly establish their
own, — a proceeding public opinion was not disposed to
tolerate.

The third obvious course was for the United States to
take the Philippines and keep them. Owing to the success
of the war, the country was not in a mood to abandon
anything, or to shrink from peril or responsibilities, and
this feeling of elation contributed more than anything else
to turn the scale. Without quite knowing how they wished
to dispose finally of the islands, the American people and
government came to the conclusion that the immediate
thing to do was to put an end to all Spanish connection
with them. Orders to this effect were sent to the com-

missioners in Paris, and were carried out in spite of the protests of Spain.

After the signing of the treaty of Paris, December 10, 1898, the Americans, from their own point of view, were in legal possession of the Philippines, which, in return for a money payment, had been formally ceded by their previous owners. Unluckily this possession much resembled what is known by the homely phrase of "getting the sow by the ears": it was equally hard to hold on or to let go. In actual fact, although the Americans commanded the sea, they controlled little on the land but the city of Manila. Nearly everything else in the islands, except where Spanish garrisons held on here and there, was in the hands of the insurgents. With them relations had already become strained, for the situation had been false from the outset. In the violent controversy which has raged over this whole subject, even the most ardent defenders of American policy have seldom maintained that the history of the transaction was wholly satisfactory, and intemperate Anti-imperialists have declared that the conduct of the United States towards its former allies was marked by black treachery and ingratitude.

It will be remembered that Aguinaldo, the leader of the last native revolt against Spanish rule, had retired to Hongkong on the conclusion of a treaty of pacification and the payment of a sum of money. Here the Americans entered into negotiations with him, and, after coming to an agreement, brought him to the islands in a ship of war, and aided him with arms and ammunition. Thus stimulated, the movement of insurrection spread with great rapidity, for the Spaniards, caught between two fires, and unable to transport troops by sea, had no means of repressing it. With Aguinaldo master of the country up to the gates of Manila and the fleet of Admiral Dewey holding the bay, the outlook for the Spanish garrison was hopeless.

For this reason, though it was capable of serious defence, it surrendered the city by agreement as soon as the place was assaulted. But for the insurgents, this would not have occurred, and we need not wonder that they were incensed at being rigorously excluded from the captured town, which some of them had hoped to pillage. As time went on, it became more and more evident that the conflicting designs of the two former allies would soon lead to open hostilities. The situation was indeed one which it was difficult to adjust by peaceful means unless one side or the other were willing to surrender its ambitions.

There has been much heated discussion about the extent to which the Americans committed themselves to the support of Aguinaldo in their original compact with him. He and his partisans have asserted that he came to the islands with the assurance of their aid in achieving the independence of his country; and the assistance actually granted him is certainly *prima facie* evidence in his favor. The American government has maintained that it gave Aguinaldo no promise whatever. Indeed, Admiral Dewey and the consul at Hongkong could in no wise commit the administration in a matter of such importance. There was nothing but a bargain for mutual aid at a moment when the interests of the two parties coincided. In trying to reconcile the different versions of what was agreed upon, it must be remembered that the negotiating was done through an interpreter. Translations of this kind, with the best intentions and every precaution, are notoriously unsafe. If many a treaty, even in recent times, has been found to differ in the two texts adopted, a verbal agreement is obviously far more liable to error. We have no proof that the words exchanged between Aguinaldo and Mr. Wildman in Hongkong, in May, 1898, were correctly rendered from one to the other. Who knows whether the interpreter even tried to be exact? And admitting that he did, a misunderstanding is easy to

conceive. We may also suspect that both sides realized
that their ulterior plans might not be in harmony, and
preferred not to look too far ahead. It was enough for
the moment that they were so situated that each was glad
of aid from the other, leaving the future to take care of
itself. This was all very well for the instant, but it now
seems extraordinary that so few Americans at the time foresaw that any kind of alliance with Aguinaldo inevitably
meant becoming involved in Spanish internal affairs from
which it would be hard to withdraw. Bringing into the
game a third party who could not be left out of account
in the dual reckoning must give rise to later complications.
At the time, the American authorities in the Far East were
doubtless thinking only of the military conditions which
confronted them, and as yet probably few of them imagined that their country would wish to retain these distant
territories.

In the events that followed, Aguinaldo had an advantage
which enabled him to act more consistently and seemingly
in a more straightforward manner than his later antagonists : he had a clear, definite aim, which he had no reason
to conceal, — the independence of the island, with himself
as the natural head of the new republic ; and he bent every
effort in this direction. The Americans were in a more
complicated position. The military commanders on the
spot were only subordinates, without much influence on
the policy of the government, and in Washington, and
indeed throughout the United States, as we know, it was
long before a decision was arrived at. By the time it was
reached, and people were ready to put it into force, the insurgents had made themselves masters of nearly all the
islands ; they had proclaimed a republic with a modern
constitution, had organized a working government, and had
despatched an agent to Washington to treat for recognition.
It may be supposed that the two armies encamped month

after month cheek by jowl with one another entertained no
friendly feelings, and the wonder is not that they finally
came to blows, but that the outbreak of hostilities did not
occur sooner. It would have done so if both sides had not
wished to avoid taking the initiative. As it was, the news
of the outbreak came just in time to influence the waverers
in the Senate to vote for the ratification of the treaty of
peace with Spain.

When fighting had once begun, there was a fresh explosion of patriotism in the United States. American blood
had been shed, and whatever might be decided about the
ultimate fate of the islands, there could be no talk of
negotiation until all armed opposition had been crushed
out. This patriotic fervor began to cool, however, when
the war degenerated into a fatiguing, inglorious, and endless guerilla contest,[1] and the Americans had to undergo
the same experience that the English had had in Burmah,
and the French in Tongking, some years before. It is not a
severe task for a well-trained army to defeat a disorganized
Asiatic host in the open field, but it is another matter to
stamp out insurrection in a land of tropical jungle, where the
seemingly peaceful villagers come out to greet the invaders
with gifts, if they arrive in force, but take to bushwhack-
ing at night, and are ever ready to massacre small detached
parties. Dacoits, Blackflags, and Ladrones, half robbers,
half patriots, have represented in varying degrees the same
sort of resistance; always apparently on the point of being
suppressed or exterminated, they reappeared again and again
to give the lie to official optimism and to weary public
opinion at home. In their exasperation the Americans
retaliated savagely, and resorted to that very policy of
reconcentration for which they had loudly condemned the
Spaniards.

[1] Annexation was not definitely decided upon until after the report
of the first Philippine Commission in its favor.

As might be expected, a reaction soon set in in the United States, and affected both political parties. Many Republicans, while insisting that the insurrection must at all costs be subdued, admitted that this was only making the best of a bad job, and they would have been only too glad to see a satisfactory way of getting rid of the islands and everything connected with them. The Democrats, not being in power, were free to criticise the acts of the government with severity. They condemned its conduct in scathing terms, and proclaimed themselves in favor of evacuating the Philippines, and turning them over to the native inhabitants. Some, it is true, conceded that order must first be restored, but a number of the more violent Anti-imperialists went so far as to give the insurgents open encouragement, — encouragement which, it is said, helped to delude them into prolonging their resistance.

Here we come upon a difficult question of ethics, which on two notable occasions in recent years has aroused intense feeling. If a nation is engaged in war, are those of its citizens who conscientiously believe that that war is unjustifiable, not to say wicked, in duty bound to conceal their opinion until the war is over and the iniquity consummated? This appears monstrous; but if, as in the case of the Philippine and the Boer wars, the attitude of the minority at home helps to encourage the official enemies of the country to prolong a hopeless struggle, what then? Excited patriots in America and England averred, with some show of reason, that these irresponsible critics were to blame for untold useless suffering, for the sacrifice of many valuable lives not only of their fellow-citizens but of the very people that they pretended to champion. It is easy to understand the exasperation of those who have lost sons and brothers in a war which they are convinced would already have come to an end but for the interposition of their compatriots, whom they brand as traitors and little short of murderers. This formidable moral question, which Nelson solved in his own simple way, — "my country, right or wrong," — is a very old one, but it has been rendered more acute by modern means of communication, which may make an imprudent speech or newspaper article known to the enemy within the space of a few hours.

Another circumstance which disgusted the American people was the reports that came back of the cruelties committed by their own troops, and notably the use of the "water cure." In peaceful communities the general public cannot appreciate the fearful strain to which soldiers are subjected when fighting against savage or even semi-civilized enemies who mutilate the dead, torture the wounded, and transform themselves from effusive friends into murderous guerillas if they can do so with safety. Under such conditions the best disciplined troops are guilty of reprisals to an extent seldom realized. Tales of harsh, not to say barbarous, treatment of Filipinos by Americans were repeated in an exaggerated form by the press, and were made the most of by the Anti-imperialists.

All this helped to make the country so tired of the affair that, if in 1900 a direct vote could have been taken on the abstract question of the retention or the surrender of the Philippines, it is certain that there would have been a large majority in favor of evacuation.[1] But complicated problems can seldom be solved in such a simple manner: there are too many outside factors to be taken into account. In the presidential campaign of 1900, the Philippine question was indeed the subject of heated debate, but there were other things to be considered, — the personality of the candidates, the possibility of bringing up again the free silver issue, the maintenance of the protective tariff. Though it is beyond doubt that

[1] The sentiment was much the same as that in France about Tongking in 1885.

the election was decided by a multitude of considerations, nevertheless, when President McKinley and his party were given a new lease of power, they felt that the country had indorsed their Philippine policy. Military operations were prosecuted steadily, Aguinaldo was captured, and one island after another was pacified, until native resistance survived only in the form of occasional outbreaks of Ladronism.

Meanwhile, the administration at Washington and its supporters, vigorously as they replied to their adversaries, could not help being moved by the criticism to which they were subjected. They were too intelligent to blind themselves to the fact that they seemed to be trampling on American traditions, and too upright not to wince under the taunt that their war, begun for the liberation of the Cubans, had ended with the enslavement of the Filipinos. Ever since the Declaration of Independence, the right of a people to control its own destinies had been too often proclaimed for any American statesman to defend the holding of subjects on the ground of mere material advantage. While unshaken in their belief that they were acting in a manner which, under the existing circumstances, was both wise and just, they knew that this justice and wisdom could only be proved by the use they made of their victory. It was for the United States to set an example unparalleled in the history of colonization. American rule must mean not only material benefit, but the moral elevation of the subject race to the level of the ruling one. The Filipinos must be treated as wards of the nation, not yet competent to manage their own affairs, but needing and enjoying protection until they should be fitted for the responsibility of ruling themselves or of taking an equal share in the life of the American republic. Thus were the older ideals to be reconciled with the new conditions. The right of self-government was not denied in theory, but was temporarily in abeyance in the case of a people too immature for complete

emancipation.   This view, that of Presidents McKinley and
Roosevelt, is the starting-point for the policy associated
chiefly with the name of Secretary Taft, — a policy novel in
many of its details, and condemned equally by the two
other schools of thought in colonial matters.

Ever since 1899 there have been three conflicting doctrines
as to the proper course for the Americans to follow in regard
to the islands.   The first and simplest is that of the Anti-
imperialists: that the Americans should simply get out as
soon as possible and hand over everything to the natives.
The arguments in favor of this course are based on moral
grounds, on the history of the republic, and on the unsatisfactory results, so far, of its colonial experiences.   The
Anti-imperialists laud the virtues of the Filipinos, whom
they pronounce quite capable of self-government, and they
fraternize openly with the most discontented elements
among them; they condemn the Taft policy as hypocritical,
or as incapable of realization, — human nature being what
it is, they say, people will always find excuses for declaring
that the natives are not yet capable of taking care of themselves, and the longer the Americans remain, the harder it
will be for them to leave.   The partisans of these views,
who are most numerous in the northeastern states, stand
on firm moral ground in their appeal to the higher principles, to the sense of justice, to the old ideal of liberty, of
the American people.   They are derided by their opponents
as visionaries, but they disturb the conscience of the nation; and their altruistic arguments are reinforced by a
widespread impression that, for purely selfish reasons, the
country would be better off without its Philippine encum-
brance.

At the other extreme from the Anti-imperialists are the
more outspoken expansionists, who laugh at sentimentality,
and declare that the Philippines are a possession fairly
acquired and worth retaining.   They admit that it is the

duty of the United States to give the islands as good government as possible, but there should be "no nonsense about it"; they would have them ruled justly but firmly, without any pretence that the inhabitants are capable of taking more than a very small part in the work. Nothing, in their opinion, could be more absurd than to talk of half-naked Orientals in the tropics as if they were Americans, with all the aptitude for self-government acquired in fifty generations. The Filipinos belong to a race which has never shown any capacity for independent civilization, and which cannot reasonably be expected to do so at any time that can now be foreseen; but under wise American domination they will enjoy such benefits as they never dreamed of before, and if they show themselves ungrateful for this, it is merely one more proof of their incapacity. There is nothing particularly new in the problems to be solved; the English have been familiar with them for a long time, and recently in the Malay protectorate, a neighboring territory inhabited by people of the same race as the Filipinos, they have set an example of almost perfect administration, a cardinal feature of their policy being the encouragement of Chinese immigration. This is just what the Philippines need as a means of supplying them with better laborers for the development of the neglected natural resources than are the lazy, shiftless natives.

In its extreme form, this opinion is probably not held by many people in the United States, but it gets its weight from the success with which the English have carried out in their colonies the principle it advocates. It also seems to gain authority from being held by the majority of the Americans living in the islands, — traders, soldiers, and even officials, — and is thus brought home by the passing traveller, who retails it as the "real truth" gathered from "those who know." We must remember that foreign colonies of a dominant race are seldom on good

terms with the people amongst whom they are called upon
to live. Even among nations of the same civilization,
groups of exiles are apt to have no affection for the
country in which they have found shelter. Between Europeans and Asiatics the antagonism is much stronger: the
Englishman in India, the Frenchman in Tongking, the
American in the Philippines, especially if he belong to
the trading class, is there to make his living, and he
is little interested in the natives except in so far as they
contribute to this object. He and they belong to two
different worlds, which he has no desire to bring closer
together. Indeed, one of the chief causes of his resentment against the missionaries is that their standpoint
is different, and he regards the white school-teacher as another enthusiast of the same type. Under such circumstances race prejudice reigns supreme. The American
commercial colony in Manila looks on the Filipino much
as the Anglo-Indian does on the Hindu, and resents almost
equally any thought of intermarriage. From the nature
of their position, the official classes are freer from such
intolerance, but they are not exempt from it.

This arrogant, but not incomprehensible, attitude cuts
to the quick the sensitive vanity of the Filipino, who, in
his heart of hearts, cares more for social than for political
recognition. A wealthy and educated citizen of Manila with
European blood in his veins, regards himself as one of the
heirs of all Latin civilization, and does not relish being
looked upon as a "nigger" by every "Yankee adventurer."
As in several of the British possessions, the presence in the
Philippines of a commercial element of the dominant people
tends, in spite of the fact that American investment and enterprise are crying needs of the islands, to embitter rather
than to improve relations between conquerors and conquered.[1]

[1] The coming of the Spaniards in greater numbers after the opening
of the Suez Canal was one of the causes of the increased discontent in
the islands in the last half of the nineteenth century.

M

Between these two extreme schools we find the opinion of Secretary Taft and those who, from the President down, support his policy. It is summed up in the phrase "the Philippines for the Filipinos." Its fundamental conception is that at the present day the people of the islands are incapable of complete self-government, and that, as long as this continues to be true, the Americans must take a part of the burden on themselves; but that it is their bounden duty not only to develop the country and insure material prosperity, but, even more, to educate the natives, who are to be given greater liberties as fast as they show themselves worthy of them. In pursuance of this idea, extensive public works have been undertaken, the laws have been revised, an efficient administration has been introduced, and capable officials of both American and Filipino origin are laboring unselfishly for the good of the lands committed to their charge. The most notable feature of the system is the extraordinary attention paid to the schools. Hundreds of teachers have come over from the United States, and they have helped to train a still larger number of native ones. With such energy has the work been pushed that there are now more than half a million children attending schools of one kind or another, and it is hoped that soon all those of school age, except among the savage tribes, will be receiving some sort of instruction. Never have the Americans given more striking evidence of the value they attach to popular education; and whatever may be the result of this first attempt to impart modern western knowledge to the whole new generation of an Asiatic community, it will be interesting to watch its fate.

One evidence of this principle of seeking the moral elevation of the natives rather than the most profitable exploitation of the islands appears in the resolve to forbid Chinese immigration. Although the prejudices of the American labor-unions were of influence here, the decision may be ascribed chiefly to solicitude for the Filipinos. If, in the midst of the arduous and delicate experiment of trying to reconstruct their system of society on a foundation of American democratic ideas and general education, they were to be exposed to an unrestricted competition of Chinese labor, the outcome might well be disastrous; for, like so many others, the pleasure-loving, indolent Filipino is no match for the hard-working, thrifty Chinese. The new dispensation, whatever may be its ultimate success, will in its early days be a hot-house plant, needing careful protection.

With characteristic promptness, the Americans began, even before the end of hostilities, to associate the Filipinos in the work of administration. The new commission of seven, which, under the governor, was to control the islands, was made to include two native members. The same practice has been pursued ever since: natives are to be found in many of the most important positions, and in an even greater proportion in the subordinate ones. There are Filipino judges in the Supreme Court; the provincial governors are Filipinos, some of whom fought under Aguinaldo; and the election of municipal officers is in the hands of the people themselves, the right to vote being subject to an education qualification. The next step has now been taken, that of creating an elective assembly, with somewhat the same power as the lower chamber in Porto Rico or in an English crown colony.

As was to be foreseen, all this is condemned by those who hold either of the other two views of the best way to treat the islands. So far it has been carried out in the face of many difficulties, mainly by the efforts of a very few men, high in authority. Many of their subordinates, who serve them from a sense of duty, have little belief in the ultimate success of the experiment. It has to overcome American prejudice and selfish interests, and at the same time, it fails to satisfy the natives, who, believing that they are competent to manage their own affairs, are not content with the promise that their great-grandchildren may perhaps be given the privileges denied to themselves. The prevalence of this discontent was shown by the victory of the partisans of independence in the elections for the new assembly.   In spite of all, American public opinion so far seems to support, if in rather a blind way, the present policy; but this support is not an assured quantity, nor is the policy itself beyond the reach of change.   By its novelty it is in keeping with the American scorn for precedents, and the belief that the United States can accomplish things impossible to other countries; by its high ideals it appeals to the best side of the American character; but for its triumph it demands a long-continued unselfishness.

Admirers of the English and Dutch colonial systems overlook certain elements of the Philippine situation which make the problem to be solved unlike any that the English or the Dutch have to deal with, and which are chiefly due to the historical development of the inhabitants.   The Filipinos are, it is true, of the same race as the natives of the Malay Peninsula and of Java, but, with the exception of the Mohammedans in Mindanao and Sulu, who may well be governed by English or Dutch methods, they are no longer on the same plane with their kinsmen.   It must not be forgotten that as the Philippine Islands have been governed for centuries by a European power which converted its subjects, the Filipinos have been for the same length of time under Christian influences, and that the upper class have the education and tradition of Latin civilization, of which they believe themselves to be the children.   It is easy enough to laugh at this assumption as childish vanity; to point out that this same upper class are not pure natives at all, but of mixed blood; to sneer at their culture as being the merest veneer; and to declare that they are nothing but a very small minority of the population, separated from the half-naked peasants by a gulf. Be all this as it may, the upper class is a representative of the people, and an expression of what they are capable of. The greatest man that the Malay race has produced, the novelist Rizal, was of almost, if not of entirely, pure Malay descent; Aguinaldo is a full-blooded native. As for the masses, they are Christians, and even admitting that they know little of the exact nature of their faith, the same is true in many countries. For centuries the Filipino peasant was under the close supervision of the church, indeed was almost completely controlled by the Friars, and though it is impossible to say exactly how this has affected his mentality, we may safely assert that his mentality is not the same as that of the savage Mohammedan of the peninsula, who has just come under British rule, or of the Javanese whom the Dutch have so scientifically exploited, rather than enlightened, for many generations. Moreover, though the claim of the Filipinos to be regarded as a Latin people may provoke a smile, it is almost as well founded as the same pretension on the part of the inhabitants of some of the so-called Latin-American states: the proportion of white blood is not so much greater in Bolivia or Ecuador than it is in the Philippines, and the American Indian can hardly look down on the Malay. Why, then, should we admit the contention of one and deny that of the other? We must remember, too, that if a people cherishes a belief of the sort, this is an important fact in itself, more important, often, than the question whether the belief is or is not well founded. Whatever our opinion may be, the educated Filipinos are imbued with the idea that they are Latins and that the Americans, with their rougher, ruder, if more efficient, culture, are in a sense barbarians. And these educated Filipinos cannot be contemptuously brushed aside, for they

are the natural leaders of the others.   One may at least be
thankful that the natives of the islands, on account of
their European affiliations, are not separated from their
conquerors by a seemingly impassable gulf, as are, for
instance, the Annamites from the French.   They are also
unlike any Asiatics that the English have to govern, and
they may perhaps best be compared to their distant kindred
in Madagascar, now under the rule of France.   The Protestant Malagasy, who have been subject to English influences,
maintain somewhat the same attitude towards the French
that the Catholic Filipinos, with Spanish culture, do towards
the Americans, but as Madagascar was never actually subject to English rule and its Christianity is recent and not
widespread, the parallel is incomplete.

One consequence of the Filipinos' Christianity and of their
quasi-European character is often overlooked.   The suggestion has been made that, in return for some compensation, the islands might be handed over to Japan; but
though this has seemed to some persons an excellent way
for the Americans to escape from an embarrassing dilemma,
in reality the idea is preposterous.   Religious sentiments
may not play in the political world so great a part as they
once did, but it requires a stretch of the imagination to suppose that Christian America would hand over some seven
million fellow-Christians against their will to the rule of
any non-Christian nation, however enlightened.   Whatever malcontents may say in the heat of passion, we may
take for granted that if such a proposal were seriously urged,
the Filipinos would protest with frantic indignation.   It
matters little that they have sufficient Asiatic sympathies
to find satisfaction in the triumph of the Japanese over the
Russians, and that they have been encouraged by this proof
that the white race is not invincible.   It means nothing that
those who hope to cast off American authority turn to Japan
as, in their opinion, their most likely ally; for they would

welcome as eagerly Germany or Mexico, if they could hope
for aid from either of those quarters. In spite of imaginary ties between the inhabitants of the two groups of
Asiatic islands, the last thing the Filipinos dream of is being
ruled by the Japanese, whom they look upon as inferior to
themselves, as representing a lower civilization.

But aside from considerations of history and religion,
the peaceable transfer of the Philippines to any one without
the consent of the inhabitants is now barely conceivable.
The people have too much national self-consciousness, and
they have been treated too long as intelligent beings with
a right to take part in shaping their own destinies, for them
to be calmly bartered off like cattle. The public conscience
in America would never permit such a transaction, and there
is no real indication that the Filipinos would prefer any
other foreign rule. They did not revolt against Spain for
the purpose of coming under the United States, and they are
not hoping for liberation from the dominion of the United
States in order to belong to some other power under whom
they might easily fare worse. What the discontented elements demand is liberty to manage their own affairs, and
the mere suggestion that their country is regarded as salable
property is enough to excite their legitimate anger.

Advocates of Philippine independence, whether Americans
or Filipinos, usually do not propose the severance of all
political connections between the United States and its
Asiatic colony, but they talk vaguely of some sort of "protectorate." This term is so loosely used that we are wont
to forget what it implies. Any state which undertakes to
protect another assumes toward the rest of the world responsibility for its good behavior, — the more complete
the protection, the more extensive the responsibility, — and
this responsibility involves a duty to interfere, if need be.
In Cuba, and to a minor degree in San Domingo, the
Americans have just had experience of this truth. It is,

indeed, one of the difficulties which the maintenance of the Monroe Doctrine may force them into in their relations with other Latin-American republics. If the United States is to be the guardian of the Philippines, it is bound to intervene in case of disorders there, and to take measures to prevent their recurrence. Moreover, there is no panacea in the word "protectorate," for a dependency may have less liberty than a colony: the "East Africa Protectorate" is a benevolent despotism; Cape Colony enjoys a large measure of self-government. In the end, the power responsible for the maintenance of order must determine the extent of the local privileges. To be sure, some declare that the Filipinos are capable of orderly self-government, and therefore will make no difficulties for the protecting power; but the American people, with the example of Cuba before them, are likely to be slow in accepting this assurance.

Another common suggestion is that the islands should be "neutralized." To which we may reply, why should they be? Where is the *quid pro quo* as far as the powers are concerned? Of course every weak state would like to be neutralized, — that is to say, to have the strong ones promise not to touch it; but only in exceptional cases have the latter found it worth while to bind themselves in this way. When they have done so, from mutual jealousy, as they have for Belgium and Switzerland, there is no certainty that the promise will be respected if there is a strong temptation to break it. Some one has to be ready to support the guarantee by force of arms. But why should the Americans do this if they retire from the Philippines themselves? Provided they keep any naval station they want, and the principle of equal opportunity for all is preserved, why should they care if England or Germany should step in? In point of fact, many of them feel to-day that, if they can only get safely and honorably out of the tangle in which they are involved, the islands, as far as they are concerned, may go to the devil.

It is still too early to sum up the results of American rule in the last eight years. In many ways it has been a disappointment, for up to the present time it has brought neither content nor general prosperity. Serious mistakes have been made in details. Taxation is heavy, and there is room for criticism about the way in which some of the money has been spent. It seems, too, as if a common mistake in French colonization had been repeated in creating an unnecessarily elaborate administrative machine. The salaries paid to the American officials appear unwarrantably high to the natives, who flatter themselves that they could do as well for much lower pay. Unfortunately, this grievance is unavoidable: if we admit that Americans are needed at all, we must also admit that what is wanted is the best, and that these can only be obtained by a remuneration which shall be some sort of recompense for the sacrifices demanded by a life in the distant tropics. Among those not in sympathy with the policy of the government there has been much criticism in regard to public education, which, it is declared, will serve only to make the natives lazier than they are now, while on the other hand the violent partisans of the Filipino condemn as both a tyranny and an absurdity the use of English as a medium of instruction in the schools. The reply to the first charge is that care is taken to make the system of popular education as practical as possible; to the second, that there is no one native Philippine tongue, but many widely differing dialects, and that it is for the advantage of the people to have the mastery of one of the great civilized languages. As between English and Spanish, it is pointed out that, in the long centuries of Spanish possession, the speech of the ruling race was never taught to the people. Previous to the nineteenth century, immigration from the mother country was discouraged; and until the end of Spanish domination, the all-powerful Friars preferred that the villagers under their charge should know nothing but their own dialect, embellished, perhaps, by a few words of Latin. The result is that at the present day only some ten per cent of the whole population know Spanish, so that there is no harshness in displacing it from its position of authority and replacing it by English, which will be a more valuable means of communication with the outside world. The Spanish language in these regions is doomed to speedy extinction.

Criticise as one may the details of the present policy, no impartial observer will deny that since 1898 the Americans have accomplished a great deal in their task of transforming the islands. Improved means of communication, public works of all kinds, modern sanitation, justice, public security, honest and efficient government, popular participation in the government, and a system of general education form a record to be proud of. In all this, good fortune has counted for but little, for in the last decade the Philippines have been sorely tried: they have suffered from war and from pestilence; from a plague which carried off great numbers of the buffalo, almost the sole source of wealth of many of the peasants; from the loss of the Spanish market; from the low price of sugar; and from the failure of the native tobacco to become popular in the United States. All these, and other evils, have borne hardly on the people. American capital has not come in in the way that was expected, partly on account of the legislation passed to protect the natives against exploitation, but more particularly because people have found it safer and more profitable to invest their money nearer home.

As in all times of distress, there have been bitter complaints against the government, though no fair-minded person would question the devotion to duty that has characterized its chief members. There is a clamor for relief measures of one kind or another. Capitalists recommend the admission of Chinese labor; but though it might be good for the Philippines, it would very possibly spell ruin for the Filipinos. What Secretary Taft has demanded with unwearied persistence is that the insular exports should be admitted into the United States free of duty, — a privilege which would be most advantageous to the islands, and might be profitable to the Union itself. The concession appeals to the sense of justice and to the generous instincts of Americans, and it has been urged upon them as their sacred duty to the weak people for whose destinies they have made themselves responsible, and whom they have deprived of their former markets without opening new ones to them. Shall it be said that the Philippines are in any way worse off now than they were under Spain?

All this cannot be gainsaid, but there are other circumstances to be considered. Such concessions cannot long be one-sided, but must mean reciprocity, and the closer the ties between any country and its clients, and the greater the number of interests in each dependent upon the other, the less will be the chance of their being separated in the future. Those who desire Philippine independence should realize that if the islands are enriched by American capital, and become a favorite field of American trade, the prospect of their ever shifting for themselves will become more remote. But there is an objection of another nature which must be taken into account. In the Philippines the Americans have given to the rest of the world practical proof that they adhere to the principle of the "open door," which they are so eager to enforce upon others. How can they continue to insist on it as fair to all, if they do not observe it themselves? Here we return to international politics.

CHAPTER IX

ECONOMIC CONSIDERATIONS

IF we would understand the attitude of the American
people after the war of 1898, we must take into account the forces which, unknown to them, had been gradually making them ready for a new departure. The policy
which they then adopted was accidental in many of its
details; it was as often dominated by events as itself
dominating them; but it was not what it had been before,
for fresh elements had entered into it. If, let us say,
President Grant had intervened in the Cuban insurrection
of 1868–1878, and had brought on a war with Spain, and
if the military successes of the United States had been
as decisive as they were later, the after effects would
not have been the same. In 1898 the country, though
unconscious of the change that had been wrought in it,
was prepared to meet the situation with a spirit quite
unlike that which would have animated it twenty years
earlier. This change was due to several causes.

One reason why the public was ready just then to run
after strange gods was that it did not happen to be pre-
occupied with other things. Many of the old issues that
had aroused it in years past had now lost their burning
character; in some cases had altogether ceased to be interesting. During the larger part of the nineteenth century
the negro question in the South had been in one form or
another a brand of discord between two sections of the

country. The prolonged struggle of the Civil War left bitter memories, and it had been followed by the period of Reconstruction, and in some states by negro rule, which had caused savage ill feeling among the whites. Not till a generation after the war did the men on either side of Mason and Dixon's line accept a settlement tolerably satisfactory to both parties. Then, on the one hand, slavery had disappeared forever, and all thought of secession had been abandoned; on the other, the North, after some hesitation, had accepted the fact that the whites of the South could not, and would not, allow themselves to be ruled by the blacks, and had acquiesced, with but few murmurs of dissent, in the virtual disfranchisement of the colored population in one state after another. The Spanish War gave an opportunity to former Confederates to serve again in the army of their country, and thus to set the seal upon the reconciliation. Proudly as the Southerners cherished the memories of their former glories, and suspicious as they were of everything that suggested interference in the race question, they were willing to let bygones be bygones, all the more as the rapid increase of their manufactures and the prosperity of their ports were creating a new South, which looked to the future and not solely to the past. In the North the Civil War was becoming a memory almost as venerable as that of the Revolution.

Another smaller trouble was also ending. The hard times and the financial crisis of 1893, with their inevitable suffering, had produced much discontent, which in some parts of the country had taken the form of sectional antagonism. The farmers of the Middle West, who, year after year, had seen the value of their crops decrease and their mortgages increase in their despair attributed their misfortune to the lack of sufficient currency, and talked of a conspiracy on the part of Eastern capitalists. The currency question became, indeed, the main issue of the presi-

dential election of 1896. But soon afterwards it lost its
acute interest. The constant growth of the output of gold
in South Africa put an end to the fear of a deficiency in the
circulating medium, and in the West a series of good years,
which enabled the farmers to pay off their mortgages,
removed their grievances.

Even the tariff issue, although it still divided, had ceased
to agitate public opinion; for after the passage of the
Dingley Bill, in 1897, foes as well as friends of protection
were disposed to leave matters alone. Within a few years
the country had seen three great tariff measures voted by
Congress; now the general cry was for stability in order that
business interests might have something on which to base
their calculations. For the while people had had enough of
uncertainty. With the return of good times, the relations
between labor and capital had improved; and the question
of trusts had not yet come to the fore. All told, internal
affairs, however important, were not at that moment either
new or very exciting, so the public was ready to turn its
attention elsewhere.

The story of the recent marvellous prosperity of the
United States has been told repeatedly, with fresh addi-
tions as the record of each year's success surpassed that
of the previous one. Never, in the history of the world,
has such a spectacle been witnessed on so tremendous a scale.
Friends and rivals were alike impressed, and among Americans themselves it awakened a sentiment often little short
of intoxication. The pessimist might shake his head over
the many evils which such circumstances created; the
economist might prove that a period of exaggerated prosperity must be followed by a reaction; but the man in the
street did not feel called upon to look so far ahead. When
he knew that he was making money, that he was successful
in his enterprises, he saw no reason why he should not succeed still better in the future. Americans had long been

accustomed to proclaim that theirs was the "greatest country on earth," and after 1898 it seemed as if facts were coming to their aid in a way that must convince all doubters. Throughout the nineteenth century the United States furnished to Europe several of the staples necessary to the support of mankind and to the development of modern industry. In the export of wheat and petroleum its sole rival was Russia; in that of cotton it had been supreme for many generations; in that of sheep and wool it came next to Australia; in the number of its cattle it was ahead even of Argentina. Of late it has taken the lead in one after another of the chief industrial commodities: in the production of both iron and coal it has surpassed Great Britain, which so long led in those staples that her primacy seemed unassailable; in copper the American output is more than a half of the world's supply. But it is not only in raw materials that the country has made such startling progress; its manufactures have developed with even more wonderful rapidity: the American silk industry is second to none but the French; the cotton is inferior to that of Great Britain only; the iron and steel leads the world. Between 1896 and 1906 American exports almost doubled in value, passing in 1901 those of England, which, since the creation of modern mechanical industry, had been the first exporting nation on the globe. The huge immigration, which has risen to over a million a year, has been insufficient to supply the demand for labor; and the railway system, though larger than that of all Europe, is inadequate to the needs of transportation. All this contributed to a prosperity which was not confined to one part of the land, or to one class of the community. Both capitalists and laborers shared in the dispensation. The Americans would, in truth, be more than human if they had not at times lost their heads in the midst of their unparalleled achievements.

In 1898 this new era had only just begun, but it had

got enough of a start for the people, with their inborn optimism, to be full of confidence in their powers. What in ordinary times might have seemed prudence now passed for cowardice; any arguments based on caution were out of keeping with the popular temper; hostile criticism from a foreign source was attributed to jealousy or fear, and was thus more flattering than praise. The whole country was bursting with a consciousness of strength. It could, then, scarcely be expected to give up its hold on the Philippines, which seemed to offer a new field for enterprise, and a base for the expansion of trade in the Far East. America was now in a position to take up her share of "the white man's burden," with all its incidental advantages.

The economic progress of the United States in the last few years has inevitably influenced the national policy in various ways, and will continue to do so. Until a short time ago the country belonged to the debtor rather than to the creditor class of states. It was well off, but it had no investments of consequence beyond its borders, and it owed the development of its resources in part to foreign capital. To-day the situation is radically different: the Americans have bought back much of their paper formerly held abroad, and, though they are continually borrowing afresh in order to carry out the countless undertakings in which they are engaged, they are no longer in the same situation as before. There is a distinction between the poor man who has to ask for a loan from a well-to-do neighbor in order to set his business going, and the wealthy financier who invites others to take shares in a profitable enterprise; and the United States is now in the position of the latter. It still needs foreign capital; but the Americans are themselves the greatest capitalists in the world, and though as yet they find uncertain ventures at a distance — as in the Philippines — less attractive than investments at home, where they do see an alluring prospect, — as in Cuba and Mexico, — they are not backward in risking their money. Of late, too, they have begun to hold the bonds of foreign governments. They may, therefore, now be regarded as belonging, and likely to belong more and more, to the class of creditor, rather than of debtor, nations, and their sympathy will go, not with the repudiation of debts, but with the payment of them. In any case where they themselves have large sums at stake, they will never permit their government to remain indifferent; witness the present occupation of Cuba. Though the United States has not been long enough in this new position to have modified profoundly its foreign policy, there has been a change: a generation or two ago it might have hailed the Drago doctrine with enthusiasm, — ten of its states have in the past repudiated their bonds, — now it has supported at The Hague only a much softened version, and it has aided San Domingo to satisfy her creditors, not to defy them. Throughout history the world has often seen communities rent by the strife between rich and poor; it may yet see the community of nations divided into creditor and debtor states, arrayed against each other by questions of financial interest potent enough to overcome ties of geography or of nationality.

Another element affecting the international relations of the United States is the transformation which is taking place in its export trade. Greatly as its exports of raw materials have increased, those of manufactured goods have grown faster still. In 1880 they formed but twelve and one-half per cent of the total, in 1896 they were twenty-six and one-half per cent, in 1906 thirty-four and one-half per cent, and the future appears to belong to them. With the growth of the population at home, the supply of wheat for exportation must diminish, and may soon disappear altogether. The development of an immense cotton industry which makes an increasing home demand on

N

the crop leaves less and less for foreign countries, several
of which are to-day making strenuous efforts to find an
independent source of supply in their own colonies.   On
the other hand, South America, Africa, and Asia produce
sufficient food for their own wants and are rich in metals,
and in raw materials — Argentine wheat, Indian and Egyptian cotton, and Burmese petroleum.   It is obvious that exports to such regions must consist chiefly of manufactured
articles.

The political consequences of this change are already
felt.   In the days when the United States sent abroad
nothing but the great staples which all the world needed,
when its rivals were mostly backward states, and it had
little to fear from hostile tariffs, it could tax as it pleased the
imports from foreign countries without much danger of
retaliation.   Now it finds itself competing on equal terms
with the highly developed industries of England, Germany,
France, and other manufacturing countries, — and every
civilized country to-day aspires to be a manufacturing
one.   Each of these countries pushes its trade by every
means in its power, and most of them protect their industries by high duties wherever they are able to impose
them.

In course of time it dawned on the minds of Americans
that they could no longer afford to look on indifferently at
the legislation or the political activity of their neighbors.
Merchants and statesmen, seeking for new markets, realized
that within a few years the greater part of Africa had been
partitioned among the European powers; that much of Asia
had undergone the same fate; and that the integrity of the
vast Chinese Empire was menaced.   This scramble for territory had been precipitated by economic reasons.   Every
power feared that, unless it acted at once, it might be antici-
pated by a rival; and where there was no agreement beforehand, all but Great Britain protected their own commerce

in their new acquisitions by duties discriminating against foreign goods. Even England, under the stress of competition, might follow the general example: mutterings were beginning to be heard of the advantage of an imperial Zollverein.[1] America was thus confronted with the prospect of being cut off from the markets which she would soon need for her rapidly growing industries. Already she was beginning to suffer from the change. She had just had, for instance, in Madagascar, an object-lesson, on a small scale, of what might be repeated elsewhere with more serious results. In 1896, when the island was annexed by France, American exports to it amounted to nearly five hundred thousand dollars; in 1899 they had sunk to eleven hundred and thirty-four dollars. It was useless to complain, for the French, in imposing a protective tariff, had acted strictly within their legal rights as owners of the place; but the incident, though too small to attract much attention, served as a warning in Washington, where it was not forgotten.

When American statesmen set themselves to face the situation, they perceived that the policy of aiding and protecting the national exports must be adapted to circumstances. In dealing with the European powers and their colonies, no originality was required: the United States was meeting equals and, in most cases, rivals. There was room for a mighty development of trade, but the government could do little to further it except by insisting on fair treatment, by improving its consular service, and lastly, by concluding profitable commercial treaties, — a matter in which it was less hampered by the demands of foreign countries than it was by the unreasonableness of the ultra-protectionists at home. Since the larger half of Asia, almost all of Africa, and the whole of Australia were in the hands of

[1] First definitely outlined by Mr. Joseph Chamberlain in a speech delivered June 8, 1896.

European peoples, a good part of the world was accounted for. There remained, however, two regions where the Americans believed they saw splendid possibilities for the future. But to make the most of those possibilities they must take decided action.

In the republics of Latin America there was no highly developed native industry to be feared as a rival. There was nothing but the competition of Europe, which had too long had the field to itself, and the Americans were convinced that they could meet this competition victoriously if only they made the best of their natural advantages. A first step was to draw closer to these fellow-republicans to the south, for the benefit of all concerned. This led to the policy known as Pan-Americanism, which we shall take up later.

The other tempting field for American enterprise was in the Far East, where hundreds of millions of human beings were just waking up, at the rude contact of the outside world, to the advantages of dealing with and imitating the hated foreigner. Here, indeed, were magnificent opportunities. Ardent imaginations pictured the countless population of the Middle Kingdom lighted by American petroleum, working with American tools, dressed in American cottons. The competition of Japan and the new activity of the Chinese themselves had not yet come to mar these fair visions. Unfortunately, even as it was, they were already threatened with destruction.

Ever since the war with Japan, China had seemed on the point of breaking up, and in danger of partition among foreign powers, who would probably introduce preferential tariffs for their own manufactures, and then — good-by to the dreams of American trade. The peril appeared extreme, and difficult to meet. Single-handed, the United States could not maintain the integrity of the Chinese Empire against the rest of the world, especially if that empire insisted on going to pieces of itself. It might, to be sure, take part in the general scramble and claim a sphere of influence of its own; but it had come into the field rather late to get a good share, and public opinion at home would never tolerate such a proceeding. The Americans' only other course was to take up and echo the newly invented British cry of the "open door." On the face of it, there was something rather ludicrous in the spectacle of the nation which had just voted the Dingley Bill waxing so enthusiastic over the justice of equal commercial opportunities for all. This attitude might be natural enough in Great Britain, which for half a century had been the free-trade power of the world, and could well assert that she had consistently stood for the "open door" policy; it was hard to see exactly how the Americans had done so, except in forcing the door open in Japan. But nations are guided in such matters not by logic, but by their interests. When the English, with intelligent appreciation of the value of American aid in the Far East, proclaimed that the two peoples had always been the defenders of the "open door," the latter cheerfully assented. It mattered not that the door which they wished to keep open was that of somebody else, not their own, and that, as in the case of most tariff doors, it was to open but one way. They did not stop for abstract considerations. Unless they were prepared to see many of the possible outlets for their trade closed against them at short notice, it behoved them to take a firm stand. Accordingly they fell into line with Great Britain and demanded the "open door" of equal chances for all, whatever territorial rearrangements might take place.

The first application of this principle came in a way that the Americans had not at all expected. When they had embraced the doctrine, they had had no thought that it might apply to them, and by the time that they had acquired colonies as a result of the Spanish War, they had committed themselves to it. How would they act now that the shoe was on their own foot? In Porto Rico and Hawaii, in spite of some grumbling on the part of their English friends, they made no pretence of observing the maxim. But there the situation was simple. In the Philippines it was more complicated. How could the United States proclaim the principle of the " open door " in the Far East, maintaining that Russia should not impose discriminating duties on American wares in Manchuria, or Germany in Shantung, if at the same time it penalized European goods in territories under its control? That it could not was too evident to be well gainsaid; and the treaty of peace with Spain, by providing that Spanish goods should for ten years be admitted on terms of equality with American, has insured an " open door " for that time. But to-day Secretary Taft and other friends of the Filipinos are anxious for free trade between the islands and the republic, — free trade which can only mean the application of the American tariff to the Philippines. Beneficial, almost necessary, as this might be, it would seriously weaken the moral authority of the American attitude. It is all very well to explain that the Philippines and China are two very different places, and that the present owners of the Philippines have inherited from the Spaniards the right to make what tariffs they please; such distinctions are seldom convincing to other nations. The Philippines were won by the sword, as Manchuria was won and lost. The sacrifices which they cost were not one tithe of those which Japan made for Korea and Southern Manchuria. The moral position is not very different, except that the United States will soon be unhampered by treaty stipulations or promises to outsiders. Though no other country is in a position to oppose the taking of the Philippines into the American customs union, the act will be resented, and may serve some others as a precedent. At any rate, it will be quoted to show the hollowness of Yankee professions when they clash with Yankee interests. And yet the advantage to seven million Filipinos appears so great that one may well hesitate before coming to any conclusion. To-day the "open door" idea is no longer confined to Asia, since it has been accepted at Algeciras as one of the conditions of Morocco. True, it is not applicable everywhere. The United States, for instance, will take good care that it never penetrates to the western hemisphere, where it might interfere with Pan-Americanism. ˙ Still, it is, within the geographical limits to which it applies, one of the cardinal principles of American policy. Its maintenance involves trouble and responsibilities; but, with the expansion of the national trade and the keen commercial rivalry which this brings, such trouble and responsibilities are unavoidable: they are part of the price which the country has to pay for its new greatness.

CHAPTER X

THE UNITED STATES AND FRANCE

IN any review of the relations between the United States and the powers of continental Europe, it is but natural to begin with France, the earliest friend of the republic. On two occasions in American history the action of the French government has been of so momentous consequence that one can hardly conceive what the destiny of the Union would have been if that action had been different. Without French aid, it is very doubtful whether the revolted thirteen colonies could have achieved their independence when they did. Without the Louisiana Purchase, the movement of Western expansion would have produced other results. Had France held Louisiana long enough to plant there a considerable French population, two rival nationalities might be struggling to-day for supremacy in the Southwest. Had she lost the territory to England, and had England joined it to her Canadian possessions, what would have been the future of the United States?

French and American writers often speak in somewhat different tones when describing the aid granted by the government of Louis XVI to the insurgent English colonies. The former point out the immense service rendered by France to the American cause, and are inclined to talk of the whole transaction as if king and nation alike had been moved by a spirit of pure generosity. American historians, on their side, dwell on the desire of the French to avenge their late humiliations, and attribute their intervention, not to love of American freedom, but to hatred of England, a sentiment for which one need owe them no particular thanks. But the masses in the United States, with more generous instinct, have recognized that whatever may have been the justifiable calculations of the statesmen at Versailles, the aid given to their country in a moment of extreme need was not wholly selfish. French sympathy for the Americans was genuine; and the Americans have shown their appreciation of this by their remembrance of Lafayette, whose fame, as a hero of the Revolution, is second in the popular memory to that of Washington only.[1] The United States has been, and is, grateful to France, even if such gratitude counts for little at moments when there is a clash of interests. In return, France has usually had for America that fondness we often feel for those who are under obligation to us, a sort of paternal pride in the greatness which, but for us, might never have existed.

The close alliance formed in 1778 between the two countries won its proudest triumph at the surrender at Yorktown, which led to the recognition of American independence by Great Britain. There was, it is true, some little friction over the peace negotiations in Paris, where the American commissioners thought they had not sufficient support from their allies in their territorial demands. Suspecting, rightly or wrongly, that the French were negotiating behind their backs, they made their own terms with England, to the anger of Vergennes when these were communicated to him. American writers in commenting on French lukewarmness at this juncture are prone to forget that France was the ally of Spain as well as of the United

[1] In the United States to-day we find one mountain, five counties, twenty-nine townships, dozens of streets and squares, and one university bearing the name of Lafayette.

States, and was justified in paying attention to Spanish wishes in determining the limits of the new republic. Vergennes could feel that he had done enough for the Americans in any case, especially as they had always made it clear that they would not tolerate a French reconquest of Canada. Here, perhaps, they were short-sighted, for a French Canada might, like Louisiana, have been sold to them some day.

After the conclusion of peace the relations between the two countries continued cordial. Their close alliance remained in force until France became involved in a new war with England under circumstances which, in the opinion of the American government, released the United States from its treaty obligations. From the point of view of international law this may be disputed; but the situation was beyond ordinary rules.

As was natural, the Americans hailed the outbreak of the French Revolution, in which they saw a continuation of their own. Thomas Jefferson at Paris was on intimate terms not only with Lafayette, but also with Barnave, the Lameths, and others of the Feuillants. To be sure, his successor, Gouverneur Morris, was in close relation with the court and the aristocracy; but Monroe, who came after Morris, went to such lengths in his demonstration of republican enthusiasm as to compromise his official dignity. American sympathy with the new revolution was so strong that if the French republic had been fortunate enough to send as its representative a more able man than the Girondist Genet, it is not improbable that the United States would have been drawn into war with England. To the injury of the cause that he served, Genet showed much more zeal than discretion. His lack of tact and his arrogant defiance of American laws helped to produce a revulsion of public feeling, and even Jefferson was obliged to reprimand him sharply. Conservative people in the United States were, moreover, soon alarmed by the increasing violence of

the French revolutionary movement.   When Americans saw
their former champion, Lafayette, in exile, and the king
who had come to their assistance sent to the scaffold, many
of them began to feel that the new France was not the
one to which they owed a debt of gratitude.
President Washington's proclamation of neutrality was
issued in 1793.   For the next twenty years American foreign
policy chiefly consisted of not very successful efforts to get
that neutrality respected.   In their prolonged and desperate struggle the two mighty combatants, France and
England, paid little heed to the rights of weak neutrals,
especially when these neutrals found the conflict lucrative
to themselves.   In 1799 hostilities actually broke out between France and the United States, but they were of short
duration and were confined to some small encounters at sea.
The difficulties with England culminated in the War of 1812.

It was in the interval of quiet which followed the peace of
Amiens in 1803 that Napoleon, after extorting Louisiana
from Spain, suddenly sold it to the United States.   The
Emperor had no particular love for the transatlantic republic, indeed there was no reason why he should have; and
Americans, on their part, owe him no gratitude, though
the benefit to them was inestimable.   Still, the transaction
constitutes another historical tie between the two nations
concerned, and as such has helped to promote good feeling
between them.

During the period of the Restoration and of the reign of
Louis Philippe, Franco-American relations were few and
unimportant.   The French conquest of Spain in 1823, by
awakening fears of European intervention in what had
once been the Spanish colonies, led to the Monroe Doctrine;
but this was not specifically directed against France.   The
long tiresome wrangle about the French Spoliation Claims
may be passed over.   Napoleon III was unfriendly to the
Union.   During the Civil War he would have recognized

the independence of the South if he could have been sure of the coöperation of the English. His Mexican expedition was a deliberate attempt to build up a Latin-American barrier, supported by France, against the preponderance of Anglo-Saxons on the continent. The complete failure of this undertaking prevented any lasting resentment in the United States, where people were inclined to look on the enterprise as the personal policy of the Emperor, for which his nation could not fairly be held responsible. Americans did not, however, forget their grievance against him, as was shown at the outbreak of the war of 1870.

Of late years, relations between the two countries have been excellent, although the Spanish War gave rise to a temporary but lively anti-American sentiment among the French. This hostility awoke a certain anger in return; but the more fair-minded among Americans recognized that, in view of the close connection between France and Spain, French disapproval of the war and sympathy with the Spaniards were to be expected. The conduct of the French government was, from first to last, irreproachable, and its representative in Washington showed much tact in the delicate task of bringing about negotiations for peace. French disapproval was further excited by what seemed an incomprehensible lack of American enthusiasm for the Boers in their struggle for freedom. At one time, too, the opposition of the United States in the Far East to Russia, the ally of France, threatened to make more ill-will between the two republics. But these clouds have now happily blown over. The American evacuation of Cuba, which very few Europeans believed would ever take place, created a favorable impression abroad; and President Roosevelt's initiative in the ending of the Russo-Japanese War was most welcome to France, as was also the friendly attitude of the Washington government during the Morocco dispute. Recent international amenities, like the Rochambeau mission, the reception of the American sailors sent to get the body of John Paul Jones, and, at an earlier date, the presentation of the Bartholdi statue of Liberty, though not very important in themselves, have helped to make good feeling. The efforts of the Alliance Française in the United States, and the frequent visits of French lecturers in recent years, have been influences in the same direction, as have the lectures at the Sorbonne of professors from Harvard University. Never during the last century have Franco-American relations been on a more satisfactory basis than they are at the present day, and, as far as we can judge, there is no good reason why they should not continue to be excellent. Small disputes will occur now and then, but in no part of the world have the two countries interests which seriously conflict.

A few years ago, one could not have said this; but certain possible causes of trouble then existed which have since disappeared. The dispute about the boundary between Brazil and French Guiana, unlike the Venezuela controversy, has been adjusted without bringing in the United States. The recent settlement of the long-standing fisheries question between France and England has put an end to the remote eventuality that the Americans, by some strengthening of their ties with Newfoundland, might become involved in the affair. Another and very real danger has been eliminated by the failure of the French Panama Canal Company, and by the sale of its property to the United States. If the canal had been constructed by a foreign corporation, the interests of the stockholders would, sooner or later, have come into conflict with the political claims of the American people. France could not well have left unprotected a company in which the savings of so many of her citizens were invested, and the result might have been a situation something like that which so long existed in regard to Egypt and the Suez Canal, and which ended in the triumph of the greater interest over the older historical right.   Such situations are extremely dangerous.   In the Egyptian question, war was barely averted; in that of Panama we may be glad that the rights of France were liquidated as they were without more ill-feeling, though we may regret that the price paid was not a little more generous.   The French may find some consolation for their failure in the thought that the cost of the enterprise, as is now evident, was too gigantic for private means.   When the canal is completed, they will be entitled to their share of glory for actually undertaking a work which others had merely talked of, and also for having met and overcome many formidable initial difficulties.

In France political writers sometimes profess fears of American aggression against her West Indian Islands. One is not surprised at this when one remembers the remarks of President Grant, Secretary Olney, and others on the unnaturalness of the connection between any European power and its American colonies; nevertheless, there is no real cause for apprehension.   If the French colonies, like Cuba some years ago, were seething with disaffection, and if exiles were trying to excite sympathy and to organize liberating expeditions in the United States, a dangerous situation might ensue; but as there is no sign of such a thing, we need not anticipate the contingency.   As long as France and the United States remain on friendly terms, the former has no cause to fear any extension of the Monroe Doctrine at her expense.   On the contrary, the doctrine is developing in a sense favorable to her; for if the Americans will not tolerate in their vicinity a transfer of territory from one European power to another, France is safeguarded against the loss of her West Indian possessions in the event of any misfortune to herself.

French authorities on the affairs of Oceanica sometimes refer to American designs on Tahiti, an island whose importance as a stopping-place will increase after the completion of the Panama Canal. American naval officers, like those of other nations, doubtless dream, as we have already said, of new coaling-stations in all regions of the world; but that is a part of their profession. Most people in the United States are hardly aware that Tahiti exists.

In the Far East, since the war between Russia and Japan, which has modified the political situation, the interests of the United States and France seem to be in harmony. Now that the partition of China, once so much talked about, has been indefinitely postponed, and foreign powers are more doubtful of holding what they have got than desirous of making fresh acquisitions, the principle of the "open door" may be regarded as reasonably secure. Some Americans may construe the recent Franco-Japanese treaty as a proof that in the rivalry between the United States and Japan in the Pacific, France must be counted on the side of the latter. Should the Americans further get it into their heads that, according to the guarantee in the treaty, France would be bound to interfere if the United States, after a successful war with Japan, should think it wise to deprive her of Formosa, then their irritation might be serious. Fortunately, this is going far afield. The Americans are not looking forward to war, and still less are the French thinking of quarrelling with them for the sake of the Japanese, treaty or no treaty; indeed their own Asiatic possessions stand in somewhat the same relation as the Philippines to Japan, who has been freely accused of coveting both.

Since both France and the United States are great manufacturing powers, they come into competition in many markets, where each does its utmost to push its own trade. Their direct dealings with one another are hampered by the many considerations which affect the policy of countries blessed with influential and highly protected industries, and which make commercial treaties complicated and thorny

matters.   And yet there should not be over many obstacles
in the way of equable concessions and profits; for the
triumph of French skill has been chiefly in articles requiring taste and care difficult to find under modern American
industrial conditions, and in the rougher productions
in which French industry cannot hold its own against
American, it has already had to give way to English and
German.

In the United States, popular ideas about foreign lands
have from the first been affected by prejudices incident
to an Anglo-Saxon heritage, and also by the English sources
from which Americans have derived much of their general
information.   Even in the days when public opinion was
most hostile to England, educated Americans, being nurtured
on English literature, unconsciously imbibed British views
on many topics and notably about the character of the
French, in spite of the facts that more of them have learned
French than any other foreign language and that the ties
between the United States and France have been not only
independent of England but actually opposed to her.   Then,
too, the press, from motives of economy and from sheer
provincialism, often took not only its news but its opinions
on foreign affairs, except in matters which concerned America
itself, from the *London Times* or from the English weeklies.
Thus there have been for generations but few native Americans who have not obtained most of their conceptions of
European questions through a British medium, which has
colored whatever has passed through it.   In recent years,
the English control of the great cables of the world and of
the news agencies has been used with effect.   In the South
African War, and even in the Russo-Japanese, the tidings that
reached the American public were likely to be as much in
conformity with English views as circumstances would
permit.   Indeed, when one considers the extent to which
the Americans have been dependent on the English for

instruction, one sometimes wonders that they have ever proved capable of disagreeing with their teachers.

This provincial condition is now being outgrown. Every year the number of Americans who visit Europe increases, and if those who take the trouble to master a foreign language are still all too few, translations are more numerous and more prompt in appearing than of old. Thanks also to the growth of the American reviews, the reader who is ignorant of French and German and is eager to instruct himself on foreign matters, is no longer confined to English sources. Several of the American newspapers now have direct communication with distant lands, and the Associated Press is competent to get its own news almost anywhere. But since the English will always be nearer to the European continent and necessarily better informed as to what is going on there, the American public will remain somewhat dependent on them for its knowledge; hence we may expect its opinions about French affairs to be favorably affected by the present *entente cordiale,* which renders English comment to-day so favorable to France.

The number of Frenchmen living in America is small, and nowhere are many gathered in one place. The American colony in France is concentrated in Paris. It includes a few business men, a good many students and artists, who are often poor, and a contingent of the idle rich. Foreign colonies of this sort seldom enjoy genuine popularity in the lands where they are settled; but the Americans in Paris seem to have made themselves about as much liked as could reasonably be expected. In many individual cases they have been very kindly received. They and their hosts do not always succeed in understanding each other, for their point of view is not always the same. To many Frenchmen the American is the typical millionnaire, rough, restless, active, in every way the parvenu, whose sole idea is money, and whose womenkind care only for the spending of it

o

with as much splurge as possible. On the other hand, it is not an uncommon belief in the United States that France is politically and morally decadent. This impression is based on doubts as to the stability of the government, on the fact that the population is stationary, and still more on the impression of moral corruption which modern French literature serves to spread abroad. It is hard for a foreigner, especially at a distance, to appreciate the extraordinary vitality and power of achievement which, though not always evident on the surface, are inherent in the French nation. Characteristically enough, both the French and the Americans (as well as others) are convinced that they themselves lead the world in civilization, and neither nation realizes that the other looks on it with a certain condescension. To tell the truth, their conceptions of what is meant by the word "civilization" are apt to be different. To the Frenchman the term suggests art and literature; to the everyday American it means efficient telephone service and improved plumbing. There is no doubt that the Americans are as superior in such important matters as public libraries, organized charities, and particularly in generous gifts on the part of private citizens, as they are inferior in the comprehension of much that goes to make life beautiful. Still, educated Americans, though sharing to a certain extent the inborn British prejudice against the Southern European, are quicker than the English to appreciate the French point of view, and some have more than an admiration, they have a real love, for France.

The influence of French thought on Americans has been great. It is true that they have not imitated French institutions, for the republic of the New World is the older of the two, but the fathers of the Constitution were steeped in Montesquieu, whom they quoted on every occasion. Rousseau did not appeal to their national temperament except in the case of certain individuals, the most notable of whom was Jefferson. Of later French political writers, the one who most affected the Americans was De Tocqueville, who furnished them with what was for long the standard philosophical study of their character and development. The influence of French literature, art, fashions, has been great from the start and shows few signs of waning. Paris has always been the Mecca of American students of the arts, and even in the field of learning there has been, of late years, something of a reaction among American scholars against German models and in favor of French ones.

Unlike most of the countries of Europe, the United States is not directly affected by the example of France in political matters, nor is it bound to her by close ties in foreign affairs. Nevertheless, it cannot be indifferent to what happens to its sister republic. France is a world power, with a territory and a population larger than those of the Union, a great army and navy, and extraordinary wealth, and, in spite of the assertions of hostile critics, her national genius seems far from exhaustion. She still plays a leading role among the peoples of mankind. Americans should not overlook, either, the immense prestige that she has, and is likely to keep, among the other Latin countries. Paris will long remain the capital of the Latin, including the Latin-American world. It is through the medium of the French mind and language that the other Latin peoples have often to be reached; and even in the political world, any state that has to deal with a Latin one will find a smoother path if it appears as the friend, rather than as the enemy, of France.

CHAPTER XI

IF history and traditional sentiment count for much in
the relations between the United States and France
and present politics for comparatively little, precisely the
reverse is true of the United States and Germany. Here the
all-important facts are the recent ones, the story of the last
ten years, the questions of the day, the aims and aspirations of the two countries. In any survey of the past we
have also to make a distinction, now ceasing to exist, between the relations of the Americans with the Germans as
a people and with the modern German Empire as a state.
The Germans have played a part in American affairs since
the early days, the German Empire is little more than a
generation old, and only within the last decade have political
relations with it become so important for the United States
that they outrank all others except those with England and
with Japan.

In America German immigrants have been welcome.
They have been preëminently steady, hard-working folk,
who have minded their own business, and who have formed
a valuable part of the population wherever they have settled. In the Civil War they played a creditable part, and
they have shown themselves ready to support their
adopted country on all occasions, even — if necessary —
against their native one. The small interest they have
taken in politics, as compared, for instance, with the Irish,
has prevented one possible cause of dislike; indeed, the

general feeling toward them has always been cordial. On
the other hand, considering their large numbers and their
excellent quality, they have had surprisingly little influence in forming American public opinion or in affecting its
attitude toward their Fatherland. It is not they, but Germans in Germany and the native Americans who have been
to Germany, who have done most to make the two nations
understand and appreciate one another.

The historical ties between the two were long slight but
friendly. The people of the United States have known
that Frederick the Great, in his resentment against England, looked with favor on their war for independence,
and that he admired the character of Washington; they
have regarded the unfortunate Hessians who, in a quarrel
not their own, were sold to fight against them, as victims
rather than enemies; and they remember that a Prussian
officer, Baron von Steuben, rendered valuable service to
the colonies by drilling and disciplining the raw revolutionary army. In their turn, the Americans sympathized
with the German struggle for liberty and with the achievement of German unity. Their dislike of Napoleon III, and
of the manner in which the Franco-German War was apparently brought about, rendered many of them pro-German
during the conflict. They admired the genius of Bismarck,
the triumphs of the German army, and the splendid energy
of the whole nation in every department of human activity.
Scholars from all parts of the world have flocked to the German universities, particularly since 1870, and have returned
singing their praises and eager to copy the methods which
have given them such preëminence. Among these visitors
have been throngs of Americans, most of whom have come
back with a very sincere enthusiasm for modern Germany as
a country which their own has much reason to respect and
none to fear.

The first slight quarrel occurred in 1888, in connection

with the far-away Samoan Islands, where both had certain claims. Overzealous local officials made the rivalry more intense, each of the home governments sent ships of war to the scene, and the situation there grew critical, until a storm destroyed the two fleets. After this, matters were patched up by an agreement signed in Berlin, that provided a hybrid form of government for the islands. Under this arrangement they continued to make trouble until, in 1899, they were divided by a new treaty which gave each side what it wanted — Germany a colony, the United States a coaling station.

The incident of 1888 was of a kind to be expected between two states whose political activities were beginning to extend far beyond their own borders. Its importance lay in its effect on the American people, who now began to think of Germany as a grasping power with ambitions that might conflict with their own. They were rather proud of having defended their claims in a dispute with the great Bismarck himself at a time when the rest of the world was inclined to bow down before the chancellor, and they were determined to maintain their rights just as vigorously on any like occasion that should occur. The episode also strengthened the demand in the country for a stronger navy. After it closed, relations with Germany resumed their normal course.

Ten years later, when the Spanish War broke out, the Americans made the unpleasant discovery that the sympathy of continental Europe was overwhelmingly on the side of Spain; so much so, in fact, that there was even rumor of a combination to restrain the United States. The result was an outburst of wrath. It is all very well to talk of the moral effect of the opinion of the outside world; but when a nation in the heat of a struggle — the United States with Spain, Great Britain with the Boers — sees that its neighbors condemn it, it ascribes their attitude to envy, hatred, and malice, and is not at all shaken in its belief in the justice of its own cause.   As might have been expected, the Americans fiercely resented all adverse criticism, and were ready to fight any one and every one rather than yield an inch. Some of them might admit that there was a certain excuse for France, owing to her close connection with Spain, but they saw none for Germany. Their anger against the latter was soon fanned into hot flame by her conduct about the Philippines.

The exact circumstances connected with the despatch of the squadron of Admiral Diedrichs to these islands have never been made public, and perhaps never will be. It is well that at the moment people in America were unaware of the relations which existed for some weeks between the American and German fleets, relations so strained that, but for the attitude of the English commander present, they might perhaps have degenerated into actual conflict; but what the people did know was enough to arouse their anger. After the battle of Manila Bay, while other countries, as is usual under such conditions, sent a few ships of war to look after the interests of their citizens, Germany, without any obvious reason, hastily despatched to the scene of action her Pacific squadron — a force equal in strength to the fleet of Admiral Dewey.   The Americans believed that this force came in no friendly spirit, but in the hope of taking advantage of the confusion to pick up something for Germany; and their distrust was intensified by the reports they heard of its behavior. Fear that the Germans might establish themselves in the Philippines was one of the motives that induced the United States to take over the islands.   When, later, they purchased from Spain the Carolines and the Ladrones, this was taken as proof that the suspicion had been well founded. From this time on, many Americans were firmly convinced that Germany was not only a covetous, greedy power, but also one that, from jealousy, was willing to do the United States an ill-turn, if she could. As this opinion was expressed by the newspapers with their usual intemperate freedom, it provoked anger on the other side and violent retorts. Indiscreet words on the part of American officers helped to envenom the situation. Naval authorities everywhere are wont to form their plans with more or less reference to some particular foreign fleet; for Americans, the German was now the one to keep in view as a standard for the strength of their own.

Here, again, the influence of the English press must not be forgotten. Since the fall of Bismarck, the relations between Great Britain and Germany, except at the moment of the Jameson raid, had in the main been cordial; but about 1899 they began to change for the worse, and they have never regained their former heartiness. As the English have been at the same time quarrelling with the Germans and cultivating their new friendship with the Americans, it was but human nature for them to strive to blacken the character of their Teutonic rivals, and to prove that the ambitions of the latter were equally dangerous to both Anglo-Saxon nations. It is true that the Germans retorted in kind, but in spite of the aid of their transatlantic kindred, they were not so well able to put their views before the American public, who can be reached more easily by the *London Times* than by the *New-Yorker Staatszeitung*.

Events in the Far East did not help to mend matters. The United States as well as England disapproved of the seizure of Kiauchau, and though the principle of Secretary Hay's famous note on the "open door" was officially accepted at Berlin, many persons were convinced that Germany was instigating Russian aggression in order to bring about the partition of China — an outcome which America was anxious to prevent. During and after the Boxer rising, the severity shown by the Germans was in opposition to the American policy of treating the Chinese as leniently as might be.

The growing alienation between two states long on amicable terms grieved and alarmed well-wishers in both. Accordingly, various means were tried to bring them together again. If we may charge the Germans with having given most of the provocation in the first instance, we must admit that the attempts at reconciliation have come from their side. The Emperor in particular has made several efforts to allay American suspicion. His most notable act of the sort was the sending of his brother, Prince Henry, to make a tour of the United States and to present a gift to the new Germanic Museum of Harvard University. The visit of the prince was in a measure successful: personally, he created a favorable impression everywhere, and the American people were amused and pleased at the attention paid them; but if any one imagined that they would take the whole thing very seriously, he misconceived the character of a nation which is too well satisfied with itself and with its own institutions to feel unduly flattered by attentions from any foreign prince. Still, the effect of the visit was good, though a little marred by an inopportune dispute between the English and the German press as to the attitude assumed by the representatives of their respective countries at Washington at the outbreak of the Spanish War. More unfortunate was the mistake in tact made by the imperial government a few months later in presenting to the United States a statue of Frederick the Great when the French Rochambeau mission was in America. The moment was ill-chosen. The Americans, without attaching too much importance to the Rochambeau festivities, which attracted less attention than the visit of Prince Henry, felt that the Germans would have done better to keep quiet for a while. It took some imagination

to believe that the services of Frederick the Great in
their behalf could be compared with those of Rochambeau. At all events, there was no good reason for an-
nouncing the gift at this juncture, when it placed the
administration at Washington in an awkward position,
and, in the eyes of the American public, looked as if
the 'Germans, after having had their fun, were trying
to spoil that of the French. Trifles of the sort were,
however, soon forgotten in the graver dissatisfaction
produced by the turn events were taking in Venezuela.

The intervention of Germany, England, and Italy in
Venezuelan waters provoked a violent irritation in the
United States. Rightly or wrongly, the Americans were
convinced that Germany was "trying it on" to test the
Monroe Doctrine, and for greater security had persuaded
the other two powers to join her. The loud and almost
universal condemnation by the English people and press
of the action of their government prevented resentment
against England, and since Italy scarcely attracted attention, all the vials of American wrath were poured
on Germany. For a while the situation was somewhat
critical, and the tone taken in Washington was serious.
Finally, after President Roosevelt had declined the request
that he should act as arbitrator, the matter was, as he suggested, referred to The Hague. The decision there pro-
nounced awoke fresh dissatisfaction in the United States;
for the lien given to the creditors on the Venezuelan customs looked like a beginning of European control of an
American state, and the recognition of the priority of the
claims of the belligerents over those of powers which, like
the United States and France, had kept quiet, might well
encourage the use of force elsewhere under similar circumstances. On their part the Germans had small cause to con-
gratulate themselves, for though victorious in the matter
in dispute, they had been taught that the United States

was determined to oppose even the slightest encroach-
ment, and that the mere suggestion of another intervention of this kind would excite American feeling to a
dangerous degree. It was also evident that public opinion
in England would never permit the government to aid
Germany against America.

Since then, passions have had time to cool down, and
though there still may be some latent resentment on the
German side and watchful suspicion on the American, the
relations between the two countries are again good.
Before deciding whether they are likely to continue so, we
must first understand why their interests may clash, and
this without the fault of any one.

To begin with, the United States and Germany are trade
rivals whose competition is keen. If we look at the great
manufacturing states of the world to-day, we see that all
are eager, as a matter of economic life and death, to
find markets for their surplus goods. England and France
appear to us like two rich, long-established, and somewhat old-fashioned commercial houses. They have com-
peted with one another for generations, they have their
specialties and their traditions, and they are often inclined
to let well-enough alone rather than to run unnecessary
risks in seeking new fields. Compared with them, Germany
and the United States are like two young pushing firms
who have their way yet to make. Confident in their own
intelligence and energy, they have little doubt that in many
branches of trade they shall be able to drive their older
competitors from the field. Already their achievements
have excited the alarm of their staid rivals, and they might
look forward joyously to more brilliant triumphs in the
future, if each were not worried by the presence of the
other.

Different as have been the methods by which the Germans
and the Americans have attained this astonishing economic

success in the last few years, the results in the two cases are similar: each has developed gigantic industries, capable of supplying goods of many kinds, and often the same goods, in almost unlimited quantities; each protects itself at home by means of a tariff, though not of equal severity; each is supremely desirous of securing new markets abroad; and each realizes that, in the fierce struggle for preëminence, the other is its most formidable rival. The Germans were slightly the first in the field, and we can well understand their deep chagrin when the Americans appeared on the scene. The situation is doubly trying, because Germany is in more pressing need of outside markets for her activity than is the United States, and is at the same time much inferior to it in natural resources. Long-cherished dreams, which had appeared not too difficult of realization, must now remain unfulfilled. The Americans, on their part, looking out for fresh commercial worlds to conquer, see almost everywhere as their chief competitors the hard-working, energetic Germans. In the Chinese Empire, both have been so successful that they had visions of dominating the markets until their ideas received a rude shock from the appearance of a still younger rival, modern Japan. In South America, the Germans were convinced that they had found a field of splendid possibilities, and their progress in recent years has been startling in its rapidity; but to South America the Americans are turning much of their attention, and with the aid of Pan-American sentiment, they hope to win the first place for themselves. Wherever on the globe there is a good opening for trade, there we may expect to find the Germans and the Americans striving in ardent rivalry. Under these circumstances, it is not surprising if the continual clash of equally legitimate interests sometimes produces ill-feeling between the competitors, which is soon reflected in the press and heightened by publicity.

A second source of difficulty between Germany and the

United States may be found in the Monroe Doctrine, in regard to which the Americans will hear of no argument or compromise, and are prepared to maintain their position at any cost. Now that England has explicitly accepted it, they are inclined to believe that Germany is the only power from whom they have anything to apprehend in this respect. They know that, although the imperial government has shown a discreet reserve, the Pan-Germanists have raged furiously against the doctrine, and that others, of a less chauvinistic stripe, regard it with lively resentment. Many Americans are convinced that Germany would jump at any safe opportunity to get a foothold in the western hemisphere, that she was taking a first step toward one in her Venezuela intervention, that she would purchase the Danish islands if she dared, and that she used secret influence to prevent their being sold to the United States in 1902. In short, they regard her whole relation with Latin America with watchful suspicion.

If this suspicion rested on any supposed wanton rapacity on the part of the Germans, we might dismiss it with scant ceremony. What is more disquieting is that we can see lawful reasons why German efforts should be directed toward South America in a way that may bring them into collision with American interests. And we can blame no one, since the trouble lies in the situation itself as nature and history have created it. We must, however, distinguish between German political dreams, often of an irresponsible nature, and legitimate commercial aspirations. It is true that the two melt into one another, and that the United States is in the way of both.

In spite of the extraordinary achievements of the modern German Empire in peace and in war, and of its splendid organized strength, if it is to keep in the future the commanding position it holds in the present, it will have to overcome grave disadvantages. Many of its leading

men, conscious of the overcrowding of its great population
on a small and not very rich territory, are convinced that
their country must either expand or stifle. Its industry,
its energy, its trained efficiency, imperatively demand
broader fields in which to display themselves. Its few
colonies, with one barren exception, — a part of Southwest Africa, — are in the tropics, and incapable of supporting any large number of white settlers. For trade with
the Far East it is less well placed than the United States,
and in China it will find it ever harder to compete with
Japan. Imperial customs preference would threaten its
commerce with the colonies of the British Empire. There
remains South America, a whole continent of vast resources,
all of whose inhabitants put together are hardly equal to
one-half of those of Germany, and many of whom are not
of the white race. Here, then, would seem to be a splendid opening for German enterprise, a unique chance for
the nation to control permanently a territory comparable
to that held by the Anglo-Saxon and the Slav. In the
last quarter of a century the Germans have made long
strides in this part of the world, not by colonization —
for few have emigrated there — but by founding steamship
lines and banking houses, by constructing public works,
by making investments, and by building up their trade in
every way. They are firmly intrenched, skilful and energetic, and are advancing steadily. Their chief obstacle to
complete success is American competition.

This competition, which bids fair to become keener every
year, fills the Germans with apprehension. They may
think they can hold their own on even terms, especially as
they have a good start; but are the terms even? Hamburg
is, it is true, little farther from the southeastern coast of
South America than is New York, and if the Germans could
get a port in Morocco, they would have an outpost nearer
than the United States to this, the most important, part of

the South American continent; but for trade further north they are relatively less well situated, and for the whole west coast their disadvantage is manifest. Their inferiority in position is, however, small compared with their inferiority in resources, and this makes the prospect of competition rather depressing. They are also justified in regarding the Pan-American movement as unfavorable to their interests; for though optimists may declare that South America offers room for the commerce of many countries, it would be hard to deny that whatever success the United States may gain there, will be to a certain extent at the expense of Europe, and particularly of Germany. This may be in the common order of things, and the fault of no one, but it will not promote mutual good feeling. And this is not the whole story. Germans have dreamed that their economic preponderance in parts of South America might be made permanent by becoming also a political one. It is not necessary to accuse them of covert designs against any South American state: what they have done is to entertain the hope that sooner or later, in the nature of things, by peaceable attraction or as a result of collision provoked by misgovernment, some of the Latin-American republics would fall into the hands of the superior race. This dream may appear fantastic to many people, even in Germany itself, but we need not wonder at its existence, or deny to it a measure of reasonableness.

When German public opinion began to recover from the exultation which followed the founding of the new Empire, gradually some unpleasant doubts asserted themselves. Men came to realize that powerful and glorious as was the new Fatherland, it occupied only a small part of the earth's surface compared with the domain of the Anglo-Saxon, the Latin, and the Slav, and that however satisfactory was the immediate situation, the prospect ahead looked less attractive. This consciousness of great actual strength coupled with anxiety about the future has led to a growing restlessness, to a feeling that something must be done. Germans no longer regard their unity as achieved, as they did in the first glow of triumph after 1871 : they now hope for a greater Germany, to include all in Europe who speak their tongue. Even this is not enough, — they have visions of a world empire, the equal of others, one that will give full play to all their energies, and furnish homes for their superabundant children, who may thus preserve their nationality instead of becoming "the fertilizer" of other peoples, and assure the sway of the German language as the idiom of hundreds of millions of human beings.

The party known as the Pan-Germanists have expressed freely the extreme of ambitions which many quieter patriots cherish in some degree. Unfortunately for such aspirations, there are but few parts of the temperate zone where it would still be possible for German colonists to transplant themselves in sufficient numbers to form new branches of the race, and those few parts are guarded by their present owners and by international jealousies. Australia, with its huge area, occupied by a small and slowly increasing population, is a British colony; in Asia Minor, the Turk is not to be lightly dispossessed, and both Russia and England may be counted on to oppose Germany; in Morocco, England and France stand in the way; in the United States, though millions of Germans have settled there, *Deutschtum* has no chance of being preserved.

There remains only South America; and here, in the three southern provinces of Brazil, is a population of some four hundred thousand Germans, who, thanks to their high birthrate, are increasing fast, and who, so far, have succeeded in maintaining their individuality. If the few thousand immigrants who wandered there more than half a century ago have grown up into so considerable a nucleus, can we wonder that enthusiasts have dreamed of the building up of a German state in this part of the New World? But how different the whole situation would be to-day if the Prussian government had not from 1856 to 1893 made the fatal mistake of forbidding the departure of colonists for this region, and if but a tenth of the swarm who in those years were lost to the Fatherland by going to the United States had made their homes in Brazil! We can well understand the despair of the German patriot when he thinks of the magnificent opportunity so wantonly sacrificed. Is *Deutschtum*, then, to be reckoned as without a future in this part of the world? Pan-Germanist writers have declared that it is not too late to hope and to act, and they have outlined possibilities magnificent enough in their eyes, but unluckily quite out of keeping with the Monroe Doctrine. Their flights of fancy, which English writers have taken care should not pass unnoticed, have sharply directed American attention to every movement of the Germans in Brazil, and there can be no doubt that German interference there would mean war between Germany and the United States.

Looking dispassionately at the situation of the German-Brazilians to-day, one cannot help thinking that, if left to themselves, they will find it difficult to maintain a separate existence. In the provinces where they have settled they are everywhere in a minority; even in Santa Catarina, where their proportion is highest, they form scarcely a quarter of the population. To-day they are receiving almost no reinforcements, partly because German emigration in any direction has decreased in the last few years, but also because the Brazilians, alarmed by the danger they have foreseen, are now discouraging, instead of favoring, newcomers from Germany. As an offset they have been bringing in large numbers of Italians, who are as prolific as Germans and more easily Brazilianized, and they are about to introduce Japanese. Finally, well as the German-Brazilians, on the

p

whole, have preserved their original type, some of them, especially in the towns, show signs of departing from it, and very few, whatever their national sympathies may be, have any desire to come under the bureaucratic rule of Berlin. If matters go on quietly, as they are doing at present, it appears probable that, in spite of the influence of consuls and merchants, of teachers and preachers and patriotic literature from the Fatherland, sooner or later here too the Germans will end by being lost in the surrounding population.

On the other hand, this may not happen. The rapid natural increase among the German settlers in the country districts may more than counterbalance losses in the towns. The old immigration may begin again, even if it is hindered by the opposition of the Brazilian authorities, and also by the fact that the population of modern Germany is increasingly urban rather than rural, and therefore less suited to the opening up of unsettled regions. Or the Brazilian Germans may hold their own and be drawn closer to their kinsmen by commercial, literary, and sentimental ties, without wishing to be under the same government. To this the United States could have no objection. The greatest danger to peace would arise from an antagonism between the Germans and other Brazilians that should lead to armed conflict, during which subjects of the Emperor might also suffer. It would then be very hard for the government at Berlin to resist the pressure of popular sentiment in favor of rendering some sort of aid to the struggling brothers across the sea. But such intervention would at once lead to action on the part of the United States. Even if the Germans felt that their navy was strong enough to risk the perils of a conflict with the United States alone, they would also have to take into account not only Brazil, but probably a South American coalition against them, and there is no one from whom they could expect help. Doubtless all this is perfectly appreciated by the statesmen at Berlin, even if it is not by the Pan-Germanists.

At all events there is no present cause for anxiety. In a study of international relations one is sometimes in danger of paying attention to irresponsible utterances in a foreign country to which one would not give a thought in one's own. There is indeed no more reason why the imperial government should let itself be led astray by Pan-Germanic clamor than that the authorities at Washington should heed the vaporings of the American yellow press. Nor should the fact that we can discern clouds on the horizon make us necessarily expect a storm. Relations between the United States and Germany are excellent, and the present trend is towards an even better understanding. In the isolation in which the Germans now find themselves in Europe, they are more desirous than they were before of American good-will, and are more disposed to second the efforts to obtain it which the Emperor has been making for some time past, — efforts the more successful because his picturesque character has always appealed to the imagination of Americans in much the same way as that of their own President, with whom he has so often been compared. They may not be much impressed by interchanges of university professors, but they do realize that the Germans are trying to be friendly, and they are disposed to be so themselves in return. They have now made their interpretation of the Monroe Doctrine so clear that no one can have any excuse for misunderstanding it, and whatever irresponsible individuals may have said, the German government since 1903 has shown no enmity to it or sign of desire to call it in question. Suspicion in the United States has in consequence subsided and given place to good-will. Then a slight sense of loneliness which the Americans feel in the midst of all these treaties concerning the Far East in none of which they are included, and uncertainty about their own future relations with the Japanese, increase their readiness to welcome German advances. They have the less difficulty in doing so because even in the days when they mistrusted the intentions of Germany the most, they could not refuse to her the tribute of their sincere admiration.

CHAPTER XII

OF all the powers of to-day, no two present a more striking example of similarity and of contrast than the United States and Russia. Their huge unbroken bulk gives them a self-sufficing continental character, which not only offers them a seemingly limitless field for internal development, but renders them, except at their extremities, almost invulnerable to outside attack. Each has been a world in itself, and both have been regarded as menaces, though in different ways, to the historic lands of older culture. From one another they can have little to fear, and they may conceivably be of great mutual service. In the past the sympathies between them have been curious and interesting, but so far their political dealings have not been highly important.

At the time of the war for American independence, the Empress Catherine II happened to be out of conceit with England. This temporary unfriendliness, combined with her high sense of the dignity of her empire, prompted her to get up the League of Armed Neutrality; but though this was directed against the English, it was of no particular service to the Americans. The Empress was not at all moved by sympathy for the revolted colonies — she had a thorough dislike of insurrection, and regarded such an example as infectious; she therefore let the agent sent to St. Petersburg by the Continental Congress wait in the city for about two years without granting him an audience.

Cordial relations were not established till the reign of Alexander I. Though the Emperor's political methods in his later years were the antithesis of American ones, and though he was the founder of the Holy Alliance, which all good Americans abhorred, he seems, at least in his earlier, liberal period, to have been well-disposed towards the United States.[1] He corresponded with Thomas Jefferson; and on two occasions he sent for a copy of the American Constitution, which was probably studied by his minister Speranski when planning a reform of the imperial government. Russia at this date was herself an American power, and it was precisely her attempts to extend her territory to the southward that called forth the protests of Secretary Adams, whose views were repeated by President Monroe in his famous message. The actual difficulty as to the boundary of Russian America was ended by the treaty of 1824. Some years later, the Russians abandoned as unprofitable the trading settlement which they had made in California, where, though they had not claimed political possession, they had remained in defiance of Spanish protest, and were looked at askance by the United States. Otherwise the connection between Russia and America was slight, but they remained on good terms, and on several occasions they acted in harmony in the Far East, where both benefited by the victories of the English and the French which opened up China. There is little further to note until the outbreak of the American Civil War.

From the very beginning of the war, Russia took her stand as the unwavering friend of the federal government. In 1861 she warned it that attempts were being made to form a coalition against the United States, and by her outspoken disapproval of all such plans she helped to discourage them. Her despatch of a fleet to American waters in 1863 attracted great attention. The

[1] American visitors to St. Petersburg were conspicuously well treated.

relations of the United States with England and France
were then so strained that they seemed likely to end in
open hostility, and many persons were convinced at the
moment, as others have been since, that the Russian squadron was not only sent as an amicable demonstration, but
was the bearer of sealed orders directing it to give aid in
the event of an appeal to arms. Though it is now generally
believed that this last impression was erroneous, there is no
gainsaying the open and emphatic friendliness of the attitude of the Russian government in contrast to that of most
of the other European ones in this the hour of sorest trial
to the United States. We may ascribe this attitude to a
disapproval of insurrections, to a cordial sentiment toward
the American republic, and, most of all, to a sympathy
with the effort to abolish slavery on the North American
continent at a time when Russia herself was freeing her
serfs. The two proclamations of emancipation were not
far from synchronous, and the men engaged in carrying
out these two social revolutions, among the most important
in history, were naturally well-disposed toward one another.
The Empire of the Tsars had also sound political reasons
for drawing close to the Union; for in this same year,
1863, a revolt in Poland led to the diplomatic intervention of England and France, which almost culminated in
a European war, and hence the idea of a Russo-American
alliance against common foes was rational enough. However, we are not called upon to go behind the fact of
the indisputable genuineness in Russian good-will at this
time.

As an expression of gratitude for this friendly behavior,
Congress, after the close of the war, seized the occasion
of the escape of Alexander II from an attempt against his
life to send a special envoy to convey to him its congratu-
lations. The mission was received with imposing cere-
monies, and in return the young Grand Duke Alexis was

despatched to America, where he was welcomed with popular enthusiasm, though trouble between the administration and the Russian minister at Washington interfered with the perfect success of the visit.

Following these international amenities came the purchase by the United States, in 1867, of the Russian territory in North America. This transaction, which was accomplished without preliminary disputes or wearisome negotiations, soon proved a good bargain to the United States; and it helped to confirm American liking for a country that had parted with its possessions on reasonable terms, and had peaceably withdrawn from the western hemisphere, thus freeing one more portion of it from European and monarchical rule.

For a generation after these events the friendship between Russia and America was an accepted commonplace in both countries; and, if not deep-rooted, it was at least sincere. Between Russians and Americans there are, alongside of many radical differences, not a few likenesses — in temperament, in the problems they have to solve, and in their relation to the rest of the civilized world. Both have regarded themselves as young peoples with the future before them, and this has led in both to a certain contempt for the "effete" nations of western Europe. The consciousness of rapid growth, of being the owners of vast territories with huge undeveloped resources, has inspired both with the same buoyant confidence that their role in the world is just beginning. In both Americans and Russians we find the same general absence of pettiness, — the "broad nature," as the Russians love to call it, — the same happy-go-lucky belief that they can make up by an effort at the critical moment for any amount of previous negligence and carelessness. For both, the questions of material development have been much the same, and both, though under different conditions, have been occupied with the task of fusing many heterogeneous peoples into one great nationality. When Russians and Americans have met, they have usually fraternized without difficulty. The Americans have found the Russians "good fellows" without that shade of condescension in their attitude which has sometimes been irritating in Englishmen, Frenchmen, or Germans. The Russians, on their side, have looked on the Americans as folk much like themselves, for they have been the quicker of the two in appreciating the resemblances between them. They have studied American progress, and have often copied American methods as those most applicable to their own conditions. Even in their high tariff they have imitated pretty directly the example of the United States; and the hopes which they founded upon it were based in a measure on the prosperity which the Americans have obtained under a similar system. Russians also used to believe that the two countries had one and the same hereditary national enemy, England, with which both had fought in the past and would some day fight again. Finally, the absence of conflicting interests has seemed to be a good guarantee against serious dispute. Such a friendship bade fair to be lasting.

Nevertheless, towards the end of the nineteenth century American sentiment about Russia began to undergo a change. In the form and in the practice of the Slav autocracy there was too much that was repugnant to the ideals of Americans for them to approve of it in the long run. Their feelings on the subject grew stronger when, after the death, in 1881, of the liberal Emperor Alexander II, a policy of reaction set in under his successor. Tidings of the ever sterner rule of the imperial government made their way across the Atlantic. In 1888–1889 the articles of Mr. George Kennan on the Siberian prison system were widely read, and created a lasting impression. Soon afterwards the repressive measures enacted against the Russian Jews

aroused a sympathy among Americans which was more than
academic, for the meaning was brought home to them by an
immense immigration of these same unfortunates. Thirty
years ago there were few Jews in the United States; to-day
there are some three-quarters of a million in and about New
York alone, and this is the direct result of the action
of Russia. As might be expected, this influx of des-
titute aliens has awakened some alarm, mingled with
resentment against the country which has unloaded
them on her neighbor. The Russian answer, that the
United States is at perfect liberty to keep out the Jews
if it doesn't like them, is perhaps sufficient from the
point of view of international law, but it is otherwise quite
unsatisfactory. If you believe in a liberal policy yourself,
it is no consolation, when the conduct of another puts a
strain upon your kindness, to be informed that you can
always protect yourself if you wish to. A reply of this
sort is nothing if not irritating.

The persecution of the Russian Jews brought its own
punishment, for wherever they went they carried with
them the tale of their suffering, and everywhere they could
count on the sympathy of their brethren. Although the
power of the Jews in the United States is of but recent
origin, it is already considerable, especially in the worlds
of finance and of journalism. Not only do they control
many of the public prints, but their strength and cohesion
are such as to make the rest afraid to offend them. It was
no slight thing for Russian popularity in the United States
to array itself against a force of this kind; for even without the inevitable exaggeration, there were too many
truths that might be told, of a kind to awaken the
indignation of the American people. Nor were the Jews
the only fugitives from Russia to spread a hatred of
the land they had left; for, whereas most of the
other immigrants into the United States are sincerely

desirous of promoting good feeling between their old and their new countries, the various Russian exiles, like the Irish, have brought with them a deep hostility to those whom they regard as their former oppressors. Very few genuine Russians, except stray revolutionists, have immigrated to America. The people classed as such in the census have been Jews, Poles, inhabitants of the Baltic provinces, Armenians, and others, for the most part animated by an intense dislike of their former masters. By means of the public press, and the tales which they have told in private, they have transmitted their sentiment to other elements of the population. And here, again, we must remember to how great an extent the Americans get their outside news, and the comment on it, from English sources which have rarely been friendly to Russia.

Profound as has been the effect of these various influences, the traditional friendship was not to be easily shaken. We may say that, in spite of everything, Russia and the United States remained on satisfactory terms until about 1898. The changed relations which characterized the next few years may be ascribed to the direction taken by the political activity of the government at St. Petersburg, both in internal and foreign affairs.

Although the American people applauded the idea of the Hague Conference, which won for Emperor Nicholas a short-lived popularity, the favorable impression which this step had produced was soon obliterated by the aggressiveness of Russian diplomacy, and by the growing tyranny of the internal administration, culminating in the régime of the late Baron von Plehve. As tales of the savage repression of everything resembling liberal tendencies reached the American public, often doubtless in a distorted form, yet with only too much truth, indignation waxed hot. The withdrawal of the liberties of Finland excited widespread compassion; the complaints from Poland and the

Baltic provinces found an echo across the water; the sufferings of the Armenians evoked pity. Above all these, the massacre of Kishinev filled millions of people in America with horror; for they believed it to be due, not to a mere outburst of mob fury, but to the instigation of the authorities. So strong was this feeling that the government at Washington took the extraordinary step of meddling in the internal affairs of another great state, by asking if a petition of American Jews would be accepted in St. Petersburg. A negative answer was, of course, returned, but the wording of the petition had been repeated in the inquiry, and was thus given the widest possible publicity.[1] The furious rejoinders of the Russian press and of its allies, calling attention to the details of lynchings in America and of the "water cure" in the Philippines, counted for nothing: the American people are not in the habit of reading foreign newspapers, least of all Russian ones. Whether the nation's horror about the Kishinev massacre was expressed in a correct diplomatic manner or not, it was genuine, and to ascribe it, as many foreigners did, to Anglo-Saxon hypocrisy, showed superficial judgment. The condemnation of the outrage at Kishinev was strongest in those parts of the United States where lynching is unknown, and where its existence in the country is regarded as a stain on the national honor. Even in the regions where it is not so generally deplored, people maintained that there was no parallelism between the two cases, and though we may perhaps question their logic, we cannot doubt their sincerity. The impression which the story of Kishinev produced was universal and profound.

In the meantime a revolution was taking place in international relations. After the Spanish War, England could no longer be looked upon as the permanent foe of the United States as well as of Russia; on the contrary, the two Anglo-

[1] President Roosevelt gave expression to the national sentiment about the massacre in his annual message of 1904.

Saxon countries were now on the best of terms. In the Far East, America had adopted the English formula of the "open door"; indeed, during the temporary effacement of England at the time of the Boer War, she had appeared as its chief champion. In 1899, when Secretary Hay demanded that the powers adhere to the doctrine, all gave at least their nominal approbation, but Russia so worded her answer as to leave its exact meaning obscure, thereby arousing American suspicion. By a curious chance it happened that it was in northern China, and especially in Manchuria, that American trade had lately grown with particular rapidity, and the political preponderance of Russia there appeared a menace to it, the more so as the advance of the Russians was accompanied by strenuous efforts, at enormous expense, to develop the resources of the country for their own sole benefit. Ordinary competition on even terms the Americans were not afraid of. They had admired the building of the Trans-Siberian railway, and they did not begrudge Russia any legitimate advantages she might derive therefrom. What they did object to was competing against subsidized industries, and, still more, being kept back by the various hindrances which a rival in control of Manchuria could easily put in their way. The conduct of the Russian authorities in the years preceding the war with Japan was most unskilful; at least, if the Russians cared to retain the good-will of the United States. Americans, when their interests are concerned, may not be more scrupulous than other people; but they are frank — not to say brutal — rather than tortuous, and they appreciate frankness in others. If, after the Boxer rising, the government at St. Petersburg had declared its intention of retaining possession of Manchuria, as the spoils of conquest, the Americans might have grumbled, but in their heart of hearts they would have accepted the decision as not extraordinary. Instead, the Russians repeatedly, and even unnecessarily, announced an intention of evacuating the territory, while at the same time they strengthened their position and made every preparation to remain. Though this contradictory behavior may be explained, in part, by a struggle of opposing opinions at court, the American public, which had long accepted the English tradition of the wiliness and unscrupulousness of Russian diplomacy, regarded the whole proceeding with unconcealed wrath, — wrath mixed with disgust aroused by tales of the boundless corruption of Russian officials in the Far East. These facts in themselves are sufficient to explain why the Americans, even apart from their old fondness for Japan, had become so thoroughly pro-Japanese by February, 1904.

When war finally broke out, to the surprise of the Russian government, and to the perfect bewilderment of the people, who had never taken the dispute in the Far East seriously, their first thought was that the Japanese would never have ventured to run such a risk without the promptings of some stronger power. Popular cartoons represented a small Japanese showing fight on the strength of the encouragement he was getting from a big Englishman and a big American in the background. That England should favor Japan was to be foreseen, — she was her ally and the constant enemy of Russia, — but that the United States, whom the Russians had supposed to be their friend, should thus desert them, was a grievous surprise, for they were unaware of any change in American sentiment and had supposed that the transatlantic republic was still their well-wisher. Their astonishment, of course, turned to anger, which was heightened by the emphatic tone taken by the American government in protecting the neutral rights of its citizens. For their part, the Japanese, as was natural, did what they could to increase the estrangement by committing their citizens in Russia not to English but to American care, during hostilities, and by giving prominence to the demonstrations of sympathy from across the water.

Since then there has been a reaction towards the old better feeling. The Japanese have shown that they did not need the help of the United States or of any one else in order to carry on a successful war. The vast majority of Russians hated the conflict, and they were thankful to President Roosevelt for taking the first step towards its termination. His act also proved that the United States was not hostile to them, but only to a policy for which no one in Russia itself now has a good word to say. American opinion is again disposed to be friendly, and particularly to sympathize with the efforts of Russian liberals in their struggle for a new system of government. The causes which have alienated the two countries have for the most part disappeared, while several of the factors which in the past made for amity still remain. In the affairs of Eastern Asia their interests ought not to clash again as they once did. To be sure, this may happen, and for the same reasons as before; but it is perhaps less probable than an understanding between them in regard not only to China but to Japan, an understanding which in case of serious complications with the latter might be of great value to the United States. Until Russia has worked out of her internal crisis, whose end no one can now foresee, her influence must remain diminished among nations. But though she is far from the proud threatening position which she held five years ago, the real sources of her strength have not been touched by war or revolution. She will remain one of the leading powers in the world, and Americans will do well to strive for a reëstablishment of the genuine good feeling which so long prevailed between the two nations.

As for the other states of continental Europe, we need not linger here over American relations with them. With all, there have been the usual interchanges of expressions of good-will and negotiations of various commercial and other treaties. The present conditions of intercourse with them are normal and satisfactory.

Now that Spain no longer owns a foot of land in the New World, Americans have towards her that kindly feeling which people are wont to cherish for those over whom they have triumphed without too much cost to themselves. It is worth noting that Americans, and in particular American officials connected with Cuba or the Philippines, appreciate better than they did of old the difficulties with which Spain had to contend in governing her possessions. They are much less inclined to sweeping condemnation of her methods than they used to be, — in truth, they find not a little to admire in them. With Spain herself the dealings of the United States are now insignificant; but with the children of Spain in the New World they are of ever growing consequence.

With Austria-Hungary the United States has never had much to do. It applauded the Hungarian insurrection of 1849; it hailed the visit of Kossuth with tremendous enthusiasm. In 1853 occurred the affair of Koszta, a Hungarian refugee who had declared his intention of becoming an American citizen. He was seized in a Turkish port, and put on an Austrian man-of-war, which was obliged to release him upon the threat of an American vessel of superior strength to take him away by force. In 1866, after the withdrawal of the French soldiers who supported Archduke Maximilian as emperor of Mexico, the American government vetoed a plan of filling their places with Austrians. Of late years Austria and Hungary have furnished a large contingent to the immigration into the United States.

For the Italians in their struggle for liberty Protestant America felt the warmest sympathy. She welcomed the new kingdom of Italy into the community of nations, and the two were long on excellent terms. This harmony was, however, rudely disturbed by the famous lynching in New Orleans, on March 15, 1891. It should be remembered that this incident cannot be compared with most of the lynchings which have done so much to disgrace the country in the eyes of foreign nations. The New Orleans "massacre" was a deliberate act of leading people in the town, who took the law into their own hands because they believed that, under the system of terrorization established by the Mafia, the courts of justice were incapable of bringing the culprits to punishment. The object aimed at was attained, for there was no more trouble with the Mafia; but the lawlessness of the episode put America in a deplorable light in the eyes of the world. It also placed her in an awkward situation when Italy made complaint of the treatment inflicted upon her citizens. The Americans had no fear of forcible measures on the part of the Italians, although the latter at that time had the stronger navy; but they realized that their form of federal government left the Washington authorities without means of defending foreigners against popular violence. Secretary Blaine made the best that he could out of the case, declaring that the United States was bound by treaty to protect Italian citizens only in so far as it could its own, and it could not protect them in New Orleans. This reply, which was rather a humiliating confession in itself, failed to satisfy the government at Rome. On both sides the ministers were withdrawn, and for some months there was a diplomatic coolness, until, in 1892, Congress voted an indemnity to the families of the Italian subjects who had been lynched, and Italy accepted this reparation. The New Orleans incident has been but one of several which have caused no little vexation to the United States. On these occasions the republic has appeared, in

q

the eyes of the outside world, as a power unable to enforce in its dominion the observance of the rights of foreigners which it has formally guaranteed, rights which it expects other nations to defend in the case of its own citizens abroad. Attention has just been sharply drawn to this state of affairs by the anti-Japanese disturbances in San Francisco, and President Roosevelt has urged legislation on the subject. In consequence of the large number of Italian laborers in the country and the dislike felt towards them by some of their competitors, outrage upon them is always possible. Its occurrence would excite justifiable indignation in Italy. Otherwise relations are pleasant enough, though some Italian chauvinists may regret the fact that the United States would as effectually prevent Italian intervention in aid of their fellow-countrymen in the Argentine Republic as it would German action in Brazil.

With the Ottoman Porte the United States has been on an amicable footing despite the openness of American sympathy with the different Christian nationalities subject to Turkey, in their desire for freedom, and notably with the Greeks in their war for independence. American indignation about the Armenian massacres was so intense that in the event of their repetition the United States might be roused to intervene, contrary to its traditions as such action would be. In the case of Turkey, as in that of China, one of the most difficult tasks for the Washington government and the officials on the spot is the protection of the American missionaries. Impartial testimony is distinctly in favor of the good work which they do. They may doubtless have lacked tact, and have yielded, from the best of motives, to the temptation to meddle in matters not of their concern; but we can well believe that the majority of the charges brought against them by the Turkish authorities have been grossly exaggerated when not wholly false. It is the clear duty of the home government to support the missionaries against persecution as long as they do not go beyond the rights guaranteed them by treaty. On the other hand, we can understand why the Turkish authorities should regard them as a dangerous nuisance. Even if they carefully refrain from teaching disloyalty, the whole spirit of their instruction cannot tend to make the dissatisfied elements of the population more content with existing Turkish rule. The mere presence of these protected strangers, the representatives of a higher and freer civilization, must stimulate aspirations which the Turks regard with aversion. We can also understand why the government of the Sultan should strongly object to the return of its native Syrian or Armenian subjects who, by emigrating, have obtained the privileges of American citizenship. In its eyes they are firebrands of the worst kind, and this belief is not without justification.

If the United States were to interpose its protection between the Turks and their subjects, it would soon be involved in the mazes of the Eastern question, which, like the various European balances of power, has hitherto possessed for it only an academic interest. Until now it has steered clear of strictly European affairs; and it has had nothing to do with the partition of Africa, except in so far as it has safeguarded its trade interests. In the future, even if it cannot always avoid entanglements which it has escaped in the past, it may well hesitate before abandoning the policy which has spared it many burdens and responsibilities.

CHAPTER XIII

THE UNITED STATES AND ENGLAND

IN the diplomatic service of any country there is usually one foreign post of prime importance and special honor, which is looked upon as the crown of a career. Until lately the United States has had no real diplomatic service, preferring to make its foreign appointments in a haphazard fashion, seldom taking the matter very seriously. One place, however, has been appreciated at its true value from the first, and has been well filled. The office of American representative to London has been one often of weighty responsibility and always of high consideration, for the relations of the United States with Great Britain have been, first and last, more important than with any other power on the globe.

The reasons for this are plain. The American republic is of English origin and inheritance. Its people, many of them of English descent, speak English as their language, and have more ideas in common with the inhabitants of England than with those of other lands. The largest foreign trade of America has always been with the British Isles. Great Britain holds in Bermuda and the West Indies outposts of the utmost strategic importance for the Atlantic seaboard of the United States, and farther north the two powers have a contiguous frontier several thousand miles long. In the past their relations have rarely been harmonious. Their interests have clashed, their passions have again and again been excited against one another; and although they have had but one actual war since the Americans established their independence, they have been several times on the verge of hostilities, indeed there has never been a period of ten years in which they have not had some prolonged controversy, not to say a heated dispute. Yet now, in the face of all this, the intercourse between the two governments is marked by an extreme cordiality, which fairly reflects the sentiment prevailing between the two peoples. The spectacle is so new that the rest of the world has not yet got quite used to it, and finds it difficult to believe that violent friendship following so fast on traditional dislike can be of long duration. But before venturing any prediction about the future relations between the two countries, we must view the circumstances which have alienated them from each other in the past, and those which have brought them together in the last few years.

After the close of the American Revolution, the causes of ill-feeling between England and her former colonies were still manifold. We need not wonder that the long years of struggle had engendered much bitterness on both sides. The Americans, who had experienced all the hardships of a war about their own homes, especially resented the use against them of Indians and of German mercenaries. The mother country, smarting under her defeat, could scarce be expected to entertain a kindly disposition toward the undutiful children who had allied themselves with her old enemies against her. On the other hand, a part of the nation had always condemned the acts which had driven the colonies to resistance, — Englishmen could put the blame for what had occurred on the blind obstinacy of the King and his counsellors, — and there was room for hope that it would be easy for the Americans, as it generally is for the victors, to forgive and forget. As soon as hostilities came to an end, a brisk trade again sprang up between the recent foes, and there seemed good prospect that with the healing influence of time their relations might become amicable.

Unluckily, the carrying out of the terms of the treaty of peace gave rise to prolonged disputes. The weak government of the American Confederation was unable to enforce the promises it had made, in not very good faith, of giving compensation to the American loyalists who had been despoiled of their property. In their turn, the English delayed the evacuation of military posts in the western territory which they had by treaty recognized as American, and this provoked sharp protest and rejoinder. These first quarrels were soon followed by others of a commercial nature, and then came complications caused by the treatment of American neutral vessels in the years of conflict between Great Britain and Napoleonic France, — complications that led to the War of 1812, which sowed a fresh crop of hatred and settled nothing.

The long list of Anglo-American dissensions between that date and this need not be repeated here in chronological order; for our purposes a clearer idea of them may be gained by grouping the most important according to the nature of the subject.

Among the first to begin and the last to end have been the boundary disputes between the United States and Canada. By the treaty of peace in 1783 the St. Croix River had been fixed as the line of division in the extreme east; but unhappily it was discovered later that people were not agreed as to what was the St. Croix River. For many years the debate dragged on to no purpose. The attempts to arrive at a solution at the peace of Ghent in 1814 ended in failure; the award made by the King of the Netherlands, in 1827, was accepted by neither side, and it was not until the Ashburton treaty of 1842 that the matter was at last disposed of. The middle section of the boundary, extending from the Great Lakes to the Rocky Mountains, had been established with little trouble in 1818, but in the regions beyond the mountains, where neither party was willing to concede the other's demands, a provisional status of joint occupation had to be accepted. This was renewed in 1827; but postponing an agreement meant keeping open a sore which steadily got worse, and finally the arrangement was denounced by the United States. Then followed threats of war, until, in 1846, the affair was compromised in the obvious and rational manner by prolonging the line of the middle section westward to the sea, a solution that might just as well have been reached in the beginning. Even this did not prevent a later disagreement about the island of San Juan da Fuca, which the United States obtained in 1871 by the arbitral award of the Emperor of Germany. With Alaska, the Americans acquired another disputed boundary, which was not settled until 1903, one hundred and twenty years after they had begun to establish the line of demarcation between their territories and those of Great Britain.

A second set of quarrels, also due to proximity, have been those connected with the fisheries. The most persistent has been the one relating to the status of the American fishermen in the waters of Nova Scotia and Newfoundland, where, as British subjects, they had enjoyed rights previous to the Revolution which they were not willing to forego afterwards, and where by the treaty of peace they had gained concessions whose extent has been wrangled over ever since. Questions of this sort are notoriously complicated, owing to the many uncertainties connected with fishing, and to difficulties about the limits of maritime jurisdiction. Until the treaty of 1904 England long had an even worse disagreement with France. That with America still continues, but, with the reference of the matter to the Hague

Tribunal, there is hope of a satisfactory termination in the near future. In the Behring Sea controversy, in which the United States supported a cause that was good morally but weak legally, it was worsted at the Paris Tribunal of 1893. The result has been the virtual extermination of the seals. Finally, among other disturbances due to proximity, we might quote the abortive and absurd Fenian raids in the sixties, of which Canada had just cause to complain.

Another batch of contentions, which the Americans carried on chiefly under the banner of the Monroe Doctrine, grew out of the interests of the British in Central America and the desire of both peoples to control the proposed isthmian canal. The Americans were not long in repenting of the Clayton-Bulwer treaty of 1850, which had brought about a temporary calm, and they chafed under the restrictions it imposed until these were done away with by the Hay-Pauncefote treaty of 1901.

During the Civil War, at the moment of the Trent affair and before the detention of the Confederate cruisers, the United States and Great Britain were on the verge of hostilities, and they might soon have been again if the latter power had not yielded in the matter of the Alabama claims. In spite of the ample satisfaction which the Americans on this occasion received by the award of the Geneva Tribunal, they were long in forgiving the unfriendliness which in their hour of need had been shown them by the English, the people who had been loudest in condemnation of slavery. As for the Southerners, they felt no gratitude for sympathy which in the end had availed them nothing, when what they wanted and had hoped to obtain was material assistance.

Remembering that all these and various other controversies between England and the United States were carried on not only in the despatches of statesmen, but even more in the public press, which envenomed them and excited passion on both sides, we cannot wonder that the two nations were constantly irritated with one another. This was particularly the case in the United States, for such quarrels loomed larger in the foreign horizon of the American republic, where they held the chief place, than among the world-wide interests of Great Britain. For a similar reason the American mind was inflamed, by popular education and by current literature, about matters which had almost ceased to attract the attention of the British public.

It is an accepted theory that a foremost duty of the school history, and of the teacher who explains it, is to imbue the youthful mind with patriotic principles, to train the child to admire the national heroes, to arouse his enthusiasm for the triumphs of his country; but such teaching carries with it the inevitable temptation to represent the enemies of the country somewhat in the character of the villain in the play. Until the Spanish War of 1898 the United States had never had a conflict with a European power except England. It had, to be sure, had a Civil War on a gigantic scale, and a war with Mexico, not to speak of many encounters with Indians; but the Indian battles had been small affairs which had long ceased to be of much account, the victories of the Mexican War had been over a weaker nation that had been forced into the conflict, and the Civil War, full as it was of heroic episodes, was a strife between brothers, a thing which good patriots should not dwell upon too much. There remained only the glories of the struggle for independence and the achievements by sea (not by land, except at New Orleans) of the War of 1812. England was thus marked out as the natural foe, defeated in the Revolution, repulsed in 1812, but ever threatening and dangerous. The effect of such teachings on millions of children is not to be lightly estimated, especially as it was reinforced by boys' stories, sensational novels, Fourth of July orations and other eloquence of the kind.

Still another element making for hostility to England was furnished by the immigrant population. For over three-quarters of a century the Irish have been coming in swarms until they and their children are now numbered in the United States by millions. With a warm affection for their own unhappy land they have brought a corresponding hatred of the people whom they have regarded as their hereditary oppressors. They have told the tale of their woes, they have continued to sympathize with the sufferings of their brethren at home, and they have never forgotten their enmity against the hated Saxon. In a measure, the loyalty to the mother country of the English and Scotch immigrants has tended to counterbalance this; but these latter have shown less interest in their former homes, have held together much less, and have not taken so prominent a place in public life. The important part which the Irish have played in American politics has given them an influence out of proportion to their numbers. It has also made it particularly worth while to win their favor; and what was an easier and cheaper way for the American politician to do this than by "twisting the lion's tail"? Naturally, the politician made the most of his opportunity. If he could gain votes in this way, that was enough for him. It is true that the largest contingent of the immigrant population, that from Germany, long had no motive for disliking England. Of late, however, owing to the changed relations between the two countries and to the effort of both to stand well with America, the German-Americans have been inclined to be anti-English. The rest of the European-born have no strong feeling on the subject, one way or the other, but most of them are recent arrivals, and in the nineteenth century all of them put together did not play on American soil a political role comparable to that of the Irish.

For long the English enjoyed one distinction which we may take as an involuntary tribute to them. They alone have been able to make the American people angry by their remarks. In times past, abuse from others rarely got across the ocean, and when it arrived it was received with indifference, or was looked on as a sign of malicious envy, which was complimentary rather than the reverse; but English criticism instantly stung the Americans to a wrath which found vent in violent answer.

The feeling of the English towards the Americans was much less marked. It was not hatred, but, rather, contemptuous dislike. Englishmen, not without reason, were inclined to think of their transatlantic kin as noisy, ill-mannered, vain, and boastful. They resented the diatribes launched against them; they objected to the aggressiveness of American policy, which so frequently came into collision with their own; and they detested the high commercial tariff in the United States, which they believed to be aimed at them especially, and to be a serious injury to their interests. It was hard for them to understand how any one could sin against the sacred doctrine of free trade except from malicious motives. All told, especially among the upper class, their opinion of the Yankees was far from flattering.

So numerous indeed were the causes of antagonism between the two English-speaking peoples that it was easy to forget the influences which were in steady operation to bring them together. The two were, after all, of one stock, with a common language, a common literature, the same system of law, the same ideals of government and well-being, the same standards of morality and taste, — in short, much the same outlook on life. Commercial and other ties brought them into continual intercourse with

one another, an intercourse which the decline of provincial
self-assertion, on one side, and of conservative prejudice,
on the other, made more easy than of old. Mr. James
Bryce's remarkable book on *The American Commonwealth* at the same time made the United States better
appreciated in England and pleased Americans by showing
that the English were capable of appreciating them. Englishmen and Americans meeting in any foreign land at
once felt they were closer to each other than to any of the
people about them. The famous saying "Blood is thicker
than water" does represent a truth, which, though it may
be forgotten for the moment, cannot help telling in the
long run. You may hate your brother, but this does not
alter the fact that you belong to the same family, and have
something in common, shared by no outsider, something
which is always there to bring you together if you can get
over the grounds for estrangement.

Since hostility had always been less active on the part of
the English, they were the first to entertain friendlier sentiments. As a race they have always had an honest admiration of success, and the Americans of late had been amaz-
ingly successful. By degrees public opinion in Great Britain
came more and more to have about the United States the
sort of feeling that a father has for a son who has often been
disobedient and is still disrespectful, but who, after all, has
grown up into a fine, lusty young fellow, a little uncouth,
but very vigorous, — in short, one a father may well be proud
of. This benevolent disposition had grown strong enough
by 1895 to survive the violent shock of the Venezuelan dispute, which, in spite of its rather humiliating termination,
left surprisingly little rancor in the English mind. People
accepted it as another bit of American assertiveness, disagreeable in itself, but showing an energy that deserved
respect.

Meanwhile American sentiment about England was going

through a somewhat similar modification. This had progressed farther than was apparent on the surface, even if it was still too weak to prevent an outburst of anti-English chauvinism in 1895. Three years later we find a very different state of affairs.

There has been much discussion about the attitude of several of the European powers at the moment of the outbreak of hostilities between the United States and Spain. We may never know the full truth on the subject, but there is reason for supposing that some sort of collective intervention to check the Americans was talked of — we cannot say how seriously. The assertion of the English that their attitude alone prevented a European coalition has been denied emphatically by other nations: no one will now admit having thought of such a thing. Whatever may be the facts in the case, there is no doubt that the general sentiment in most of the European countries, especially at first, was altogether in favor of Spain, while the sympathy of Great Britain — of both government and people — was with America. English neutrality throughout the war was of the friendliest kind, and Americans felt that, in case of need, they could rely on English goodwill and moral support, if not on something more. The impression which all this produced in the United States was decisive. The national pride had been lashed to fury at the mere suggestion of a hostile league of the European powers, and the very different tone taken by the English awakened a lively sense of gratitude. The American people, all at once, abandoned the tradition that the British were their natural enemies, and acclaimed them instead their friends and brothers. It was a rather violent transformation, but this new era of cordiality between two peoples whose sentiments towards one another had been the reverse of cordial has lasted to the present day.

The reasons for the pro-American attitude of Great

Britain in 1898 appear to have been twofold. First, there was a very genuine popular feeling that the Americans were kinsmen, to whom, in their struggle with a decaying power and an unenlightened government, English sympathy should go out. The new war was only one more in the long series of contests between the Anglo-Saxon and the Spaniard, which had followed one after another since the days of Philip II, and which had done so much to change the face of the world. Secondly, there were sound practical considerations to guide the instincts of the masses as well as to determine the conduct of statesmen. The position of Great Britain during the closing years of the nineteenth century was difficult. Her policy of "splendid isolation" had thus far failed to produce satisfactory results. In the Near East she had found herself reduced to helplessness, at the time of the Armenian massacres, by the combination of Russia, Germany, and France, and in the middle of this crisis America had threatened her with war from another direction. In Persia and China, the Russians were ominously active, and England might be called upon at almost any moment to oppose them by force of arms. In the Sudan, Colonel Marchand was already approaching Fashoda, and the British government, which more than suspected this fact, was fully determined to fight France rather than permit him to remain. It was certain that a fresh crisis would occur before long in South Africa, and recollecting the German Emperor's telegram to President Kruger after the Jameson raid, Englishmen might well doubt whether a Boer war would not soon lead to a general European one, in which the British Empire would have to fight for its life. Vast as were England's resources, she could not face the whole world at once. In view of the menacing questions which pressed for solution in Europe, Asia, and Africa, what could be wiser than for her to free herself from all apprehension in at least one quarter? The friendship of the United States at this moment was well worth serious sacrifices, not only of pride but of material interests.

Seldom has the wisdom of a policy of concession been so fully justified in so short a time. When the South African War broke out in the autumn of 1899, public opinion on the European continent was overwhelmingly pro-Boer. Europe expected, too, that American sympathy would, as a matter of course, be enlisted on the same side — an expectation that was quite justifiable. If we look at the whole history of American ideals, since the earliest days of the independence of the nation, we may say that there never was a cause more calculated to arouse the enthusiasm of the people than that of the handful of Dutchmen fighting heroically for their freedom against the infinite resources of the greatest empire of the world. The Boers were more like the "embattled farmers" of Lexington and Bunker Hill than any other insurgents in the last hundred and twenty years, and the enemy they had to face was the same. The analogy of the two struggles was so obvious that it seemed as if it must appeal to the American imagination; and in truth, it did so appeal, but it was met and neutralized by counter-considerations. If the Boer War had occurred a few years earlier, there can be little doubt that sympathy in the United States would have gone out unreservedly to the Dutch farmers, who would have been continually compared to the heroes of the Revolution. Now the situation was changed. Young as the new Anglo-American friendship was, it had already struck deep root. When England had stood by the United States against the enmity, and — as the English declared — against a coalition, of the European powers, was the United States to combine with those same powers when England in her turn found herself isolated? Such an act would look like the blackest ingratitude. If the English and the Americans were

brothers, as had just been so loudly trumpeted, should
not brothers support each other in time of need? It
may be imagined that the English were not sparing in
their use of this argument, of which the Americans recognized the force.

There was also another crucial reason why the American
public did not feel free to declaim about English oppression in the good old way: the insurrection in the Philippines
was just then in full blast, and though it was all very well
to declare that the Filipinos and the Boers were very different people, and that the senseless revolt of the Malay
islanders against their benevolent protectors was quite
another matter from the heroic struggle of the Dutch
pioneers to maintain their independence, nevertheless an
uncomfortable consciousness remained. If one lectured
the English on their sins, the retort was too obvious. Altogether, it was not a happy moment for the Americans to
hold forth on the sacred right of "government with the
consent of the governed."

The cause of Great Britain would in any case have found
partisans in the United States. The struggle in South
Africa could be depicted as one for Anglo-Saxon supremacy
or as one between modern progress and hide-bound con-
servatism. The contention of England that all she had
demanded was fair treatment for her citizens settled in the
Transvaal appealed to American love of justice. In consequence of all these opposing claims on their sympathy the
attitude of the Americans on the subject of the South
African War was singularly hesitating. There were warm
friends of both combatants; still more people condemned
neither of them, and all were glad when the wearisome conflict came to an end. But this attitude of hesitation was
of immense service to England. If the United States had
from the outset shown itself in favor of the Boers, the
European powers who wished to intervene might well have

taken heart to do so, and have brought on a war whose results would have been incalculable.

From this time on nothing occurred to ruffle the good relations between the two English-speaking people, except the short episode of Anglo-German intervention in Venezuela in 1902, which indeed angered the Americans; but when English public opinion unanimously, as well as vociferously, condemned the action of the ministry, they turned all their ire against the Germans. Since then Great Britain has continued her policy of "graceful concessions." By the second Hay-Pauncefote treaty she consented to release the Americans from the irksome Clayton-Bulwer agreement, and to give them a free hand on the isthmus for the construction of an interoceanic canal. In the settlement of the Alaska boundary dispute, they again got the better of the bargain, either on account of English desire to be conciliatory, as the Canadians have charged, or because they really had the better case, as is more likely; for the high character of the English arbitrator, the only impartial member of the commission, appears a sufficient guarantee that the decision was just. To be sure, it would be foolish to expect the Americans to be grateful for what they have obtained in this way, — the winner in any controversy believes that his success is but a proof of the righteousness of his cause, — still, they appreciate the fact that the English in the last few years have gone out of their way to be agreeable to them, and they are themselves well disposed in consequence. At the present day, the two peoples are on the friendliest footing, and both believe that there is every reason why they should remain so.

Most foreigners are inclined to doubt this, and to point to their many quarrels in the past; but the causes of the majority of these quarrels have now, in one way or another, been removed: the boundaries are at last fixed, the canal question is settled, England has accepted the Monroe

R

Doctrine even to the extent of withdrawing most of her forces from American waters, all but a few of the seals in Behring Sea have been killed off; only the fisheries question remains, and this last is soon to be adjudicated by the Hague Tribunal. The patriotic imagination of young America no longer needs to look on England as the hereditary foe. Romances can now deal with the Spanish-American War, or the contest in the Philippines, or the march on Peking. New subjects of dispute may spring up, but to-day the horizon is serene. In the Far East the two countries have followed of late the same policy, for their interests have coincided. Grave complications between the United States and Japan might put Great Britain in an awkward position, but Great Britain herself is not entirely free from difficulties with Japan. Although trade rivalry will continue to exist, it is not so keen between England and the United States as it is between each of them and Germany. Even the American tariff is no longer looked on as a specifically anti-English invention; some Englishmen indeed are envious of it, and there can be no doubt that the prosperity of the Union under a highly protective system has done much to stimulate the movement in Great Britain for "tariff reform." [1]

Meanwhile, the progress of time and the improvement of means of communication are having their influence. Mere proximity, whether physical or intellectual, is not necessarily a reason for affection, and it may be just the reverse; but where good feeling already exists, it makes for mutual understanding. Every year more people travel and interchange ideas between England and America;

---

[1] If this movement should triumph, the Americans will not be the gainers. So far they have enjoyed unrestricted access to British markets, but an imperial customs union or high preferential duties would almost certainly be unfavorable to them.

already there is a considerable American colony in London, and international marriages are not infrequent; the Rhodes scholarships bring some American students to Oxford (though most prefer the continent); there are international races and tournaments of various kinds; important books appear simultaneously in Great Britain and the United States, and any really successful play is sure to be seen in both, — in short, visible, as well as invisible, ties bind the two countries ever closer together.

One last question to be considered in judging of the permanence of Anglo-American harmony is whether the present friendship is in keeping with the general trend of the modern world. We can affirm without hesitation that it is.

At different periods in the history of mankind nations have shown a tendency to group themselves according to one or another common sentiment. At times it has been the religious motive: witness the Christian coalition of the Crusades against the Mohammedan East, and again the hostile Catholic and Protestant leagues in the sixteenth and seventeenth centuries. At other moments similar principles of government have led to political groupings, as when, after 1815, monarchical Europe gathered about the Holy Alliance, while the idea that the free republics of the West have a natural community of interests was the basis of the Monroe Doctrine. But in the nineteenth century the feeling of nationality was the most potent instrument in uniting peoples, notably in the case of Italy and Germany. This last sentiment is still in full force, as is shown by the present Pan-Germanic and other movements, and it is coming to include not merely members of the same nationality, but, in some vague way, the people of kindred nationalities. We thus have the Pan-Slavic agitation, the dreams of Latin union, Pan-Iberianism, and even some Pan-Teutonic aspirations, although the last named are not flourishing just now. Whether any of these broader

movements will lead to permanent political results may
perhaps be doubted, but, taken together, they prove that
at present kinship, real or imaginary, is potent in determining the sympathies of nations. Looked at from this
point of view, the recent revolution in the feeling of the
two English-speaking peoples, instead of being an isolated
event, is but a manifestation of a general tendency. The
discovery that "blood is thicker than water" is but the
Anglo-Saxon way of expressing a belief which has affected
most civilized peoples in recent times. It matters not
that American blood in the future will be quite a different mixture from English — children by adoption count as
members of the same family. Many people in Italy and
France hail the South American republics as "Latin sisters,"
though some of them are rather black or brown ones.

To sum up, we may say that there seems to be good
reason for optimism about future relations between England and the United States. We must not forget, however, that if the disappearance of past causes of dissen-
sion, on the one hand, and the strengthening of natural
ties, on the other, promise well for the continuance of the
present cordiality, they cannot guarantee it. There may
again be such sharp divergences of interest as to reawaken
former animosities, if not to lead to actual conflict. Englishmen and Americans would equally deprecate any such
occurrence, and, as far as they alone are concerned, there
is small ground for apprehension. But in the dealings of
the United States with Great Britain, the Dominion of Canada must be of increasing importance. Before many years
elapse, Americans may be called upon to put their relations
with the Dominion in the forefront of their national interests and cares. If this should happen, it could not fail to
affect their attitude toward the mother country, which protects Canada; and it would be additional ground for desiring her good-will.

CHAPTER XIV

THE UNITED STATES AND CANADA

IN any consideration of the political future of the Dominion of Canada, and particularly in a survey of its relations with the United States, we should begin by recalling two fundamental facts. They are sometimes lost sight of by Canadians, and they are, we may admit, less important than they once were, but they are permanent, and will always exert an influence.

The first of these facts is that, as has been well said by an eminent Canadian writer, "whoever wishes to know what Canada is, and to understand the Canadian question, should begin by turning from the political to the natural map. The political map displays a vast and unbroken area of territory, extending from the boundary of the United States up to the North Pole and equalling or surpassing the United States in magnitude. The physical map displays four separate projections of the cultivatable and habitable part of the continent into arctic waste." These four "projections" are the Maritime Provinces, Old Canada, the Northwest, and British Columbia. They are separated from each other by thinly inhabited wildernesses or by mountain ranges, and though this separation is less marked than it was when Mr. Goldwin Smith wrote the above words and will become less marked still as Canada fills up, nevertheless it remains true that the Dominion consists and will consist of four separate geographical regions. This might not matter in itself, were it not that each of these regions has a closer natural connection with the American territory to the south of it than it has with the nearest Canadian section.

Secondly, along the four thousand odd miles of frontier, for the most part accidental and artificial, the population north and south of the dividing line is largely the same. An exception must be made in the east, where, in spite of the large Canadian colonies south of the boundary, there exists a national as well as a fairly satisfactory geographical separation between the French Canadians and their neighbors of New England and northern New York.   Everywhere else we find essentially the same folk on both sides: they speak the same language; they have the same laws, ideas, and general characteristics.   The Nova Scotian is more like the New Englander than the New Englander is like the Virginian; between the people of Ontario and those south of the Lakes the difference is slight; and from Lake Superior to the Pacific there is virtually none anywhere.   From one ocean to the other the differences between the English-speaking population on the two sides of this far-flung line are smaller than those between the inhabitants of northern and southern France, Germany, or Italy, and are insignificant compared with those between the dwellers in English and French Canada.

In view of these truths, and that they are such is hardly to be gainsaid, we cannot avoid the double conclusion that the union of Canada into one Dominion, less than half a century ago, was a somewhat artificial process, and that the present separation of Canada and the United States is the result, not of natural forces, but of historical accident.   Both the union and the separation may, none the less, be permanent.   Modern science has overcome many obstacles, and, thanks to transcontinental railways, the Canadian provinces are now bound to one another in a way that would have been impossible a century ago.   Moreover, in the last few years, there have grown up a sentiment for Canada and a pride in her which have created, over and above the old common loyalty to the British crown, a new, stronger bond of common patriotism, felt in all the Dominion, by French as well as English. There is, then, a Canadian nationality, as there is a Swiss and a Belgian, and this nationality, when not actually hostile to the Americanism of the United States, is at least consciously differentiated from it. The question of the future is, Which are going to prevail in the long run, the geographical and ethnographical influences that tend, and must tend, to draw Americans and Canadians together, or the historical circumstances which keep them apart?

After the cession of Canada to Great Britain by the peace of 1763, most of the colonists who had the means to return to France left the New World. There remained only some seventy thousand peasants, with no one to guide them save their priests. These held them firmly together, and have remained their leaders till the present day. At first the English government tried to Anglicize its new subjects; but later it abandoned this policy, to the regret of ardent patriots to-day, who declare that a little persistent firmness would in time have made Canada English in every respect. This assertion appears hazardous when we remember the tenacity shown by the French Canadians in the maintenance of their own nationality. If they had been oppressed, they might in their discontent have thrown in their lot with their neighbors across the border. As it was, when the American Revolution broke out, they did nothing of the kind. They had no reason to love Great Britain, but the British American colonists were their particular hereditary enemies, for the colonial wars of the eighteenth century had been carried on less by the regular troops from home than by the settlers on both sides, and had left a legacy of ill-feeling behind. What the Canadians would have preferred was a return to

French rule, but this the Americans would not consent to under any circumstances. It was clearly understood in the treaty of alliance of 1778 that France might regain all that she could in the West Indies, but was not to claim her former possessions in the North. The readiness with which she agreed to this — the Americans were not in a position to enforce such terms — may be ascribed to the exaggerated importance attributed to the West Indies in the eighteenth century, and to the absurdly inadequate understanding of the value of Canada. It is not certain that the Americans have not lost by this policy. As has been said, if Canada had become French in 1783, it would not improbably have fallen to the United States ere now.

English and Canadian writers have descanted eloquently on the aid rendered by the Canadians to Great Britain during the American war for independence. There is exaggeration in this, for in the critical days when Montgomery and Arnold attacked Quebec in 1775 and 1776, the local population remained almost neutral. Later, it is true, they took a more active part, when they had been embittered by the lack of respect shown by the colonial troops to the Catholic churches, and by the fact that the soldiers perforce paid for the stores they took with the continental currency, which was worthless to the recipients. The failure of Arnold decided that Canada should not be a part of the United States. The defeat of Burgoyne, on his counter-invasion of New York, assured American independence. In the peace negotiations at Paris, Franklin asked for Canada, in order to avoid further dispute between England and America; but when his suggestion was rejected, he did not press the matter, feeling doubtless that, as the region was wholly in English hands, he had no tenable claim. The Americans did succeed in obtaining the Ohio Valley, which, in spite of the protests of the colonies after its cession by France, had been united to Canada, but

THE UNITED STATES AND CANADA

had been conquered by the Americans during the war. Patriotic Canadians have deplored this as the first of the series of England's "surrenders" of their welfare to "Yankee claims."

For Canada, the most immediate result of the Revolution was that she received all at once a larger accession of English population than she would otherwise have got for many years. The Revolution had been a prolonged civil war, in which, as happens in such cases, the defeated party had suffered severely at the hands of their neighbors. First and last, some fifty thousand Loyalists, or Tories, fled to Canada, where the British government did its best for them, settling them in the Maritime Provinces, and more especially in the present province of Ontario. They brought with them the memory of their sufferings, and the intense bitterness against their oppressors which is peculiar to exiles who have been driven from their homes by political strife. The story of their hardships has been handed down to later generations, and must be taken into account in any study of the causes of Canadian hostility to the United States. By the Canada Act of 1790 the home government divided its territory into the two provinces of Upper and Lower, or English and French, Canada, which were equally unfriendly to the new republic.

The War of 1812 is recounted very differently in American and Canadian histories. American writers describe it as having been brought about by a succession of British outrages on the high seas. They devote comparatively little space to the rather insignificant battles by land, except to the defeat of the attack on New Orleans. Their attention is taken up with the gallant exploits of the young American navy. Canadians depict the war as a mean attempt of the United States to grab their country at a time when Great Britain was engaged in a life-and-death struggle with Napoleon. They show slight interest in the battle of New Orleans and none at all in the sea-fights. Instead, they dwell on the patriotism of the Canadian population of both nationalities, the gallantry of their militia, the brilliant and successful defence of a long line of frontier against a foe of greater power. They look back on the conflict with a proud satisfaction, seldom suspected by most people in the United States, who are unaware of the importance their neighbors attach to it, and fail to realize that north of the frontier the memories of the war are still cherished and help to keep the two nations apart.

It was inevitable that the long-spun boundary disputes, beginning with the one about the northern frontier of Maine, too ambiguously determined in 1783, and ending with the establishment of the boundary of Alaska in 1903, should make bad blood between the two parties. The Canadians, as the weaker, have felt a more vital interest in these contentions, and having, on the whole, got the worst of the agreements, they have attributed their ill fortune to the readiness of England to sacrifice them in order to avoid trouble with the United States; and they have been correspondingly embittered. This belief, we may remark, rests on the comfortable assumption that they were in the right on every occasion, and that whatever they lost in the final decision was a "surrender."

During the nineteenth century the growth of Canada, though steady, was not rapid. In 1841 the two provinces were united, and in time immigration from Great Britain made the English-speaking inhabitants a majority. The number of settlers from Scotland and from the North of Ireland has been so great that this sturdy, loyal element forms a much more considerable ingredient of the population than it does farther south. As for the Irish Catholics, circumstances have assigned to them an especially important role, not wholly in keeping with their behavior elsewhere, that of moderators; for it is they who prevent national and religious antagonism in the provinces from coinciding. The extreme Protestants of Ontario and the devoted French Catholics of Quebec are separated from each other by a deep religious hostility, as well as by their differences of speech and of racial characteristics. It is most fortunate, then, that there is a strong Irish contingent to lean to one side in questions of language, to the other in matters relating to the church.

With Lord Elgin's treaty, in 1854, a new period began in the history of the trade between Canada and her southern neighbor. So profitable did this prove to the former country that the latter came to feel that it had got the worst of the bargain. It was also incensed by the sympathy which Canada showed for the South during the Civil War. In consequence, when the period for which the trade treaty was made came to an end in 1865, the agreement was not renewed. Justifiable as such action may have been from a commercial point of view, it was none the less short-sighted. If the Americans believed that Canada would one day come into the Union, they should have prepared the way for the event by cultivating close trade relations, even if the weaker state did in the meantime get the greater profit from them. Wise foresight would have dictated the same sort of policy in the United States as was shown by Prussia in her formation of the German Zollverein,—a willingness to sacrifice small temporary advantages in favor of large aims for the future. But a popular government is seldom guided by such long views if they mean immediate loss.

The purchase of Alaska by the United States, in 1867, was an unwelcome stroke to the Canadians. Thanks to it, the Americans, especially since the boundary dispute was settled to their advantage, have held British Columbia, with her small sea-coast, as it were in a vice. The steady attraction of the same neighbors to the south, the north, and, for half her extent, to the west of her must exert an influence in uniting territories so obviously belonging together.

In the same year, 1867, the present form of the Canadian federal union was established. In Washington, the House of Representatives protested against the step in an extraordinary resolution, declaring it to be contrary to the spirit of the Monroe Doctrine, a piece of gratuitous impertinence which Canadians have not forgotten. The Dominion was at first an artificial creation, favored by the home government, and acceded to slowly and unwillingly by the Maritime Provinces, and by British Columbia, the latter joining in 1871. Prince Edward's Island came in in 1873; Newfoundland still holds aloof.

For a generation the new Dominion grew but slowly; and until the building of the Canadian Pacific its constituent parts had little to do with one another. We must remember that British Columbia, lying beyond the Rocky Mountains, was far distant from Canada proper and by sea in direct communication with England from the opposite direction; and Manitoba was naturally much more closely connected with Dakota and Minnesota than with Ontario. At each Canadian census the slow progress of a country with such splendid possibilities awoke fresh disappointment. Contrasted with the rapid growth of the republic to the south, it was painful to national pride. Then, too, the desire for American markets was strong in the minds of many Canadians, and as the years softened the memories of former disputes, there was for a time a considerable, though never active, feeling in favor of annexation. With a little fostering care the Americans might have nursed this sentiment into a real force, instead of which they never troubled their heads about it.

One thing above all others grieved patriotic Canadians — the steady emigration across the border. Settlers were attracted to the southward by the greater activity and prosperity which they found there, and year after year they went over in thousands, obtained profitable employment and remained permanently. According to the United States census of 1900, there were then nearly twelve hundred thousand people of Canadian birth in the United States. If we add to them the children born in the United States of Canadian parents, we get a total of some two million, two hundred thousand lost to the Dominion, or about thirty per cent of what its total population would have been at that date if they had remained at home. Even this does not tell the whole story, for it leaves out of account many immigrants to Canada from Great Britain who have afterwards gone southward. The English-speaking Canadians have scattered throughout the Northern States, and have followed occupations of all kinds. In most cases, they have soon had themselves naturalized, and are not to be distinguished from the Americans about them. The French Canadians also, in spite of the efforts of the clergy to keep them back, have wandered away in large numbers, and have settled chiefly in the mill towns of New England. At first they left Quebec with the intention of returning, as many have done, but most have come to stay in their new homes. To counterbalance this terrific loss, the Canadian census of 1901 could show only 127,899 Americans in the whole Dominion.

With the opening years of the twentieth century, the tide at last began to turn. Although the population of the Maritime Provinces remains almost stationary, and that of the central region is not increasing very fast, the new western part of the Dominion is advancing by leaps and bounds. Men have discovered that wheat can be cultivated much farther north than had previously been supposed; indeed, the conditions of climate and soil appear to be more favorable to its growth in Canada than in the territory immediately to the south of her. Moreover, as the United States is daily getting more crowded, and as it has now no great new regions left to open up, it may before long cease to produce more than enough grain for its own consumption. Its place as the chief wheat-exporting country in the world is coveted by Canada. And grain is not her sole reliance: her forests will be called on more and more to supply the lumber which their depleted American rivals will be unable to furnish; her fisheries, both in the east and in the west, are of untold value; she has copper north of Lake Superior, coal in Nova Scotia and elsewhere, mineral wealth of all kinds in her Rocky Mountains only waiting to be exploited, and near the Alaska frontier the gold of the Klondike. These resources, which are just beginning to be developed, hold forth a brilliant promise for the future. Thanks to all this, and also to very strenuous advertising, immigration, which in 1901 was still under fifty thousand, in 1906 had risen to 215,912; and, a greater triumph still, the number who came from the United States had risen in these years from less than eighteen thousand to nearly sixty-four thousand. The Canadians are tasting the sweets of revenge.

One need not wonder if this new-born prosperity has had an almost intoxicating effect on their imagination. Their dreams are indeed of the rosiest kind. They see no limit to their growth, and talk of the day when their land shall support hundreds of millions of inhabitants. As they put it, "The United States has been the country of the nineteenth century, Canada will be that of the twentieth." Even the climate, which is rather dreaded by people at a distance, is lauded as one of the attractions of the Dominion.

Of course, we must not take the words of such enthusiasts too seriously. Americans, in particular, are so familiar at home with the buoyant optimism which revels in a fair future, while overlooking some of the ugly realities of the present, that they can afford to be indulgent when they find it in others, especially when there is so much justification. There is no doubt that Canada is at last developing rapidly, that she has immense unexplored resources, and is capable of supporting a population several times larger than the one now living within her borders. We may not share all her admiration for her climate, — it has been well said that the heat of the stove is as debilitating as that of the sun, — yet the winter is not only endurable for the white race, but it is, on the whole, healthful and bracing. In character and resources Canada resembles Siberia more than she does any other territory; but her climate is less rigorous, her scenery finer, and the proportion of her good land is somewhat greater. Granting that her wheat-fields, like Siberia's, extend much farther north than was once supposed possible, she has, after all, a vast extent of barren wilderness which can never be of much value. Wheat lands, too, desirable as they are, do not need a very large population to work them in our day of improved machines and extensive cultivation. Canada can never possess the variety of staples produced by the United States with its much more varied conditions. Cotton, silk, tobacco, sugar-cane, rice, many kinds of fruit, and other Southern products are, in the nature of things, impossible of cultivation there. The mineral wealth is immense, but we may well doubt whether it is equal to that of the United States, — at present the output is not a fifteenth of the American. When all is said and done, Quebec was founded before New York, and if the resources of Canada were greater than those of her southern neighbor, the world would have discovered the fact before now.

There is also nothing in the beginning of an emigration to ' the northward that need alarm, or even astonish, Americans, especially while it is still only a twentieth of what they themselves are receiving from outside. It is true that this

emigration is made up of excellent elements, — perhaps the
best that Canada is getting, — but the movement in itself
is natural, and is the continuation of one that has run
through the history of the United States.   With every
decade the frontier line of colonization was pushed farther
and farther to the westward, until, toward the end of the
nineteenth century, there were no new tracts to open up,
except Oklahoma, and no part of Canada has grown in the
last ten years as Oklahoma has.   But as the frontier which
has played such a part in the history of the American
West disappeared, men discovered that in Canada there
were yet unopened regions, and the old movement set
in again, this time to the northward.   The original settlers
who have pressed on after finishing their pioneer work
in their first homes, have not, however, left a waste behind them: their place has been filled by newcomers, who
have increased with the development of the country.   The
farmer who has sold his land in Iowa to seek virgin soil
in Alberta may be the son of a man who parted with his
acres in Ohio to go to Iowa, and the grandson of one who
left New York or Pennsylvania for Ohio.   And far from
being left vacant, New York and Pennsylvania have each
to-day a larger population than that of the whole Dominion.   Americans, then, have no cause to be alarmed at the
prosperity of their neighbors any more than they have to
depreciate it.   Unluckily they must put up with the fact
that one of its effects has been to heighten national consciousness and a sense of rivalry with them.

It is in the nature of things that there should be much
more hostility to the United States among Canadians
than there is to Canada among Americans.   This is to be
expected between two peoples of unequal strength, when
the weaker has a succession of grievances against the
stronger, and is suspicious of its designs for the future.
For instance, we might conceive of the Belgians hating

the French when the French were innocent of hostile feeling, or perhaps of any feeling at all, toward the Belgians. Canada is as large as the United States, but the difference between them in population and developed resources is greater than that between France and Belgium. We need not be surprised, therefore, if Canadian newspapers abound in hits at America, while the American ones bother themselves little about Canadian affairs. But in order to get a complete understanding of the attitude of the Canadians, we must examine separately the several elements that make up the population.

Of all the inhabitants of the Dominion, the Irish Catholics are probably the most friendly to the United States. They have inherited little loyalty to England and her King, and they know that millions of their fellow-countrymen have found a happy home south of the border. They have nothing to lose by annexation, nor have they cause for sentimental repugnance to it; they may therefore be counted as an influence tending to draw the two countries closer to one another.

The French Canadians are in a different position. Although they are still affected by inherited national and religious antipathy to the Americans, the old reasons for hostility have in great measure disappeared. Time has softened the memories of the colonial feuds, and the United States now counts among its inhabitants some fifteen million thriving and contented people of their faith. Hundreds of thousands of the French Canadians themselves have found a home and a living in the New England States. To-day the prejudice of the French Canadians is hardly stronger against Americans than it is against their fellow-Canadians of English stock. Nevertheless we find among the leaders of the French an invincible repugnance to the idea of annexation, a repugnance based no longer on prejudice but on a simple calculation.

s

They believe that annexation would be fatal to their future. It is true that their old dream that the French element in the Dominion might in time outnumber the English, is now impossible of fulfilment; still, the French bid fair to be an important fraction of the population as long as Canada remains independent. But if she should be annexed to the American republic, they would at once be reduced to a position of hopeless insignificance, so hopeless that one may doubt whether, in the long run, they could preserve their nationality. The clergy, too, are fearful of the more liberal spirit of the Catholic church in the United States. They have already noticed that their flocks in New England are less docile than at home, where the payment of tithes is enforced by law. Considerations like these explain the well-known saying that the last shot in defence of British sovereignty on the American continent will be fired by a Frenchman.

The English and the Scotch of the central Province of Ontario are the full embodiment of the typical Canadian and old anti-American sentiment. In the Maritime Provinces this feeling is less strong, and the new West, with its mixed population, is subject to other influences; but in Ontario there is still the inherited antagonism of the Loyalists who fled from the revolted colonies. Memories of their wrongs and sufferings, as well as later ones of the glorious repulse of the invaders in the War of 1812, have been perpetuated in legend and in popular literature. Traditions of the sort are not easily forgotten.

The patriotism of Canadians has besides been kept warm by their knowledge that any fresh war between the United States and England — and we know how often one has been threatened — must begin with an invasion of their territory, which they would have the utmost difficulty in repelling. In truth, the calm way in which the Americans have taken for granted — wrongly or rightly — that they could occupy Canada without much trouble whenever they tried, has caused natural resentment across the border. It must be admitted, too, that the general tone of careless condescension which has marked both the public and the private utterances of Americans when speaking of their kinsmen in the Dominion is a sufficient cause for anger in itself; such phrases as "manifest destiny" and "paramount position in the western hemisphere" are highly irritating. This has long been endured, but the national pride of the Canadians, always well developed, has at last something substantial to feed upon. The present growth and prosperity of their country and its brilliant outlook for the future are a consolation for the slights they have had to put up with. They are cured of all desire for annexation or feeling of dependence, and they were never less in a mood to make concessions.

By a certain poetic justice, now that the Canadians are no longer seeking for American favor, people in the United States are beginning to regret their own previous indifference towards Canada. Throughout the nineteenth century they held the comfortable belief that somehow or other, as a result of a war with England or, more probably, of "peaceful attraction," the northern half of the continent would come to them by "manifest destiny." Although this opinion has been expressed with the frankness characteristic of American utterances, nothing has been done to aid destiny: the treaty of 1854 was not renewed, only a futile protest was made against the formation of the Dominion, and the increasing American tariff duties have never taken Canadian wishes into account. Of late, however, men have perceived that the United States, in its dealings with its northern sister, has not made the most of its favorable position. Canada has suffered from American tariff restrictions, but so far from having been brought to her knees by them, she has artificially built up her native industries under the shelter of a high tariff of her own, first under the government of the Conservative party, and now under that of the Liberals, who used to be the sworn partisans of free trade. To-day, on both sides of the border there are powerful influences opposed to closer trade relations.

In these days of popular government and protected interests, the making of commercial treaties is getting more and more difficult. No one interest shows any readiness to let itself be sacrificed for the general good, and each can exact the support of others by threatening to desert them in turn. Again, the selfish opposition of a minority to every measure that threatens to be to their disadvantage is usually much more determined and persistent than the action of a majority inspired only by zeal for the general welfare. Both Canada and the United States now have high duties on each other's goods, and neither seems to be in a temper to yield anything. It is true that some persons in the States are becoming convinced that closer connection with the Dominion is most desirable. This is particularly the case in New England, where the manufacturers are eager for the free importation of leather, wool, and Nova Scotia coal. But it does not look at the present moment as if the efforts of New England were likely to lead to much — especially as they meet with little encouragement from any quarter. And yet Boston is the natural port of eastern Canada.

Since the Canadians do not receive for their exports to the United States one-half the money they expend on their imports from there, they are convinced that they are in a position to strike the harder of the two in the event of an actual tariff conflict. On the other hand, the Americans have always in reserve, in case of financial war, the suspension of the bonding privilege. As the St. Lawrence is frozen in winter, and Halifax and St. John are foggy and, if the passage through Maine were closed, would be far away, this is a weapon of considerable potency, but one to be used only at last resort.[1]

To Americans the relations between Canada and other British possessions are not without importance. It was at Canadian instigation that, in 1890, the Blaine-Bond Convention of the United States and Newfoundland was disapproved by the imperial government. Newfoundland may, sooner or later, enter the Dominion; but the Americans have no reason to be eager for a consummation which, among other things, will hardly tend to make the fisheries dispute easier. Another possible contingency that would affect them is the union which has been suggested between the Dominion and the British West Indies. Now that England has abandoned her old rivalry for the predominant position in the Caribbean Sea, and has withdrawn from there most of her soldiers and ships, the Americans would not welcome newcomers upon the scene. We should hear before long of Canadian interests in the Panama Canal. Indeed, the annexation of the British West Indian Islands would give Canada somewhat the same advantage of position as regards the United States, though in a lesser degree, that the Americans obtained over her by the purchase of Alaska. It would also provide her with a tropical territory of her own, whose prosperity she might, and probably would, stimulate by a bonus on its sugar and other exports. In rejoinder the United States could, if it wished, hit back very hard; an import on fruit from Jamaica would pretty nearly ruin the island. Finally, it is worthy of note that, though the Dominion is the largest of the American countries, it is still only a foreign colony, not a free republic, and it has therefore not been invited to send representatives to the Pan-American congresses.

---

[1] The suspension might be applied in part; as, for instance, against goods from another country benefiting by preferential duties denied the United States.

At present, the political situation of Canada offers her many advantages; for she enjoys almost complete self-government, and is at the same time protected by the power of the British Empire. This arrangement cannot, however, last indefinitely. In a generation or two, when the Dominion comes to contain a population approaching and then surpassing in numbers that of the mother country, it will scarcely remain contented with the status of a mere possession, whose official head is appointed from abroad, whose acts are liable to the veto of the home government, and whose diplomatic relations with foreign powers are directed from London. It is in the last particular that changes may first be expected. Where and how they will end cannot as yet be foretold, but there are three possible, and not unlikely, solutions to the problem of the future of the country; namely, imperial federation, complete independence, and annexation to the United States. Which of these shall prevail is a question of supreme interest to Americans.

The arguments in favor of an imperial federation — of a Greater Britain, of which Canada shall be a vital part — are both sentimental and practical. The devotion to England of her children in the western hemisphere has been manifested on more than one occasion, and notably at the time of the South African War. Even admitting that the contingent which Canada sent into the field was hardly large enough to warrant the stir made about it, we need not doubt that if the mother country were engaged in a more desperate struggle, one putting a greater strain on her resources, — for instance, the protection of India against invasion, — the colonies would give far more aid than was necessary against a handful of Boers. Recently Canada has afforded another proof of her pro-British sentiment — and that under a French premier — in the preferential tariff, amounting on some goods to thirty-three and one-third per cent, granted to England and to some of the other British colonies. There is no doubt that the idea of being an equal member in the community of the largest and most populous empire in the world is one to appeal to the imagination, a magnificent dream capable of rousing the utmost enthusiasm in those who glory in the greatness of the English name. It is also one which has for the Canadian farmer attractions of a more prosaic kind. Such an empire would pretty certainly be bound together by preferential duties, if not actual free trade between the members and a protective tariff against outsiders, and this would give Canadian wheat a decided advantage on the London market over rival grain from Russia or Argentina. There is no valid reason for regarding this dream as chimerical simply because the principles which it embodies received a check at the last English election. In one form or another the federation of Greater Britain is quite possible, and, though the issue will not be settled in a day, it bids fair to become within a generation one of the most momentous in politics.

From the point of view of the United States there would be no cause to welcome this federation. If it should be based on internal reciprocity with protection against other nations, American exports, both raw materials and manufactured goods, would suffer. So vast are the markets included in the domain of Greater Britain, so imposing is its situation almost everywhere, that if this greatest of empires were to follow a policy of exclusion toward others, it might provoke a league to break its power. In such a league, too, the United States might conceivably have a place; for, from the closeness of its relations with British America, it might be forced either to become a part of this Greater Britain or, as a matter of self-preservation, to oppose it. This may be fanciful speculation about the distant future, but it is a fact of the present that the drawing together of Great Britain and Canada is in no sense to the benefit of the United States.

So far, however, Canadian public opinion is inclined to look forward not to absorption, but to ultimate independence, with friendship, and perhaps an alliance, with Greater Britain. Canadians to-day are so full of life and confidence, so proud of their resources, and so entranced with their dreams of their own future that nothing could seem more glorious to them than the destiny of Canada herself. The prospect of her being merged in a larger empire does not appeal to them. Above all, it possesses no attraction for the French Canadians, who would be an even more insignificant minority in Greater Britain than in the American Union. Besides, though traditional fealty to the old country and to the crown is strong (except among the Irish) in Ontario and the Maritime Provinces, in the far West it is an exotic plant, too delicate to flourish in such soil. In these new regions, with their mixed population imbued with the materialism of frontier life, the whole tone is latter-day American rather than English.[1] The people are too matter-of-fact, too much taken up with their every-day affairs, to indulge in such luxuries as loyalty to a distant throne; to them it seems very unreal sentimentality.

From an independent Canada the United States would have little to fear. Strong and respected as such a state might be, it could hardly be dangerous. Canadians who believe that their interests have repeatedly been sacrificed by the mother country are wont to declare that they could manage their foreign affairs better themselves. Once independent, they would have full liberty in this respect. But the Americans would certainly not complain if, in future discussions with their northern neighbors, they no longer had to think of such contingencies as the blockading of New York and San Francisco by English fleets.

[1] The English immigrants in Canada are far from being generally popular.

There remains the third possibility for the Dominion: direct annexation to the United States, or union of some kind with it, either with or without a previous period of complete independence. This possibility, which for over a century most people in the United States and not a few in Canada expected soon to be realized, never seemed farther off than at the present day. Annexation is for the moment a dead issue. The United States is not eager for it, and Canadians are almost unanimously opposed to it. They no longer care even for reciprocity, which they once longed for. In each country the community as a whole is well satisfied with the present, and confident of the future, and it feels no need of a combination which must demand some concessions, not to say sacrifices. In each country, too, there is a protective tariff, whose beneficiaries will not of themselves give up a jot of their individual advantage in order to help along some general political idea. Why, then, should the Dominion and the republic ever unite, when each is so well off alone?

The answer is, to-day is not eternity or even to-morrow. Men, parties, protective tariffs, national ambitions, change, and change suddenly: the forces of nature remain. Nothing can alter the fact that the natural connection of every part of Canada is with the lands to the south of it rather than with those to the east or the west. Railways and tariffs may turn the channels of trade in other directions, but with what difficulty is shown by the much more rapid increase of American than of English importations into the Dominion in the last few years, in spite of a tariff hostile to the United States and favorable to Great Britain. And even if political reasons can prevent men from dealing freely with their most obvious customers, such hindrances must be but for a time.[1] In the end, other interests will

---

[1] "The action of the great forces is often suspended by that of secondary forces; but in the end the great forces prevail." — GOLDWIN SMITH.

win the day. Remembering, too, the essential similarity between the populations on the two sides of a purely artificial boundary, we can not conceive of their always remaining separated. Every new railway, every new wagon road, that crosses this line of four thousand miles, makes it a restriction harder to observe. If aërial navigation should so improve in the next few years that people could go with ease in any direction they wished, the difficulty of maintaining a customs line, and particularly one so long as that between the United States and Canada, would become almost insuperable. Even without this improved means of locomotion, as American and Canadian towns grow up within a stone's throw of one another the task of keeping them separate will be ever more complicated. We need not take overseriously the bickerings of the moment. Political and commercial unions are not always preceded by an era of good feeling; on the contrary, two nations, like two rival trading companies, may quarrel with and hurt one another until it becomes evident to both that the only wise course is to sink their differences. If we restrict our observations to present political conditions, we may see no reason why either the United States or Canada should ever wish to be merged in one larger whole; but if we take into account the great permanent forces of geography and nationality, we may well feel disposed to repeat the words of the marriage service, — "Those whom God hath joined together, let no man put asunder."

CHAPTER XV

THE relations of the United States with England in the western hemisphere have not been confined to questions concerning Canada. Even without the Dominion, Great Britain occupies a position in the New World which Americans have always to take into account. In the fortified and almost impregnable coral islands of Bermuda, she possesses an ideal base of operations from which a hostile fleet could threaten the whole coast from Maine to Florida. Farther south, the Bahama group commands the entrance to the Florida channel, Jamaica watches over Nicaragua and Panama, British possessions in Guiana and the Lesser Antilles guard the eastern entrances to the Caribbean Sea. The chain of posts is a formidable one. The strongest of them, the Bermudas, stand by themselves, and have given rise to no dispute. Although the United States may not relish their being in British hands, there is nothing to be done in the matter. It has therefore turned its attention all the more to the waters in and about the Caribbean Sea, where, during most of the nineteenth century, it found itself in fierce rivalry with England, — a rivalry which has only just come to an end.

The great American Mediterranean is composed, like the European one, of two distinct halves, the Gulf of Mexico and the Caribbean Sea, which are connected with each other by only a narrow passage, somewhat similar to that between Sicily and Tunis. The Gulf of Mexico has but two outlets: to the east the Florida channel, leading into the Atlantic; to the southeast the straits of Yucatan, which open into the Caribbean Sea. Between them, and dominating them both, is the western end of the splendid island of Cuba. The Caribbean Sea is landlocked on the west and the south; at the north is the broken barrier formed by Cuba, Haiti, and Porto Rico, with Jamaica as an advanced post; at the east is the chain of the Lesser Antilles, a line of small islands pierced by divers passages, and belonging to various powers. Along the coasts of the American Mediterranean are many points of strategic and commercial advantage, but two surpass all others: New Orleans, on the north shore of the Gulf of Mexico, at the mouth of the Mississippi, which drains the huge inland plain of the United States; and secondly, on the southern edge of the Caribbean Sea, the canal which will connect two oceans. From the earliest days of their independence the Americans coveted New Orleans; they acquired it in 1803. A century later, after several generations of dispute with Great Britain, they obtained definite control of the site of the future canal.

The West Indian Islands were the first part of the New World discovered by Columbus, and the first territories to be settled by the Spaniards. In time they were invaded by other nations, and during the seventeenth and eighteenth centuries they were the scene not only of the exploits of the buccaneers, but of many a fight by land and sea between the regular forces of rival powers. The English were the first intruders to establish themselves in this Spanish domain by their conquest, in 1655, of Jamaica, to-day their oldest colony. The French, the Dutch, and even the Danes and the Swedes soon followed, all striving to get what they could of this favored part of the world; for in early days an extraordinary value was attached to the possession of these islands, most of which have now sunk into insignificance. With the fortunes of war several of them changed hands more than once.

In 1783, after the conclusion of the peace of Paris, Spain, who had won back Florida and kept Louisiana, held all the shores of the Gulf of Mexico as well as the continental ones of the Caribbean Sea, besides Cuba, Porto Rico, San Domingo, and Trinidad. Her grasp was weak, but she had an overwhelming superiority of position. Compared with her territories in this quarter of the globe, those of the other European nations were mere outposts, although Haiti and Jamaica were proverbially wealthy and flourishing. The new American power, the United States, did not as yet possess a foot of land on the Gulf, but as the owner of the eastern head waters of the Mississippi it was already interested in Gulf affairs.

Here, as elsewhere, the next sixty years witnessed great changes. Spain, during the first quarter of the nineteenth century, lost all her continental possessions in the New World, which went to form a number of weak independent republics or passed into American hands. France, during the wars of the French Revolution and the Empire, let slip her fine colony of Haiti, which became an independent negro republic, as did later San Domingo. England gained several more West Indian Islands, planted herself on the South American continent, at the expense of Holland in Guiana, and began to get a footing in Central America. The United States obtained its first foothold on the Gulf by the purchase of Louisiana, to which it soon added West Florida, then East Florida, and finally Texas, so that it came to own the whole northern coast. The rapid development of these lands, and, still more, the strength of the nation as a whole, assured to the North American republic an importance on the Gulf much superior to that of the feeble Spanish-American states, or, in spite of the matchless situation of Cuba, of Spain herself. Its only real rival was Great Britain, who, though holding a comparatively small area of territory, nevertheless was firmly intrenched in certain choice positions, from which, as ruler of the waves, she could sweep these seas with her fleets. On the other hand, the economic decay of her West Indian possessions in the nineteenth century lessened their value in her eyes.

A curious fact about the rivalry between the two English-speaking powers in West Indian waters was that it was concerned not so much with any actual opposing interests as with an object that did not yet exist, — namely, the canal which should connect the Atlantic and Pacific oceans and become one of the chief highways of the world. The idea of such a canal is as old as the days of Philip II, and ever since his time people have taken for granted that sooner or later it would be dug. Indeed, many have kept expecting that it would be begun, not to say finished, before long, for the tremendous difficulties of the undertaking have only very lately been grasped. To the old mistress of the seas, and to young America, the question of the control of the future thoroughfare seemed equally vital. No one knew for certain where it would be made; but whether it was to go through Nicaragua, or Panama, or was to take some other route, the interest remained the same, and both countries were keenly alive to it.

In their contentions on this subject we find two sharply defined periods, separated from one another by the calm that followed the Clayton-Bulwer treaty of 1850. We need not cite the details of the various manœuvres and negotiations that were entered into, but we must note the different standpoint of the United States in the first and in the last half of the nineteenth century. During the first period, while England was trying to strengthen her position in such a way that the canal, which men commonly supposed would be dug through Nicaragua, should be as much as possible within her reach, the United States watched every movement of hers with the utmost suspicion, protested violently in the name of the Monroe Doctrine against her action, and upheld the theory that this international waterway should not be under the control of any one country. Its whole attitude was the defensive one of the weaker power.

The interest of America in any passage connecting the two oceans was obvious from the start, and the whole course of her development tended to make it ever greater. Her trade with the Pacific, which had begun immediately after the establishment of her independence, soon became flourishing. In 1803, as a result of the expedition of Lewis and Clark, she first laid claim to land on its shores. That she kept vigilant watch in this part of the world was shown by her sharp protest in 1823 against Russian advance. In 1846 the Oregon treaty defined her Pacific territory in its northern limits, and the acquisition of California extended it to the south. Since these possessions of the republic could be reached only by long weeks of travelling overland, amidst many hardships, the necessity of a quicker, easier route was evident, and it kept the desire for a canal constantly before the American mind. The discovery of gold in California, with the ensuing rush of people there from all parts of the world, brought the question of transport more to the front than ever, and lines of vessels were started from the principal United States ports to the two sides of the isthmus.

There was thus reason enough why the United States should view with alarm each step of Great Britain's which seemed likely to strengthen her already dangerous hold on the line of a future interoceanic route. The story of the moves and the counter-moves of the two powers is long and intricate, and was brought to a close, men hoped, by the Clayton-Bulwer treaty, which provided that neither should have control over the waterway, or build fortifications along it, but that it was to remain open to all. Much as the Americans repented later of having signed the compact, at the time they got the best of the bargain; for they attained their main object, which was a defensive one. In return for their recognition of English possession of British Honduras, which they had vainly protested against, they obtained a sufficient guarantee that England would not build and dominate the future canal. It is true that the United States bound itself in like manner, but at this time it was scarcely in a position where it could hope for supremacy.

In spite of some misunderstanding as to the exact meaning of the treaty, and discussion about the so-called Mosquito Coast of Nicaragua, — where England had certain claims which she did not surrender until 1860, — the Clayton-Bulwer agreement was successful in producing at least a lull in the dispute. For other reasons, too, the agitation in favor of the immediate construction of a canal subsided for a while. The building of the Panama railway lessened the immediate need of one, and the completion of the Union Pacific, in 1869, made California more accessible. Moreover, the United States was soon engrossed by the Civil War and its after effects, and England, upon the opening in 1869 of the Suez Canal, which gave her a short route to the East, became less eager for a western passage. Thus the matter slumbered, although various plans were evolved, in one of which the Emperor Napoleon III was interested. Meanwhile public opinion was beginning to turn away from the Nicaragua route in favor of the Panama.

With the organization of the French Panama Company by M. Ferdinand de Lesseps, flushed by his achievement in Egypt, the question became once more a live one. But American sentiment had changed: a feeling had grown that the future canal should be controlled by the United States. President Grant had held this belief, and during his administration various government surveys of the isthmus had been undertaken, and negotiations for a concession had been entered into with the United States of Colombia. The de Lesseps Panama plan was therefore looked at askance. President Hayes, in his message of March 8, 1889, declared that " The policy of this country is a canal under American control. The United States cannot consent to the surrender of their control to any European power. . . . If existing treaties between the United States and other nations, or if the right of sovereignty or property of other nations, stand in the way of this policy, — a contingency which is not apprehended, — suitable steps should be taken by just and liberal negotiations to promote and establish the American policy, on this subject, consistently with the rights of the nations to be affected by it. . . . An interoceanic canal across the American Isthmus will essentially change the geographical relations between the Atlantic and Pacific coasts of the United States and between the United States and the rest of the world. It will be the great ocean thoroughfare between our Atlantic and our Pacific shores, and virtually a part of the coast-line of the United States."

M. de Lesseps met the situation with much tact. Constantly insisting on the private nature of his company, he formed a special American committee to interest the American public and obtain support in favor of his plan. Still, what really prevented opposition in the United States from assuming an active form was the widespread doubt whether his enterprise would succeed. Had it done so, there would have been trouble.

President Hayes's declaration had formulated the new policy of his country, but his assurance that any interference arising from the rights of other nations was "a contingency

T

which is not apprehended" was, to say the least, optimistic; for by the Clayton-Bulwer treaty the United States had expressly given up all right to "American control" of any proposed interoceanic canal. In 1881, Secretary Blaine took up the matter, and began "liberal negotiations" to get over this obstacle. Unfortunately, his ingenious arguments were refuted without much difficulty by Lord Granville, and those of Secretary Frelinghuysen, who succeeded Mr. Blaine and continued the discussion, fared no better. The wording of the treaty was clear enough; there was no date set on which it should expire; and the English government evinced no desire to abandon or to change it. When the negotiations came to an end, the Americans felt that they had not only been worsted in debate, but had been left in a most unsatisfactory position, from which they saw no way of escape except by denunciation of the treaty. Although this course was urged by irresponsible individuals in and out of Congress, soberer men felt that it would be a breaking of the national word, and an act of the most serious character.

Another lull of some years followed. The increasing difficulty and final failure of the French Panama Company rather dampened the enthusiasm of would-be canal builders, and also helped to bring people over to the Nicaragua route, which, in contrast to the Panama, was recommended to patriotic sentiment as an American enterprise.

During the Spanish War the spectacular cruise of the *Oregon* from the distant waters of the Pacific to join the blockading squadron before Santiago, while it thrilled the nation with pride, at the same time brought vividly before it the disadvantage under which the American navy labored owing to the immense détour that had to be made to transport its forces from one ocean to the other. By the terms of the treaty of peace Spain forfeited her last foot of land in the New World, which she had discovered. In her stead, the United States greatly strengthened its position in both the Gulf of Mexico and the Caribbean Sea, and in reference to any future canal. It was now in a situation, as well as in a mood, to take up the canal question with an energy it had never before shown. If it had still been on as unfriendly terms with England as it was, with little interruption, from the Declaration of Independence to the Spanish War, there would have been danger of friction almost at once; but English sympathy with the United States during the war had produced a revolution in American feeling. Never had such cordiality reigned between the two nations. This was all very well for the moment; the question was, would it last? Fortunately the British government grasped the situation. For good and sufficient reasons it had determined to win American friendship, and it had succeeded; but it saw that that friendship would not endure if England placed herself squarely on the ground of the Clayton-Bulwer treaty, and, by refusing all modifications, thwarted a plan on which the Americans had set their hearts. Permanent good-will between the two countries could only be obtained by putting an end to the rivalry between them in West Indian waters, — a rivalry all the more difficult for England to maintain since her power in this part of the world had stood still, if it had not declined, during the greater part of the nineteenth century, whereas that of the United States had progressed immeasurably. English statesmen had made up their minds that the time had come for England to adopt a different policy, and that the benefits she would gain by it would more than compensate her for sacrifices she might be called upon to make. The events of the next few years in Africa and the Far East were to prove that they were right.

Having once decided on its course of action, the London government did not allow itself to be influenced by the laments of a few people at home, or by the sneers of foreigners at British weakness. Not only did it consent to negotiations for a revision of the Clayton-Bulwer treaty, but when a new agreement, the first Hay-Lansdowne treaty, proved unsatisfactory to the American Senate, it consented to a second one, which satisfied all American demands; for it provided that the United States might not only construct the canal, but control and fortify it. Following this, British garrisons were reduced in the West Indies, and British ships withdrawn. In a word, England virtually recognized American supremacy in this long-disputed region.

With this, the greatest, obstacle removed from their path, the Americans could now go ahead with their canal projects. The first thing to do was to decide upon the best route. While the majority of the people, for sentimental reasons, still believed in Nicaragua, expert engineers had quietly come to the conclusion that the Panama course would be the better one. The government at Washington accepted their opinion, and, using the Nicaragua project to bring the French Company to terms, made an offer, not characterized by generosity, to buy it out. Thus pressed, the old Panama Company accepted the hard bargain, and a treaty was negotiated with a representative of the Republic of Colombia to determine the status of the future canal. The rejection of this document by the Colombian Senate led to the Panama Revolution and the establishment of a new republic, which hastened to agree to a fresh compact, the Hay-Bunau Varilla treaty. In return for the payment of ten million dollars — previously promised to Columbia — and a later annual subsidy, the United States acquired practical sovereignty over the two ends of the route, and a strip of five miles breadth on each side of it.

The morality of American action in this affair has been often questioned. There is no doubt that, though the government at Washington was not an actual party to the plans concerted in New York and elsewhere which resulted in the overthrow of Colombian sovereignty, it may have had more than a suspicion of their existence, and it did nothing to interfere with their success. To forbid the landing of Colombian troops was to stretch the meaning of the old American right to maintain order along the line of the railway to an extent hardly justifiable in dealing with a friendly nation, and the haste with which the administration at Washington recognized the independence of the new republic and concluded a treaty with it appeared to many people indecent. The truth was the Americans did not feel that they were dealing with a friendly nation. They looked upon the rejection of the Hay-Herran treaty by the Colombian Senate as what they would call a "hold-up" — a scheme to interfere, for the sake of personal profit, with a work which was to benefit all humanity. It must be remembered that the relations between the Colombian President and Senate were such as to preclude the belief that the government of Bogota had been acting in an honorable way in the negotiation of the treaty and its subsequent refusal. It happened, too, that the political circumstances at Panama were such that the United States was able to get all it wanted, almost without moving a finger. It had little more remorse about brushing away Colombian opposition in this manner than a railway company would feel in disposing of the claims of an Indian squatter which happened to interfere with its line.

For some time after the signing of the Hay-Bunau Varilla treaty and the taking over of the Panama Canal by the Americans, matters did not proceed so well as it had been hoped they would. American optimism and self-confidence had underestimated the difficulties to be dealt with, — difficulties which seem to increase rather than to diminish as time goes on. But, whatever they are, they are at the worst only of a temporary nature, and at present it seems that they are being met with success. No one can doubt that sooner or later the Panama Canal will be dug: the wealth of the United States is in itself a sufficient guarantee that, though the cost may be enormous, the undertaking will be pushed to a successful conclusion. The difference of a year or two in the date of its completion, or of a score or two of million dollars, more or less, in the outlay, is insignificant compared with the importance of the result. We can see now that no private company could have met the necessary expenses; for a company must pay returns to its investors, whereas a government may rest satisfied with indirect profits. One smiles as one recalls the confident underestimation of all the earlier plans.

When the Panama Canal is at last completed, the advantages to the United States must be great. Even if it disappoints the expectations of those who think it will equal its rival at Suez in the traffic which it carries, it cannot but stimulate American trade. New York, as well as the Gulf ports, will be brought within a short distance of the western coast of South America, and will also be able to communicate with Australia and the Far East to more advantage than at present. How much this will amount to it is hard to say, — greater distance does not prevent Bremen from competing successfully with Marseilles in the same regions, — yet it must count for something. The gain to the American navy is still more evident; for the canal, by giving it a safe line of inner communication, will enable it to concentrate at short notice its whole strength in either ocean.

The supremacy of the Americans in the Gulf of Mexico and the Caribbean Sea is to-day firmly established. Great Britain is no longer in a position to renew her former rivalry in this part of the world, even if she would; the other European powers count for but little here; and though the appearance of Canada might be annoying, it need not be taken tragically. And there are indications that the United States will not rest content with its present situation, satisfactory as it is, but that, guided by natural forces and inherited traditions rather than by any set purposes, it will be led still further to fortify its position. The fate of the Danish West Indies is, we may believe, not yet finally settled. San Domingo is likely to come under American supervision, and perhaps Haiti. The connection of Cuba with her protector seems to be destined to grow closer, rather than looser, as the years go by.

When thinking of the future of these West Indian Islands, we must always remember the immense temptation which the prospect of free access for their tropical productions to the protected American market holds out to them. The prosperity of Porto Rico is in itself an object-lesson; and the economic advantage of free trade with the United States is enough to explain the strong sentiment of the property holders in Cuba in favor of annexation. Again, in the case of Jamaica, the recent welfare of the island is due to its fruit-trade, which the United States could destroy by adverse tariff legislation. So great indeed is the attraction which the American market, the wealthiest in the world, exercises on the West Indian Islands that there is scarcely one of them, of whatever nationality, which would not welcome annexation if it were accompanied by complete freedom of trade. As long as this state of affairs continues, — and we can see no reason why it should soon come to an end, — American preponderance in these regions rests on a firm basis.

But political expansion in the West Indies, following upon economic, raises a host of difficult questions. To begin with, it will be hard, without violating American traditions, to treat any parts of the New World as subject colonies, especially if they have already enjoyed self-government. How, then, are we to reconcile the annexation of new territories inhabited chiefly by negroes with the present position of the same people in the Southern States? Are the blacks in the islands more worthy of the ballot than those who have grown up under Anglo-Saxon institutions? If not, why should they enjoy greater privileges? The dilemma is evident. And there are other considerations which cannot be left out of account. It must not be forgotten that Cuba, Porto Rico, San Domingo, and Panama belong to what we call Spanish America, and the United States cannot separate its dealings with them from the broad question of its relations with all the Latin republics of the western hemisphere.

CHAPTER XVI

THE UNITED STATES AND LATIN AMERICA

A MONG all the foreign questions with which the government at Washington has to deal, none are of more far-reaching consequence than those that concern the relations of the United States with the different republics of Latin America. And none require more tact and patience in small matters or more clear-sightedness in large ones. The situation is in some respects new; for though the affairs of South America have always had a certain importance for the northern power, and have called forth the most characteristic expression of its policy, the connection between the two continents has not been close until recent years. We can sum up the chief historical facts in a few words.

As was natural, the inhabitants of the United States sympathized with the Latin Americans when they rose against the long-continued misgovernment of the mother country. The movement was a counterpart to their own successful revolution, and could not fail to enlist the approval of a people who had fought for and won their freedom from European rule. Accordingly, they furnished volunteers to the insurgent armies, and they were the first to recognize officially the independence of the revolted Spanish colonies. The enunciation of the Monroe Doctrine was, it is true, made primarily in the interests of the United States, but it was at the same time an act of extreme friendliness to the

weak republics of the South.   All this was logical, even if
the two struggles for freedom were unlike in many ways
and the parallel which has been drawn between George Washington and Bolivar serves to bring out differences rather
than resemblances.   American sympathy, however, did not
go far enough to produce a desire for joint action: witness
the tardy and hesitating despatch of delegates from Washington to the first attempt at a Pan-American Congress, the
abortive conference of Panama in 1826.   After this, for
more than half a century relations, in most cases, were
unimportant, amicable but distant.   In general, the Anglo-
Saxon republic, while protecting its weaker sisters in virtue
of the Monroe Doctrine, has been content to leave them
to their own devices, and most of its citizens have known
little and cared less about what was going on in the territories south of the isthmus.

With Mexico, its immediate southern neighbor, the dealings of the United States have not been of a kind to reassure
the other American republics, or make them desire its approach.   It is to be expected that Mexicans will never
entirely forgive or forget the treatment they received, and
that their fate will be held up as a warning to others.   But
there is no real reason for them to dread a repetition of the
events of two generations ago.   The Gadsden Purchase,
following a territorial dispute, was not perhaps an entirely
voluntary cession on the part of Mexico, but since that time
the relations of the two republics have been untroubled and
as cordial as could be hoped for.   By compelling the withdrawal of the French troops who supported the Emperor
Maximilian, the United States, while enforcing a principle
whose maintenance it believed to be necessary to its own
security, also did the Mexicans a service in freeing them
from foreign domination.   For that service it made no
attempt to exact compensation.   With the disappearance of
slavery north of the Rio Grande, and with the increase of

population and the achievement of order south of the river, the former causes of American aggression have disappeared. For forty years, Mexico, under the strong rule of President Diaz, has enjoyed a political tranquillity unknown in her previous history; she is in a peaceful, prosperous condition, and on excellent terms with her northern sister.

Central America has in the past attracted the attention of the United States chiefly by its proximity to the site of the future interoceanic canal.[1] Thus, the Americans supported the claims of Nicaragua against Great Britain for the possession of the Mosquito Coast, and long refused to recognize the English occupation of Belize. They also did much negotiating with Nicaragua on their own account; but this chapter of canal history has come to a close.

The story of the political relations between the United States and the different republics of South America since the establishment of their independence is brief enough. In regard to Ecuador, Peru, Bolivia, and Uruguay, there is nothing to be noted here. The Argentine Republic asserts that it has actually lost territory to a European power by American intervention, and has vainly demanded an indemnity therefor. In 1831, owing to the seizure of three American sailing vessels for violating fishing regulations in the Falkland Islands, the ship of war *Lexington*, sent by President Jackson, removed the Argentine colony settled there. Two years later the islands were occupied by Great Britain, which had claims upon them, and the Argentine Republic has ever since maintained that her loss of this possession was the direct consequence of American action.

With Paraguay the United States had a more serious difficulty. In 1850 it was obliged to send an armed expedition to exact satisfaction for hostile treatment of a ship sailing

---

[1] Walker, the American filibuster, whose exploits as a would-be dictator were brought to an end by his execution in 1860, never obtained official countenance, though he had many partisans in the South.

under its flag in the Paraguay River, but this small show of force was enough to bring about a peaceful settlement of the affair.

In the case of Brazil, we need only mention that in 1893, during a civil war, the American fleet present in the harbor of Rio Janeiro almost came into conflict with the Brazilian vessels which were blockading the port. As the Brazilian navy was then in the hands of the party who were in the end unsuccessful, harmony between the United States and Brazil was not disturbed.

With Chile, the chief South American power on the Pacific, and one of the most enterprising on the continent, there have been a number of unfortunate incidents, due not to any necessary divergence of interests between Americans and Chileans, but to a succession of accidental circumstances. In 1881, the attempt of Secretary Blaine to moderate the demands of Chile after her triumphs over Bolivia and Peru angered the victorious belligerent. Ten years later it so happened that, during the civil war between President Balmaceda and the Chilean Congress, the American minister in Santiago was friendly to Balmaceda, whereas the sympathy of most Europeans was on ʻthe side of the Congress. The affair of the *Itata*, in which the United States government was prepared to use force, if need be, to get back a fugitive vessel loaded with supplies for the troops of the Congress, increased the anger of that party, whose subsequent triumph gave the occurrence a semi-international character. While feeling in Chile was still sore on this subject, a riot occurred in Valparaiso, in which sailors of the American cruiser *Baltimore* were attacked by a Chilean mob. An unsatisfactory correspondence ensued, till a circular note of the Chilean foreign minister, couched in undiplomatic language, led to an ultimatum from Washington. Chile submitted, but the incident has rankled.

When the United States supported Venezuela against

Great Britain in 1895, the Latin Americans were jubilant over this defence of the Monroe Doctrine. Shortly afterwards, however, when war broke out between the United States and Spain, their emotions were conflicting. They sympathized with Cuba in her revolt, which was but the last of the series by which they had freed themselves from Spanish rule; but on the whole, the bonds of common language and civilization, and, still more, fear of the expansion of the all-too-powerful Anglo-Saxon republic, outweighed their enthusiasm for Cuba and for Pan-American ideals. Their apprehension seemed to be justified by the annexation of Porto Rico, and again by the events that took place in Panama in 1904. It was not that they cared for Colombia rather than for her revolted province, but they were alarmed by the spectacle of the United States summarily getting rid of the opposition of a sister republic, abetting the dismemberment of her territory, and securing for itself practical sovereignty over the canal zone. Finally, the arrangement made with San Domingo, however good the reasons were that might be urged in its defence, suggested a disguised protectorate, or one more step toward extending Anglo-Saxon sovereignty over Latin-American territory.

In order to still the fears thus excited, the United States has repeated its assurances of friendly intentions, pointing out that, in Panama, all it has desired is the requisite control of a canal which it is ready to build at its own expense for the benefit of the whole world; and that in San Domingo it is endeavoring to maintain the independence of a bankrupt state, threatened with foreign interference. But it has had a more convincing argument than these: it has been able to dwell on the fact that the Americans, in spite of all temptation to the contrary, kept their promise to evacuate Cuba, when the rest of the world believed they would never surrender so valuable a possession. Their faithfulness to this promise, though somewhat marred by the Platt Amendment, did indeed produce an excellent effect in Latin America as well as in Europe. For some years the island was quiet and prosperous, presenting a spectacle they could well point to with pride as a refutation of the charge that they coveted further territory in the New World.

Under these circumstances, the recent troubles in Cuba have a significance that goes far beyond the immediate limits of the island. Much turns on the success of the experiment being tried there. We must remember that to-day people in the United States are hesitating over the question whether those of the so-called Latin-American countries in which there is a large proportion of colored blood are capable of satisfactory self-government. As long as this question remained an outside one, men did not need to make up their minds decidedly, one way or the other; but with Porto Rico eager for statehood, and with the Philippines clamoring for independence or, at any rate, extensive autonomy, the matter has become pressing. President Roosevelt has recommended further privileges for Porto Rico, the first Philippine assembly has already met, and before long the American people must come to some decision about the future of these territories. Since the conditions in them are, in most respects, so nearly the same that what is true of one is likely to be so of the others, the conduct of the Cubans, who have been given a fair start, cannot help affecting public sentiment in the United States about the whole question of the ability of the Latin-American population of mixed blood to rule themselves without disturbance.

No fair-minded observer can doubt the honesty of President Roosevelt's administration in its dealings with Cuban affairs. American troops were landed on the island only after the government collapsed, when it was obvious that something must be done to prevent anarchy; and they will be withdrawn if there is a reasonable hope that the Cubans can keep the peace among themselves. The outlook, however, is very discouraging; for though we may take for granted that the majority of the natives prefer independence, and may even be ready to fight for it, the property holders of all nationalities appear to desire a union with the United States, which would, they hope, bring them not only protection, but free access to the American markets, with resulting financial profit. The mass of the inhabitants — more of whom are of negro blood than are acknowledged as such in the statistics — are densely ignorant, they have the tradition of insurrection, and they live in a country in which sleeping out-of-doors is no hardship, and which, with its alternation of field and forest, mountain and plain, is ideally suited to guerilla warfare. To the insurgents who took part in the movement that caused the resignation of President Palma, the whole affair was one long picnic : for a month they lived at the expense of others; they had no fighting to do; and in the end they were allowed to keep for their own use the horses which they had appropriated, for it would have been worse than useless to try to get them back. And even if the masses are of themselves disposed to keep quiet, it is not inconceivable that some of the property holders may think it worth their while to stir them to mischief, in order to force American intervention.

Feel about Cuba as we may, it is certain that the American government will and must interfere in the event of a menace to the foreign property in the island. Not only are there probably more than one hundred and fifty million dollars' worth of American investments there, but there are English, German, French, and Spanish holdings of value, which cannot be left exposed to the whim of a few half-clad negroes who in a few hours can work vast damage. Already, before the troops were sent to Cuba this last time, several foreign governments had inquired at Washington what steps the United States was prepared to take. Now, no nation will go to the trouble and expense of continually occupying and then evacuating an unruly region. As history runs, we may wonder that the Americans ever evacuated Cuba at all. If they do it a second time, they will deserve still more credit. But if the Cubans rise in insurrection before the Americans leave, and have to be repressed, perhaps at the cost of a long and arduous campaign, or if they soon force the American army to return once more, the occupation may be a long one, and the days of Cuban independence numbered.

The effect of the Cuban situation on public opinion in the United States is already evident. Those who have always declared that the abandonment of the island was a mistake, and that half-breed Latin Americans are incapable of governing themselves, now repeat triumphantly, "I told you so." Others who have approved with some reservations the policy of Pan-Americanism, cannot help being confirmed in their doubts.

On the other hand, the Latin-American republics are disposed to accept the policy of the United States in Cuba as the touchstone of its sincerity. Annexation, however veiled, and however justified, could not fail to excite their fears. They would believe it to be dictated at bottom by greed and by lust of dominion, and would regard it as full of menace to themselves. They, too, are liable to internal troubles which might endanger the property of foreigners, and which could furnish reasons enough for intervention. In spite of the special circumstances which may demand that the Cubans should be treated as children who, for the moment at least, are incapable of taking care of themselves, the fact remains that whatever policy is adopted toward them will react, not only on Porto Rico and the Philippines, but on the whole of Latin America in its relation to the United States.

By virtue of the Monroe Doctrine, even the weakest and the most disorderly of the American republics have hitherto been shielded against foreign aggression without having to render any service in return, whereas their protector, in the maintenance of the doctrine, has been called upon to meet without flinching the complications with European states which this policy has entailed. Of late, however, questions of a new order have arisen, which threaten to involve it in difficulties with its protégés rather than with the European powers. Secretary Olney declared in 1895 that the United States was "paramount" — whatever that may mean — on the American continent, and that it would defend its weaker sisters. This is all very well, but suppose — as has happened in the past — foreign nations have legitimate grievances to be righted. Then, of course, the United States does not pretend to interfere, unless the righting of these grievances leads to results that violate the Monroe Doctrine. But every dispute has two sides to it, with something to be said for each, and who is to determine which way the balance inclines? The United States has no desire to assume the position of arbiter in matters of this kind, even if the other great powers were willing, as they are not, to recognize its right to pass judgment on every controversy between a European and an American country. And if it should act as arbiter, how would its decisions be carried out? Would the European plaintiff, if in the right, be allowed to take any method he pleased to enforce the verdict, or would the United States serve also as sheriff, and carry out its own decrees against refractory American republics? Neither prospect is at all alluring.

President Roosevelt deserves praise for the admirable way in which he has recognized and faced the diffi-

u

culties of the situation. In his message of February 7,
1905, to the Senate, he declared: "It has for some time
been obvious that those who profit by the Monroe Doctrine
must accept certain responsibilities along with the rights
which it confers, and that the same statement applies to
those who uphold the doctrine. . . . An aggrieved nation
can, without interfering with the Monroe Doctrine, take
what action it sees fit in the adjustment of its disputes with
American states, provided that action does not take the
shape of interference with their form of government or of
the despoilment of their territory under any disguise. But
short of this, when the question is one of a money claim, the
only way which remains, finally, to collect it is a blockade
or bombardment or seizure of the custom-houses, and this
means . . . what is in effect a possession, even though
only a temporary possession of territory. The United
States then becomes a party in interest, because under the
Monroe Doctrine it cannot see any European power seize
and permanently occupy the territory of one of these
republics, and yet such seizure of territory, disguised or
undisguised, may eventually offer the only way in which
the power in question can collect any debts; unless there
is interference on the part of the United States." Returning to the subject in his message of December 5, of the
same year, he wrote: —

"We must make it evident that we do not intend the
Monroe Doctrine to be used by any nation on this continent
as a shield to protect it from the consequences of its own
misdeeds against foreign nations. If a republic to the south
of us commits a tort against a foreign nation, such as an
outrage against a citizen of that nation, then the Monroe
Doctrine does not force us to interfere to prevent punishment of the tort, save to see that the punishment does not
assume the form of territorial occupation in any shape.
The case is more difficult when it refers to a contractual

obligation. Our own government has always refused to
enforce such contractual obligations on behalf of its citizens
by an appeal to arms.

"It is much to be wished that all foreign nations would
take the same view. But they do not; and in consequence
we are liable at any time to be brought face to face with
disagreeable alternatives. On the one hand, this country
would certainly decline to go to war to prevent a foreign
government from collecting a just debt; on the other hand,
it is very inadvisable to permit any foreign power to take
possession, even temporarily, of the custom-houses of an
American republic in order to enforce the payment of its
obligations; for such temporary occupation might turn into
a permanent occupation. The only escape from these
alternatives may at any time be that we must ourselves
undertake to bring about some arrangement by which so
much as possible of a just obligation shall be paid. It is
far better that this country should put through such an
arrangement, rather than allow any foreign country to
undertake it."

It will be noticed that the President emphasizes the distinction between torts and contractual obligations, and recognizes the right of the European powers to take action in
the former cases. Indeed, unless the United States were to
declare a protectorate over Latin America, this is the only
tenable ground; for we cannot expect that any great self-
respecting nation will submit to another's meddling in its
disputes unless that other is willing squarely to accept all
the responsibilities involved. But, in practice, the President's distinction does not help much. Contractual disputes may easily be complicated by torts,[1] and it will be
hard to make the American people appreciate the difference between the two. They are inclined to view with

[1] For instance, the treatment by President Castro of the French Chargé
a'Affaires in Venezuela.

increasing impatience and suspicion all military action of European powers in the New World, and yet they are unwilling to substitute themselves for the injured party. This is easy to understand. Apart from their natural disinclination to put themselves out for matters which do not interest them, they know well that, if they undertake to enforce justice against a Latin-American delinquent, they will immediately be regarded as tyrants who, under cover of the Monroe Doctrine, are trying to become dominant over the whole western hemisphere. The role of forcible mediator is a most uncomfortable one. The Americans have shown a creditable willingness to defer to arbitration the controversies in which they themselves have been engaged, and they have good reason to desire that the practice should be adopted in all the disputes in which Latin America is concerned. Nothing could do more to relieve them of their present embarrassments.

In the particular case with which President Roosevelt was dealing in his message, that of San Domingo, he recommended a remedy which consisted in playing the part of both judge and benevolent policeman. The American government had brought about an agreement between San Domingo and her creditors as to the proportion of the Dominican customs-duties that should be devoted to settling their claims; and, in order to insure that the payments should really be made, American officials were appointed to take charge of the Dominican custom-house. The arrangement seems equitable enough in itself, and avoids immediate trouble. But who can blame the outside world, and especially the Latin Americans, for regarding it as a sort of disguised protectorate over San Domingo? No wonder that the Senate hesitated to approve the measure, which had to be twice modified before it was confirmed. No wonder, too, that it produced some disturbances in San Domingo itself, and although it is in active operation, has

not yet been ratified there. If the next of the many Dominican insurrections should start in the orthodox way with
a seizure of the custom-house (the only place where there
are available funds), the United States might be forced to
act at once. It is easier to see the beginning than the end
of such interventions.

In its policy toward San Domingo the administration at
Washington was doubtless influenced by the recollection of
the blockade of Venezuelan ports in 1902. The incident
had produced so great irritation in the United States
that the international situation was, for a moment, pre-
carious; and the outcome left American public opinion
profoundly dissatisfied. The guarantee of thirty per cent
of the Venezuelan customs to the creditor powers gives
them a hold on the country which may be menacing;
it also may easily lead to trouble with the native government. To make matters worse, the decision of the Hague
Tribunal, granting priority to the claims of those nations
which had taken steps to enforce them, was a distinct invi-
tation to creditor powers to press their demands without
delay, for fear of being forestalled by the action of others.
It was to preclude another crisis of the sort that the San
Domingo arrangement was entered into; but the question
arises, What next? [1]

The whole subject of the relations between debtor and
creditor states is big with possibilities of trouble for the
future. The modern development of capital among civilized nations, and its investment in all parts of the globe,
have greatly complicated the situation; the more so, as
international law has not yet expressed itself clearly on
some of the points at issue. So far, strength alone has

[1] In the still unfinished dispute between France and Venezuela, it has
looked as if France were remaining quiet on the assurance that the United
States, which has grievances of its own against Venezuela, will not forget
the French ones when the day of reckoning comes.

decided such cases. Take, for instance, the question of repudiation. When a community has been strong enough,
like the Ottoman Empire, or in a safe enough position, like
some of the American states, to repudiate its debts, the
creditors have had to suffer without redress; when it has,
been weak, like Egypt, it has been exposed to the danger
of seeing itself deprived of independence for the benefit of
those who hold its bonds. If the Russian Empire were to
go into bankruptcy to-day, France could do nothing to save
herself from enormous loss; but if Persia were to repudiate
the debt she has contracted with English and Russian banks,
she would be taken in hand at once.

The matter of private investment in foreign lands is more
difficult still. Civilized states have protected the interests
of their citizens abroad by treaties insuring to them, as far
as possible, the rights enjoyed by the native population.
When they have had cause of complaint on this score, they
have had to remain content with protests if opposed by
equals, but if dealing with weaker or barbarous communities, they have often resorted to force. Never have people
been emigrating so freely as to-day; never has capital been
invested in foreign lands to the same extent; hence opportunities for conflicts are being multiplied. At present,
owing to the disappearance, within a generation, of many
Asiatic and African states where Europe has had to interfere in the past, danger from those quarters is less to be
feared. It is in some of the Latin-American countries
that we meet the conditions best suited to produce international difficulties of a financial kind, frequently complicated by ill-treatment of resident foreigners. When we
find an ignorant mixed population, a government consisting of a few greedy politicians grouped about a dictator soon to be overthrown by some rival and his band,
and this in regions whose splendid natural resources inevitably tempt foreign capital, which is now scanning the

whole world for chances of profitable investment, we have almost ideal conditions for trouble. What makes matters worse is that the parties to such a dispute are often not those who made the original transaction. An irresponsible Eastern prince or Latin-American president may profit by his brief lease of power to conclude a loan with foreign bankers on terms which constitute a crushing burden for the future of the unfortunate people over whom he is momentarily ruling. He disappears, and they are left to pay the bill. On the other side, a group of shady capitalists, advancing money under these circumstances, will hasten to unload their bonds on the unsuspecting public of investors, to whom the transaction is represented as a reasonable and normal one. The debtor country objects to suffering indefinitely for the caprices of some conscienceless Khedive, as in Egypt, or dictator, as in parts of Latin America; but the state where the bond-holders reside feels obliged to do its utmost to protect the interests of its citizens, who have believed that their legitimate investment was guaranteed by the honor of an established government. It is notorious, too, that the decisions of the courts of some Latin-American states, owing to corruption or to subservience to the Executive, cannot be accepted as final by the rest of the world. To cap the climax, in some of these same countries legislation has been made, forbidding foreigners to appeal to their home governments for protection. All this helps to make the outlook rather discouraging from the point of view of the United States, which is trying to keep the peace without shielding the wrong-doer.

The last few years have witnessed the birth of the so-called Drago Doctrine, according to which all states should be forbidden by international law from collecting debts from one another by force. As was to be expected, this principle has met with much scorn in Europe, but has been hailed as a new gospel by many Latin-American countries.

There may well be two opinions as to its inherent justice. If, after many centuries of contention, the world has not yet made up its mind as to the exact limits of the rights of debtors and creditors among individuals, we need not expect any prompt agreement when in the place of individuals we have states, or collections of individuals, often less responsible than are private citizens. The Latin-American republics look at the question from their point of view, that of comparatively weak communities owing money. It is not surprising that at the recent conference of Rio Janeiro, many of the delegates desired to see the new creed adopted by the powers represented, and above all by the United States.

The position of the latter is delicate. It is evident that it would be relieved of much responsibility if the European powers were prevented by international law from trying to compel American republics to pay their debts. Incidents like the latest Venezuela one would then be impossible, and the burden of the Monroe Doctrine would be appreciably lightened. But, as we know, the United States is becoming more and more a creditor itself, and its interests are not in favor of protecting irresponsible debtors. In the course of time, if Pan-American dreams are realized, it may have more money than any other country invested in the domains of the sister republics, and in that case it will be more solicitous than any other that such investments receive fair treatment. At Rio Janeiro its representatives carefully avoided expressing an opinion on the Drago Doctrine, which was referred to The Hague. There its commissioners succeeded in putting through a resolution — one of the few tangible achievements of the Conference — that no nation should attempt to collect debts by force till arbitration had been tried and had failed.

As far as it goes the principle is sound, and its adoption at this juncture was a brilliant stroke of diplomacy.

The debtor Latin-American states, while not obtaining all they wanted, did acquire a certain protection for cases in which they should act in good faith, and the creditor European powers did not abdicate the right to enforce the payment of claims justly due them, but only consented to try peaceable means first. The United States was able to appear as the friend of both, and of abstract justice, without having to commit itself in one way or the other on the theories of Señor Drago.

If, at the time of the promulgation of the Monroe Doctrine, it appeared to Americans that the New World differed from the Old chiefly in being the home of free governments in contrast to the lands ruled by the principle of authority, to-day, at the opening of the twentieth century, one of the main distinctions between Latin America and western Europe is that between debtor and creditor nations, but the interests of the Anglo-Saxon republic are no longer entirely on the side of the former.

Secretary Root's declaration in Rio Janeiro that the United States "does not and will not collect private debts," though received with enthusiasm as meaning adherence to the Drago idea, does not dispose of the question. We may be sure that the United States will do its best to protect the property of its citizens wherever circumstances so demand. The causes which have forced it to intervention in Cuba would lead to similar action in Haiti or Nicaragua, if American interests there were of equal magnitude; and it would never tolerate either wanton destruction or confiscation, even if confiscation were sanctioned by the verdict of some Latin-American court. Already, American investments in Mexico are so great that we cannot conceive that the government at Washington would remain inactive in case they were menaced; and what is true of Mexico to-day may be equally so of Venezuela to-morrow. As matters stand, if the United States should formally accept the Drago Doctrine, it could not be with the understanding that it was thereby precluded from defending the large present and prospective interests of its citizens in the regions in which it is so eager to promote them to-day. And, on the other hand, we must not forget that, from the Latin-American point of view, the intervention of the United States would be regarded as perhaps more dangerous to the independence of the southern republics than that of any European power, and that forcible measures against one would almost certainly alarm them all. Even such salutary discipline as compelling the turbulent little communities of Central America to keep the peace with one another must be enforced with all possible tact, and the United States government has been wisely inspired in seeking the coöperation of Mexico in its recent efforts in this direction.

The idea that all the republics of the New World should draw closer together was first taken up with energy by Secretary Blaine. In many ways it is a development of the Monroe Doctrine, — one to which Bolivar had already tried to give premature expression. We may say that Pan-Americanism, as the conception is usually called, is based on two considerations. The first is the sentimental one, which is dwelt upon chiefly on state occasions. It proclaims the natural community of ideals and aspirations of the American republics. This community, be it remembered, applies only to the self-governing nations of English or Latin tongue: it was applicable to Brazil when it had just ceased to be a monarchy, and to Cuba when it became independent of Spain, but it does not apply to Canada even now, although the Dominion, if we take into account its Arctic domains, is the largest of all American states.

The second consideration is of a more practical nature, of a kind to appeal not merely to enthusiasts, but to hard-headed business men. In spite of natural sympathies, of the workings of the Monroe Doctrine, and other forces of the

sort, the trade between the Anglo-Saxon republic and the
Latin ones of the western hemisphere has been, and is,
unreasonably small. European critics declare that South
America, a new country, has preferred intercourse with
those lands from which she has had most to gain, the
lands of historical traditions and aged civilization, rather
than with a new and comparatively crude nation in much
the same state as herself. The American explanation is,
of course, different. It is, in substance, that the manufacturers and merchants of the United States have been so
busy elsewhere that they have neglected the regions to the
south of them. Without denying that there is some truth
in each of these theories, we may accept as more satisfactory
the explanation that, until lately, the United States has been
an exporter almost entirely of raw materials, many of which
South America either possesses herself, or has not felt the
lack of. American wheat is not needed in Argentina, nor
can it be expected to compete in the long run with the
wheat of Argentina in the markets of Brazil. And South
American industry has not been sufficient in the past
to make much demand on the United States for cotton.
But to-day conditions are changed; for the manufacturing
industries of the United States have developed, and are
developing, at such a rate that the Americans are not afraid
to meet their European rivals in almost any branch of trade.
It was to be expected that they should turn their gaze to
the southern half of their own hemisphere, where, as yet,
they are only beginning to get a good commercial foothold, but where the future appears to offer them golden
opportunities. Why should the American merchant leave
this splendid field to be exploited by the Englishman or the
German? Is it not the plain duty of his government to aid
and encourage his enterprise in every possible way? As for
the easy sneer that Pan-Americanism combines business
and sentimentality, we may answer that the same is true

of most national friendships, as well as of many private
ones. An obvious initial step to bring about amity between
people, especially in these modern days, is to bind them
by commercial ties which shall be to the advantage of
both.

The first Pan-American Congress was held at Washington
in the winter of 1889–1890. It lasted many weeks, some
of which were devoted to a special trip for the purpose of
showing the United States to the Latin delegates. Numerous speeches were made, and expressions of good-will were
freely exchanged. In so far as the object of the Conference
was to promote harmonious relations, it may be called successful; but its concrete achievements were not imposing.
All thought of a customs-union was soon abandoned, and
most of the various resolutions and recommendations that
were passed did not lead to action on the part of the governments represented. The most definite creation of the
Congress was the Bureau of American Republics, an institution which has had a career of modest usefulness. At its
headquarters in Washington it has gathered a library of
some fourteen thousand volumes; it has published, besides
its regular bulletins, a series of monographs on the conditions
and the resources of the different Latin-American countries,
and also a commercial directory. So far, its work has been
chiefly that of a bureau of information.

In accordance with the spirit of the Congress as well as
with Secretary Blaine's own policy, the Secretary and his
successors negotiated a number of reciprocity treaties with
different Latin-American states; but the moment chosen
was an unfortunate one. The McKinley Tariff Bill, by
which the American government committed itself to a
principle of extreme protection, was just going into effect,
and the highly protected industries had no thought of allow-
ing their profits to suffer for the sake of promoting friendship and closer relations with Latin America. So strong

was their influence that these treaties, like certain later ones with European countries, fell to the ground without even being submitted to the Senate for ratification. The manufacturer in the United States means to conquer the Latin-American market, if possible, but he does not intend to sacrifice any of his own advantages, if he can help himself. This attitude is comprehensible, but it limits the ideal of Pan-Americanism. After the high hopes that had been cherished, and the exaggerated language in which enthusiasts had indulged, such a result was meagre. Foreign writers proclaimed the whole movement a fiasco, and they have joyfully held that opinion ever since, although each new congress has awakened fresh trepidation. Some Americans, on the other hand, have attempted to conceal the smallness of the results by fine language about the moral effect produced by the conferences and the affection which the republics of the New World have come to entertain for one another. Stripped of rhetoric, this view has some truth in it: the Pan-American congresses have tended to produce good feeling between the United States and its sister republics. Even the actual creations have been of value, if for nothing else, as stepping-stones toward future progress. But progress has been slow. The second Congress, that of Mexico, in 1901–1902, accomplished very little.

When the third meeting was called in Rio Janeiro in 1906, men had profited by experience. In a session which lasted but six weeks this Congress achieved more than its predecessors. Avoiding general discussions, it did its real work in committees, and, laying aside all ambitious dreams, it confined itself to a modest programme of practical objects which were attainable.

The Bureau of American Republics was made an executive organization, entitled to correspond with the different American governments; to call their attention to the necessity of ratifying treaties or recommendations, —

in general, to take action in Pan-American matters. The
Bureau will also prepare the programmes for future Congresses, its scope as purveyor of information is to be
enlarged, and it is to make investigations of common
American interests. It is to have a building of its own,
which, thanks to a private gift, is to be a considerable
one, and which will probably become a club for Latin
Americans in the city of Washington. Each of the governments represented has been called upon to appoint for
its country a permanent Pan-American commission, and
certain bureaus dealing with special subjects are to be
established in some of the South American cities. Even
this total is not startling, but it represents distinct progress. In connection with the Congress, Secretary Root's
journey to South America made an excellent impression,
and one can only regret that the unfortunate outbreak
in Cuba which threatened to undo much of what he had
accomplished, occurred even before he got home. To sum
up, we can say that the Pan-American movement, which
is being wisely kept within moderate limits, has so far
achieved satisfactory if not brilliant results, and promises
well for the future.

Many foreigners have declared that Pan-Americanism
is nothing but militant Monroeism and the beginning of
an attempt to impose Yankee domination, political and
commercial, on the whole western hemisphere. Kindliness
is not to be looked for in the judgments of those who
feel that their interests are menaced by unwelcome competition, and we may expect that most Europeans will
regard this part of the policy of the United States as
a cloak for covert designs. We also need not wonder
that many people in the Latin-American republics entertain suspicions of the same kind. No fair-minded observer
can, however, deny that the aims of Pan-Americanism
have so far been legitimate, and the means of carrying

them out unobjectionable. Like the Triple Alliance or the
entente cordiale, Pan-Americanism can claim that it is not
directed against any one, but is an association for mutual
benefit, of which no one has a right to complain. It is
the business of other nations to make the most, in their
turn, of such ties as may be beneficial to themselves.

This is true as far as it goes, but though in theory the
commerce of Latin America may develop to such an extent
that all the peoples trading there may sell more goods than
they do at present, in practice some of them are likely to
suffer by competition. It would therefore be idle to pretend
that American rivalry in these regions is not a menace to
the commerce of several European countries. This may be
deplored by the philanthropist, but in the present stage of
industrial competition it seems unavoidable. If my shop
sells better or cheaper goods than any other, my rivals are
likely to be disagreeably affected, but not through my fault.
All we can ask is that competition shall be fair. Among
nations, reciprocity treaties with mutual concessions are regarded as within the rights of all. If the European powers
were to join together in a customs-union, the United States
would have no ground for protest, even if it suffered by the
combination; but it would be perfectly justified in trying
to detach any member from that union, just as Germany
is at liberty to make a better commercial treaty than the
United States, if she can. In many cases the odds are not
all on one side; for instance, it is not probable that American friendship will lead Mexico and Argentina to forget that
Spain was their mother country, any more than there is an
immediate prospect that the literary and æsthetic standards
of New York will supplant those of Paris at Rio Janeiro or
Buenos Ayres.

The gravest difficulties in the way of Pan-Americanism are those which are inherent in the social and political conditions of the New World itself. To begin with,

although such topics are avoided in public discussion, it is useless to blink the fact that the average citizens of the United States and of the Latin-American republics are not overcongenial to one another. There are, of course, numerous exceptions to this rule, but not enough to affect the general truth that the people of the United States have a rough contempt for the Latin Americans, especially when they are of mixed blood, and the latter suspect and dislike their Anglo-Saxon brothers. To the Latin Americans, the Yankee frequently appears brutal, egotistical, arrogant, and lacking in appreciation of the æsthetic side of civilization. To the citizen of the United States, his Southern neighbors, when he stops to think of them at all, often seem vain, childish, and, above all, incompetent to maintain decent self-government. Time and better acquaintance will, let us hope, do much to eradicate these mutual prejudices; but we must recognize, as one of the obstacles to good feeling to-day, the fact that the two races do not find it easy to understand and appreciate each other. In Paris, for instance, where there is a large colony of both, they seldom flock together: both have far more to do with the French than with one another. We must remember, however, that comparatively few people of the Anglo-Saxon republic and the Latin-American ones come into actual contact, hence their lack of natural affinities may not prove a serious obstacle to good relations. Then, too, nations can esteem those of very different character from themselves: the great masses on both sides do not know each other sufficiently to appreciate how much they differ.

It is the political suspicion which many Latin Americans entertain of their Northern neighbors, and which Europeans will always be ready to keep alive, that is perhaps the greatest bar to closer connections. Without paying attention to irresponsible writers who have declared that it is the destiny of the United States to rule the whole western hemisphere, and without questioning the sincerity of the American people any more than that of the government at Washington in seeking the friendship of the Latin-American countries, we must, nevertheless, admit that this suspicion is not without foundation. History shows that the close association of weak states and strong ones may be dangerous, sooner or later, to the independence of the former. At the present moment, the United States, as regards strength, is in somewhat the same position as was Prussia toward the other members of the German Zollverein, that is to say, it has a larger population, greater actual wealth, more available resources, — in a word, is stronger in almost every respect, not only than any one of the Latin American republics, but than all of them put together. Such a disproportion is formidable to the weaker states, and though with the growth of Argentina and Brazil it will diminish before long, the day when any likely combination of the Latin republics will be the equal of the Anglo-Saxon one is still far ahead. We must admit, too, that the history of the growth of the United States is not entirely reassuring to the Latin Americans; in particular the story of the Mexican War will always frighten them. With such fears in their minds, they are prone to scrutinize closely each act of their powerful neighbor, to take offence at any semblance of a slight to their dignity, and to view with angry alarm every step which can in any way be interpreted as menacing to their independence. Incidents which in the United States have hardly attracted a moment's attention, careless words of public men to which people at home have never thought of attaching weight, — these, repeated abroad and magnified, are capable of producing among a sensitive people a resentment dangerous to all friendly relations. To make matters worse, public men in the United States, as well as private citizens, are by disposition notoriously reckless of possible consequences of their words and deeds, and often quite indifferent to the

x

opinion of any persons but those to whom their remarks are immediately addressed.

American statesmen who have been trying to bring about better relations between the countries of the New World appreciate all this, and are aware that the first task for the government at Washington must be to convince the Latin Americans that they have nothing to fear. This was one object of the circular voyage of Secretary Root already mentioned. In his speech at Rio Janeiro he declared, with equal tact and emphasis: "We deem the independence and equal rights of the smallest and weakest members of the family of nations entitled to as much respect as those of the greatest empire, and we deem the observance of that respect the chief guaranty of the weak against the oppression of the strong. We neither claim nor desire any rights or privileges or powers that we do not freely concede to every American Republic." This idea Americans will have to repeat without ceasing if they wish to dispel the suspicions which their superior strength cannot help exciting. They will also have to act in such a manner that their conduct shall not give cause to doubt the sincerity of their words.

For their part, enlightened Latin Americans find much to admire and imitate in the history, institutions, and character of their Northern neighbors; they admit that they owe a debt of gratitude to the United States for protection in the past, and they realize that the intention of its government is excellent. On the other hand, they are beginning to feel pretty well able to defend themselves against European attacks, which they do not now dread as much as they do North American preponderance. They are very touchy on the subject of their own dignity, and they wish to see their nations treated on an equal footing with all others. Perhaps the most important result of the recent Congress at The Hague was the new prominence it has given to the Latin-American countries. They appeared there not at all as quiet followers in the train of the United States: on the contrary, they assumed an independent attitude, — one that on certain occasions brought them into open collision with the United States in a way ill-suited to further the cause of Pan-Americanism. We may consider them as having for the first time thoroughly established their equality and obtained a recognized status in world politics. They are ceasing to feel the need of a protector, much less of a guardian.

Against Pan-Americanism some persons in the southern republics have set up the standard of Pan-Iberianism, in furtherance of which a congress was held, in 1904, in Madrid. In the course of eloquent speeches, former feuds were consigned to oblivion, bonds of blood and language were exalted, and the dangers of Anglo-Saxon predominance were more than hinted at. Yet nothing more practical than a flow of soul was sought for, and so far, the first effusion has had no successor. Pan-Iberianism is a comprehensible ideal, and we can understand why many a man in Mexico or Chile should prefer it to Pan-Americanism: many people in the United States care more about friendship with Great Britain than with the sister republics. But however elevated a sentiment in itself, Pan-Iberianism scarcely belongs to the domain of practical politics. Close alliance with Spain and Portugal would do little to fortify the Latin-American countries against the United States. Though nothing can be more proper than that they should do all they can to strengthen the intellectual and moral ties which bind them to their old mother countries, their salvation must come from themselves.

When we come to examine in detail the present dealings of the separate Latin-American republics with the Anglo-Saxon one, and the outlook for the future, we perceive that underneath a certain general resemblance in the relations there are great differences, and tha' these are likely to increase rather than to diminish. Without entering into the considerations affecting each particular case, we may divide these republics into three or four groups as regards their connection with the United States.

The most important of these groups is composed of four states — Brazil, Uruguay, Argentina, and Chile. Together they include two-thirds of the South American continent, and almost the whole of its non-tropical portion. They have great undeveloped resources, nearly three-quarters of the total population, and nineteen-twentieths of the white blood; and with the exception of Chile, they are receiving a large immigration, that ought to continue. They are modern organized communities, which, if not yet free from the danger of revolutions such as have troubled them in the past, at least seem to be settling down to orderly government and good progress, and, individually or in combination, they should be able to take care of themselves, and to play their fair part in the world. To all intents and purposes, they are about as far from the United States as from Europe, so far, in fact, that some persons maintain that it is absurd to include them in the scope of the Monroe Doctrine. Nevertheless, the doctrine is certainly an advantage to them, for it insures them against perils to which, owing to the presence of many foreigners within their borders, they might otherwise be exposed. The Americans, on their side, hope for better relations. The United States which to-day receives more than half of the exports of Brazil furnishes in return only about eleven per cent of its imports, — less than Germany, and far less than Great Britain. Even in the case of Chile, which after the completion of the Panama Canal will be much nearer than it now is to the eastern coast, there is, in spite of past difficulties, no ground for permanent estrangement; the disputes of a few years ago were due to chance events, not to permanent opposition of interest. As for Brazil and Argentina, unless they compromise their future through some fault of their own, they should enjoy before long a much more prominent international position than they have to-day. And none of these four southern republics need entertain the slightest fear of their North American sister.

Since Paraguay and Bolivia have no sea-coast, it is not likely that the United States will ever have very much to do with them.

The northern republics of South America, those of Central America, and the two insular ones of Haiti and San Domingo may, for convenience, be grouped together; they differ in size and population, but they have many characteristics in common: all are situated in the tropics and have but few white inhabitants compared with the colored; all have been the homes of revolution; most are burdened with debt, and in danger of financial disputes with foreign creditors. Although they have in their splendid natural resources a promise of better days, they are not making rapid progress at present, and they attract but little immigration. Here are the lands that threaten to make trouble for the United States, which has come into more immediate contact with them since it has established itself in the waters of the Caribbean Sea, and will come into closer contact still when the Panama Canal is completed. In none of them are the governments stable enough as yet to give permanent assurance of law and order, and several are likely at almost any moment to break the peace, or to become involved in dispute with European nations whose citizens have made investments in their territories. The United States may at any time be called upon, as it has already been in San Domingo, to perform police duty the ultimate consequences of which will be hard to limit. A first task will be to keep the peace between them. This applies particularly to Central America, whose miniature states are ready to fly at each other's throats with or without provocation. The time will soon be past when small nations in any part of the world will be allowed to settle their quarrels by force: this will become a privilege of those countries which are strong enough to fight, not only their immediate enemy, but whoever tries to stop them. Just as Europe would not tolerate to-day hostilities between, let us say, Holland and Portugal, so very soon America will compel the smaller Latin-American states to live at peace, whether they like it or not. It is here, if anywhere, that the "big stick" of the United States should be used when the occasion demands.

The republic of Mexico must be considered by itself. Along a boundary of many hundred miles it is in direct proximity to a far stronger power, and such a position cannot be quite free from danger, — a danger which the memories of the Mexican War will never allow to be quite forgotten. It is a land in which the native Indian element is more numerous than the white, and which as yet attracts but few foreigners. Its resources are extraordinary, as American capitalists have of late been discovering. Although the American colony in the country numbers less than fifty thousand (not one-third of one per cent of the population), more than half the imports of Mexico are from the United States, nearly three-quarters of its exports go there, and the investment of American capital in Mexican enterprises of many sorts is already very extensive, and likely to increase. It cannot be denied that this peaceful taking possession constitutes a peril to the independence of the Mexican republic. Not that the American capitalists are working in favor of annexation, — on the contrary, they are well satisfied with conditions as they are; but if Mexico were to fall back again into her old slough of revolutions, and especially if these were complicated by anti-foreign policy, we may feel sure that, in view of the immense interests involved, intervention from the North would come sooner or later. It would be the story of Cuba again on a larger scale. The best, indeed the only, way for Mexico to avoid this peril, is to maintain orderly government. For more than a generation now she has been peaceful, in striking contrast to her condition at earlier periods in the history of the country. Whether this stability is permanent or not, it is still too soon to say; it is so much the work of one man. Not until some time after President Diaz has disappeared from the scene, can we judge whether the order which he has established will be lasting. As long as it holds, Mexico need have little fear, for the United States is not meditating unprovoked aggression against her.

Stable government is the first condition which all the Latin-American republics must accept, if they wish to keep clear of difficulties. The more responsible they become, the more they will win the respect of the world, and the more secure they will be against interference from outside. They have, too, another means of self-defence which no one could deny them, and which might go far to insure their safety: they can combine into larger units. Although these new countries could treat with the United States more as equals than their individual components are able to do now, American public opinion, far from opposing such unions, would regard them as thoroughly sensible; for nothing could be further from its conceptions than the idea of playing one Latin-American power against another, or of fearing any combination of them. The North American republic is too conscious of its own strength to stoop to thoughts of this kind. If, for instance, Bolivia, Uruguay, and Paraguay should unite with Argentina; if the old United States of Colombia should be reconstructed to include, as once before, Venezuela and Ecuador, with the possible addition of Peru; if the Central American republics should at last succeed in forming a stable federation, and perhaps joining with Mexico; Latin America would then consist of a few large states, each of sufficient importance to claim a dignified place in the modern world, and to be safe against aggression on the part of any outside power. It is one of the clearest proofs of the political backwardness of the Latin-American people, as well as an unfortunate inheritance of Spanish temperament, that where there are so many essential similarities between them, they persist in political divisions which are but historical accidents. In spite of the obstacles in the way of such combinations as the above, — the difficulties of communication, diversity of interest, inherited feuds and jealousies, — we may hope that some day the natural forces which make for union will prevail. The formation of these larger Latin republics would be applauded by the world, and by no country more cordially than by the United States. Their birth would relieve it of cares from which it would gladly be free.

CHAPTER XVII

THE UNITED STATES IN THE PACIFIC

IN the days when the Americans first assumed their place among nations, neither they nor others foresaw how soon they would turn their attention towards the distant Pacific Ocean, and play a leading part on its shores. Not only had they no territory there, but they did not even send their first exploring party across the continent until nearly a generation later. The thirteen original states were all situated on the North Atlantic. Boston was farther in actual time from China or Japan than were London and Paris, or St. Petersburg; and yet, scarcely had the treaty of peace with Great Britain been signed, when American vessels made their way to the South Seas. Since then, in a century and a quarter, the United States has acquired a coast line of some thousand miles on the eastern side of the Great Ocean, it has established itself firmly in the middle and in the west, and has proclaimed to the world its dream of the dominion of the whole. In all history such momentous changes have rarely taken place in so short a time.

If we examine the reason why American ships penetrated so early into these remote waters, we find that their hardihood is easier to explain than it would seem at first glance. The people of New England had been active in commercial and maritime affairs in the old days of British rule. As colonists, they had carried on a thriving trade, much of which was closed to them when they became foreigners, cut off by the English shipping laws from their former privileges. They were too energetic not to look elsewhere for compensation. Like Scandinavia, if in less measure, their rocky, wooded country, with its severe climate and many excellent harbors, afforded little temptation to agriculture, but pushed its inhabitants to shipbuilding and a maritime life. In 1784, within a year after the conclusion of peace with Great Britain, the first American vessel reached Canton.[1] So successful were its operations that, two years later, the number of ships from the United States had risen to five, and three years after that to fifteen, a number exceeded by those from Great Britain only.

The situation was indeed very favorable to the Americans in their commerce with the Far East, and though they encountered many risks and hardships, they reaped enormous profits, for they had marked advantages over their rivals. The English were hampered by the fact that their China trade was in the hands of the East India Company, which did not deal in furs, the most profitable articles that could be sold in China. The French and others soon suffered by the European wars which broke out in 1792 and lasted until 1815. The Russians, who had almost a monopoly of the fur trade in the Northern Pacific, were fettered by the Chinese regulations which excluded them from Canton, and confined their commerce to Kiakhta on the borders of Mongolia. In consequence, the furs they had obtained were obliged to make a long, expensive journey overland before they even crossed the Chinese frontier. The Americans were free from such restrictions. After killing their fur-bearing animals in the South Seas or on the northwest coast of America, or, oftener still, buying the skins from the natives, they sold them at Canton, and returned home with a cargo of tea, silks, and other valuable Chinese goods. In 1801 we find them importing into Canton four hundred and twenty-seven thousand sealskins

[1] During the last part of its voyage, it was escorted and aided by two French men-of-war, which it had met on its way.

alone, besides skins of otter and other animals.   It is true
their own country did not as yet produce much that the Chinese wanted, nor was it rich in gold and silver; but some
vessels carried goods which they were able to dispose of in
Persia or the Indies, where they loaded up with others that
found a market in China.

In their wanderings through the length and breadth of
the Pacific Ocean, American skippers felt the need of a
convenient stopping-place where they could repair damages
to their craft, dry the skins they had on board, and pass
the worst of the winter months.   As a haven of this kind, no
place was so well situated as the Hawaiian Islands, which
had been discovered by Captain Cook in 1778.   So obvious
were their attractions, with their equable climate, gentle
natives, and plentiful resources, that Cook's successor,
Vancouver, found Americans already located there in 1792.
The newcomers soon discovered a fresh source of profit for
their commerce.   Sandalwood was abundant in the islands,
and as it was much in demand among the Chinese, the
Americans exported it in large quantities.   From the first,
they were the largest and most influential foreign element
in Hawaii, which they looked upon as, in a way, their own
domain.   Thus, by one means or another, their trade in
the Pacific grew, till, within a few years of the time when
they made their appearance there, it formed an important part of the national commerce, and their influence
had become dominant in the only convenient stopping-
place in mid-ocean.

Overland their progress was slower, for they did not
cross the continent until 1803, and Astoria, their first trading station on the Pacific, was swept away by the War of
1812.   When peace was restored, they returned, and in
time their numbers increased.   It was not, however, until
the compromise treaty of 1846 that they secured undis-
puted possession of the whole territory south of the forty-

ninth parallel. California they took from Mexico just before
the discovery of gold, which brought into it such a rush of
population that it soon became a full-fledged state. Nevertheless, until the completion of the first transcontinental
railway, California was in many respects more like a distinct
self-governing colony than an integral part of the republic.
To-day the Pacific coast is bound to the rest of the Union
by five lines of rail, the land behind it is no longer vacant,
and though the Pacific States retain certain characteristics
of their own, they are not a detached portion of the country,
but the western front. As their resources develop and their
population increases the United States will be assured an
ever firmer position on the Great Ocean. Without Alaska,
the actual Pacific coast-line of the republic is shorter than
that of Chile, but it is backed by a much larger territory,
and it faces directly towards China and Japan, instead of
towards the South Sea Islands. The acquisition of Alaska
has nipped in the bud Canadian rivalry in this part of
the world, and when the Panama Canal shall have brought
the Atlantic and Gulf coasts into easy communication by
water with the Pacific, through a passage which the United
States can close at will, its situation will be unassailable.
Even the unfortunate break in continuity caused by British
Columbia does not seriously weaken its strength.

Toward the end of the first quarter of the nineteenth century, when the fur-bearing animals had become less abundant and the sandalwood of Hawaii was almost exhausted,
American vessels in the Pacific began to devote themselves chiefly to whaling, an occupation which they had
followed in the days when the colonies belonged to Great
Britain. Hawaii, however, remained as important a centre
as ever for resting and refitting. In 1822, twenty-four
whaling vessels were in the harbor of Honolulu at one time;
in 1845, according to the local records, 497 whalers, manned
by 14,905 sailors, visited the islands, and, of the total, some

three-fourths flew the flag of the United States. But earlier in the nineteenth century, another class of Americans, the Protestant missionaries, had found their way there. Before long they succeeded in converting the King and the principal chiefs, and the larger part of the population, over whom henceforth they exercised much influence. French Catholic priests, it is true, came afterwards, and also made many converts; but, as later arrivals, they never were so successful as the Protestants in bringing the natives into their fold. As usual, the missionary element and the foreign commercial one bore little love to each other.

So thoroughly had the United States become interested in Hawaiian affairs that in 1842, five years before the acquisition of California, and before the Oregon dispute with Great Britain was settled, — that is to say, before the Americans held a foot of uncontested territory on the Pacific coast, — the President declared in a message to Congress that the republic would oppose the seizure of the islands by any foreign power, and in 1851 this assurance was repeated by Daniel Webster as Secretary of State. In 1874, and again in 1889, when there were local disturbances, American marines were landed to guard the legation. After the acquisition of California, a direct trade had sprung up between San Francisco and the Far East, in consequence of which the unique position of Hawaii as a stopping-place and as a strategic point became more evident than ever. The Americans, without as yet wishing to possess it, were determined that it should never become a hostile outpost in the hands of someone else to menace their Pacific coast, in the way that Bermuda does their Atlantic.

On the high seas, and in Chinese waters, the United States continued to be well represented until after the middle of the nineteenth century. In its diplomatic intercourse with China, it followed in the wake of England and France, but in the opening up of Japan it took the lead. Soon after this, however, it met with reverses. During the Civil War, owing to the depredations of Confederate cruisers, and to the fear of them, American vessels almost disappeared from the Pacific. At another moment the misfortune might have been short-lived; but it occurred just at the period when sailing vessels were giving way to steam, and wooden ships to iron ones. In the construction of wooden sailing vessels, the New England builders feared no competitors; but the American iron and steel industry at that date was not sufficiently developed to compete with the European, and the registration laws of the United States forbade the purchase of foreign ships. At just about this time, too, the whaling industry declined, owing to the decrease in the number of whales, and the substitution of mineral oil for whale oil for lighting purposes. From these and other causes, the American flag, once so common all over the Pacific, became rarer, and in many regions almost unknown, for the navy long shared in the decay of the merchant marine. Politically, too, for some thirty years the influence of the United States in the Far East remained stationary, or declined. But the country itself grew and prospered; its different parts became more closely knit together, and the purchase of Alaska doubled the American coast-line in the Pacific, and, through the Aleutian Islands, first brought it near to Japan. Meanwhile, relations with Hawaii became more intimate as the years went on. In 1876 the islands were granted a reciprocity treaty which bound them close to the continent by economic ties; for with free access to the American market, the exportation of sugar to San Francisco increased enormously. In 1884 the United States obtained a lease of Pearl Harbor for a naval station.

It has been generally supposed that, in the event of a war with England, the American navy would make the destruction of British commerce its chief object. But if it possessed no base of operations beyond San Francisco, it could hardly inflict much damage on British trade in the East. To overcome this difficulty, American seamen were desirous of securing more advanced posts, which they believed would be invaluable to the country for successful warfare, either offensive or defensive. Hawaii was unrivalled as a first stopping-place; and, still farther away, though the American public scarcely realized the fact, the United States had acquired claims in Samoa.

The primary cause of the annexation of Hawaii in 1898 was the change that had taken place in its population, which rendered the old system of government impossible to maintain in the long run. As is well known, the Hawaiians, like their kindred, the Tahitians, and the Maoris in New Zealand, belong to a race which, though unusually attractive, has so far not shown the ability to adapt itself to civilization. The relations between the whites and the islanders had been good. Indeed, from the first coming of the foreigners, the natives had followed their advice, and under the guidance of the missionaries had made creditable progress. They remained children in character, yet, if they could have held their own in numbers, they might have kept in power for some time longer. But they have been diminishing at a fearful rate. In 1830 they numbered about one hundred and thirty thousand, already considerably less than when the islands were discovered; by 1850, they had sunk to eighty-four thousand, and by 1890 to thirty-nine thousand; to-day, with less than thirty thousand, they do not make more than fifteen per cent of the total population of their own country. On the other hand, ever since the treaty with the United States had procured a free entrance for Hawaiian sugar, the whites, who had ended by acquiring most of the land, had been importing laborers by the thousands to work on the plantations. The natives were too indolent for this toilsome labor; Polynesians from other islands also proved unsuitable; Portuguese from the Azores soon left the fields and took to occupations like market-gardening, in which they have since thriven. The Chinese did well, as usual, but promptly began to flock into the towns and to go into shopkeeping in such numbers that the supply on the plantations could be kept up only by further importations that would threaten the rest of the inhabitants with being submerged. Partly under the influence of anti-Chinese sentiment in the United States, the immigration from China was restricted, and Japanese were next tried, again with success in the beginning, but with somewhat the same disadvantage as in the case of the Chinese, aggravated by the fact that they had the support of a watchful government at home which was determined to secure to them their rights.

In this state of unstable equilibrium, the kindly, indolent natives, reduced to ever greater insignificance between white capitalists and Asiatic laborers, could not maintain for long even a show of political domination. The very fact that the Hawaiian sovereigns had, as a rule, followed wise foreign advice and governed well made it certain that, when a less intelligent ruler should act differently, a rising of some sort could not fail to take place. The actual circumstances that led to the revolution of 1893, the attempt of the Queen to change the constitution and her overthrow, are unimportant. The much-debated question, whether the landing of the American marines who were in the harbor did or did not render aid to the movement, is also idle to-day. Admitting that the prompt appearance of the American force gave such moral backing to the insurgents that the party of the Queen was terrified into submission, we may still feel sure that the marines would in any case have been obliged to land within a few hours. Whatever we may think of the way in which the revolution was brought about, we can see that something of the sort was inevitable. The well-meant attempt of President Cleveland to restore the sovereignty of the Queen proved abortive. The republic which was then constituted, during its short existence, ruled wisely and well. From the natives, after one feeble attempt at revolt, it had little to fear; but the growing strength of the Japanese, coupled with a readiness on the part of the government at Tokio to uphold their demands, made the whites on the islands feel that they must have American protection. The outbreak of the Spanish War brought the question once more to an issue. In the prosecution of hostilities the Hawaiian Islands were almost indispensable as a halting-place on the long journey from San Francisco to the Philippines. Had they remained neutral, the task of supplying Dewey's squadron would have been much more burdensome; but as it was, they made no pretence of neutrality. They were definitely annexed to the Union on July 7, 1898.

In the case of Samoa, the United States was drawn into unexpected complications, partly through the zeal of its own officials there, and partly through anger at the overbearing conduct of the Germans, who, it is fair to remember, had the largest interests in the islands. The result was a situation that no one for a time knew just how to get out of. In 1872, Admiral Meade had concluded a treaty with the native chiefs which granted to the United States as a coaling-station the excellent harbor of Pago Pago in the island of Tutuila. Although the Senate never took action on the document, it included this stipulation in a commercial treaty which it ratified half a dozen years later, while at the same time it refused the request of the natives for a protectorate.

Small as the Samoan group was, its politics were seldom quiet. The intrigues and disputes of ambitious local

Y

chiefs, stimulated by ultra-patriotic and overzealous foreigners, led to repeated disturbances, culminating in 1887
and 1888 in conflicts that brought about intervention.
Irritated by the high-handed action of the Germans, the
United States despatched three war vessels to the scene;
but they, like their German rivals, were destroyed in the
harbor of Apia by a typhoon. This disaster cooled down
all parties, and after a conference in Berlin, a provisional
arrangement was made for a mixed system of government,
which for ten years worked badly, as such systems do.
Then followed fresh trouble, in which the English and the
Americans were the ones to use force against the natives,
while the Germans protested. Each of the three powers
sent a commissioner to investigate matters, a new agreement was made, and finally, by the treaty of December,
1899, the English, in return for compensation elsewhere,
withdrew altogether from the islands, which were divided
between the other two claimants. Although Germany got
the larger part, the United States was satisfied with its
share, Tutuila, which contained the best harbor in the
archipelago.

Already, before this agreement was arrived at, the treaty
of peace with Spain had given the Americans another Pacific station by the cession of Guam in the Ladrones. Here,
again, the territory acquired was too small to have any value
except as a good stopping-place.

In the Philippines, the situation was very different.
There the question of a naval base was so distinct from that
of the retention and government of the islands that some
Anti-imperialists, who were violently opposed to keeping the
whole group, with its seven million inhabitants, were willing
to retain a particular spot for naval purposes. This was
thought of in Washington, and though in the end everything was kept, the importance of a strategic position in
the western Pacific is nevertheless a subject that can be

considered apart from the problems involved in the treatment of the native population.

That this interest alone would justify the United States in retaining possession of the Philippines is an opinion sometimes advanced. However extreme we may regard such a tenet, we cannot deny that the acquisition of the islands, for better or for worse, has radically changed the situation of the Americans in the Far East. They are no longer a mere trading nation, come to-day and gone to-morrow, but like other great powers, they are a land-holding one with populations to govern, local interests to see to, and territories to defend. They are now not only the near neighbors of the French, the English, the Germans, and the Dutch, and as such interested in whatever affects these; they are also in close proximity to the two Asiatic empires of China and Japan, in both of which they are deeply concerned.

Although we may not go so far as those who declare that Manila is the natural distributing point of the trade of the whole western Pacific, it is evident that, with the possession of the Philippines, the Americans have come into immediate contact with the Chinese and Japanese in their own part of the world. There are drawbacks to propinquity, but as long as China is weak, the Americans are far better placed to bring pressure on the Middle Kingdom, as well as to hold their own against other powers in affairs relating to it, than if they did not occupy a strong position in the immediate vicinity. If, for instance, they had not had a powerful army near by in 1900, they would never have been able to send the troops they did in time to take part in the Peking expedition, nor would they have had the authority which was theirs in the councils of the assembled nations, and which they have enjoyed in the Far East ever since.

On the other hand, we must admit that, by making these distant acquisitions, the United States has forfeited part of

its former invulnerability.   But, though its real strength
might be little affected by losing them to some victorious
enemy, the wound to its pride would be so intolerable
that it will defend them at any cost.   To heed warnings
as to the dangers they bring with them would seem like
listening to the counsels of cowardice.   It is too confident
in itself to fear other powers, and it is willing to accept
the responsibilities of its new greatness.

Whatever pertains to the Pacific Ocean appeals strongly
to Americans at the present day.   There is something in
the very immensity of the field which makes it seem appropriate for the display of their superabundant energy.   They
believe that they have an unequalled advantage, and are
entitled to the foremost place.   As early as the middle of
the nineteenth century, Mr. (later Secretary) Seward declared: "The Pacific Ocean, its shores, its islands, and the
vast region beyond, will become the chief theatre of events
in the world's great Hereafter."   According to Mr. Seward,
and to many others who have since shared his opinion, the
United States is to play the leading role in this theatre of
the Hereafter.

This idea has always been firmly held in the states of the
Pacific coast, and the more they have grown, the more it
has appeared justified.   In 1903, President Roosevelt proclaimed, at San Francisco, in a speech of lofty imperialism,
that to the United States must belong the dominion of
the Pacific.   Such terms are vague, and we may suspect
that if the Russo-Japanese War had then taken place, the
President might have been more guarded in his phrase.
Nevertheless the conviction which it embodies is an article
of faith to many, and it has found much in recent events
to confirm it.   Everywhere the minds of men have turned
towards the Pacific as never before; all five of the world
powers hold territory on its shores, and are vitally interested in its concerns.   Within a few years it has witnessed

a succession of startling events, which have followed each other with bewildering rapidity — two wars and several minor conflicts, the appearance of Germany as a power in the East, the sudden menacing growth of Russia and her sanguinary discomfiture, the threatened dissolution and the present awakening of China, and the transformation of Japan. We can understand why President Roosevelt should have called the period of the world's history which is just beginning, "the Pacific Era," though not in the sense of the peaceful one.

Among these startling events, the stretching out of the United States to the farther shores of the Great Ocean is second to almost none in its wide importance. No one can wonder that it has fired the American imagination, especially in the Pacific States; it has also interested the whole people as never before in the broader questions of world politics. Many who would be glad to get rid of the Philippines are none the less unwilling to see the new prestige of their country diminished by one tittle. This feeling has given stimulus to the desire to build up a mighty navy. In the Atlantic, the American fleet remains chiefly in its own waters, where, now that most of the English vessels are withdrawn, it does not come into direct competition with that of any other country. But in the Pacific it is kept on the farther side of the ocean, at the great gathering place of the fleets of all nations. American pride demands that the United States shall be well represented there, and the sending of a formidable squadron of battle ships to show the might of the republic in Pacific waters as it has never been shown before, is an impressive demonstration which thrills popular patriotism. The Americans are already disposed to regard themselves as more than the equal of any other people in this part of the world, and they are convinced that when the Panama Canal has been dug, and New York and New Orleans have been brought into quicker water communication with the Far East than London and Hamburg, and when their fleet can pass at will from one ocean to the other, then their supremacy will be beyond question.

But the Pacific is not for any one nation to take exclusively to itself; and American boasts about domination, besides being irritating to others, are premature. Every one of the world powers has territories in this domain, and interests which it will defend to the best of its ability. Not only has imperial Britain widespread possessions in this ocean world, but it has a merchant marine many times larger than that of the United States, and a far stronger navy; and it has also great and growing children, Canada and Australia, who will have to be taken into account by their American kindred. And there are others to be considered. Both China and Japan, if in different ways, have entered into the drama of world politics, which they have already profoundly affected, and on which their further influence is incalculable. With both of them the present relations of the United States exceed in intricacy and in difficulty, when not in actual importance, those with any state in Europe.

CHAPTER XVIII

THE historian of the relations between the United States and China is confronted at the outset of his task with a curious fact. He has to recognize that the tale of the dealings of the American government with the Chinese Empire and with its inhabitants in their own homes is one story, and that of the treatment of Chinese immigrants to the land of liberty, by both government and people, is quite another. What is stranger still is that until very recently the two phenomena had almost as little influence on each other as if they concerned separate groups of nations. In the first case the Americans can point with pride to their record; in the second they can feel no pride whatever; at best, they can fall back only on the plea of self-defence and of disagreeable necessity.

The American traders who made their way to Canton in the last years of the eighteenth century and the first of the nineteenth, suffered from the same disabilities as other foreigners bartering at that port, but, on the whole, they seem to have been successful, as such success went, in getting on with the local authorities. In one respect their government took moral ground from the first; not only did it prohibit its citizens by law from sharing in the opium traffic, but it declared that those guilty of so doing should thereby forfeit their claim to the protection of their country, and be left to the tender mercies of the Chinese courts. Even if we admit that there are two sides to the opium question, and that the English have not deserved

all the blame which has been cast upon them in this connection, the stand of the Americans is to their credit, in
spite of the sneers it has provoked from some foreign
writers, who regard it as a bid for Chinese favor.[1] Like
other powers, the United States profited by the successes
of the English and the French in wringing from the rulers
in Peking concessions in behalf of foreign trade. Its policy,
if a little inglorious, was prudent and successful; but the
decline of the national commerce in the East in the period
following 1860 left to American diplomats and consuls in
China, as their chief occupation, the protection, not of
traders, but of missionaries.

The first American missionaries reached Canton in February, 1830, and were soon followed by others who established themselves at many distant points. Their activity
has been great, but its results have been the cause of prolonged dispute. This is not, however, the place to enter
into the complicated and thorny question of the value of
Christian missions in heathen lands, and especially in the
Far East. In judging the evidence on the subject, we must
remember that the witnesses are rarely unprejudiced, and
that owing to the permanent antagonism between the business community and the missionaries, the oral testimony
of the former has little more claim to impartiality than the
official reports of the latter. They can be used indeed, to
a certain extent, to counterbalance one another. To the
diplomat and to the consul, unless they happen to have
personal sympathy with efforts to spread Christianity, the
missionaries appear chiefly as the makers of endless trouble.
Without passing a summary judgment on so many-sided
a controversy, we can understand the point of view of
those who declare that the coming of strangers to convert
a people of ancient civilization from long-inherited beliefs
with which they are satisfied, is an impertinence in itself;

[1] Of late the prohibition of opium has been extended to morphine.

that the missionaries frequently lack tact, and by their meddlesomeness get into unnecessary difficulties, and that what good they have accomplished has been incommensurate with the money spent in doing it. All this may be more or less true, but unprejudiced observers bear witness that, notwithstanding the jibes of the foreign settlements about the missionaries' comfortable mode of life, the latter often set a fine example of unselfishness; that they have alleviated much suffering, and in many cases they have done great good to individuals if not to nations as a whole. They have also more than once been helpful to their own government, and they have promoted civilization by adding to our knowledge of the lands where they have worked, often at the price of untold hardships and perils, and sometimes at the cost of their lives. Finally, it should be noted, that at the present day the Protestant missionary of the older type, whose single idea was that of preaching the Gospel to the recalcitrant heathen in season and out of season, is dying out. In his place we find the practical, efficient representative of Christianity, who gives more time to looking after the material wants of his flock, and in particular to the cure of their diseases, than he does to direct propaganda.

Whatever might be the personal opinions of the official representatives of the United States in the Far East, they were obliged to protect their missionary fellow-citizens in the rights which treaties had accorded to them. Beyond this duty, the American ministers in Peking had, for many years, little to do. In one respect they pursued a course different from that observed by their government in every other part of the world. Few principles have been more characteristic of American policy than the avoidance of "entangling alliances," and the maintenance of the perfect independence of the United States in all its dealings with other powers. The only marked exceptions to this rule have been made in the East where, by the necessities of the situation, the American representatives have been forced to associate themselves with their European colleagues in the making of joint demands upon the imperial government. This association has even gone to the extent of taking common military action, as in 1900, when the allied troops marched on Peking to rescue the besieged legations.

For a whole generation after the Civil War there is little to tell about the conduct of the United States in Asiatic affairs. In 1894, when the war between China and Japan broke out, the sympathy of the Americans at home, though not of those on the spot, was generally on the side of Japan. The American government did not put itself forward at the time, but it received a unique tribute to its fairness by being charged by each of the warring empires with the protection of its subjects who were resident in the domain of the other, — always a difficult and delicate task and here doubly complicated. It was through the American minister at Peking that the first overtures for peace were made by the Chinese, and a former American Secretary of State, Mr. John W. Foster, was one of the commissioners appointed by China to negotiate the treaty. Nevertheless, the role of the United States in this part of the world remained a platonic one, exercising slight influence on the course of events, till the results of the Spanish War brought American warships and armies into the scene.

Up to the outbreak of the Chinese-Japanese conflict, the interest of the American people in the politics of the Far East had been languid. Now it became keener, and it was quickly stimulated by the acquisition of the Philippines, and by the independent revival of American trade. The United States had never ceased to make large purchases from China, and in 1880 its imports from that country amounted to almost twenty-two million dollars, but its exports thither were barely over one million. In 1890, the imports came to about sixteen million and a quarter, the exports to just under three million; in 1900, when the imports had risen to almost twenty-seven million, the exports had grown to over five times what they were ten years before, and were now fifteen and a quarter million; in 1902, the exports at last exceeded the imports. This rapid increase in the sale of American goods, an increase which bade fair to continue, made it incumbent on the nation to follow with more attention what was going on in the Far East, and above all to determine what course to adopt in reference to the break-up of the Chinese Empire which then seemed imminent.

The situation was not easy. Something had to be done, and done promptly, lest a trade which, in the popular imagination, offered unlimited possibilities for the future should be lost just as it was coming into existence. Several of the European powers seemed bent on the partition of China, and even Great Britain and Japan, who were opposed to it, had taken care to mark off a sphere of interest for themselves in order that, if the worst should befall, they might not come out empty-handed. Unable to prevent and unwilling to take part in a division of this sort, the United States fell back on the principle of the "open door." The move was successful; for not only did it serve to steady the somewhat wavering attitude of Great Britain, but it elicited at least the nominal approbation of the states to which Secretary Hay's circular was addressed. However little some of them might sympathize with the doctrine it enunciated, none dared oppose it openly; for to do so would have been to proclaim to the world an intention of taking over Chinese territory for purely selfish purposes. Secretary Hay was too shrewd to put unlimited trust in the assurances he received, but the United States had now ground to stand on, a principle formally accepted by other countries, and one which it could maintain with all the weight of its influence. The declaration had the additional merit that, though prompted by interested motives, it did not set forth a selfish theory, but one of fair play for all; and it was likewise advantageous to the Chinese themselves.

The American policy towards China was, indeed, one of consistent friendliness. Even during the Boxer troubles and the siege of the legations, the United States announced that it had no war with the Empire as such. The American troops in the Peking exposition may have looted as much as the others, but they treated the native population with more humanity than some of them did. When order was restored, the government at Washington, disclaiming all thoughts of revenge, exacted an indemnity that was moderate compared with what was demanded by most of the other powers; and to-day, after revising the estimates, it proposes to release China from all payments in excess of the loss actually suffered by the United States and its citizens at that time, or from more than half of the total amount.[1] After the suppression of the Boxer revolt, when China was bolstered up, with her territory intact, American influence at Peking was exerted in favor of treating her as leniently and trusting her as much as possible.

There still remained for the Americans the difficulty of protecting their trade in Manchuria, where the Russians, in spite of promises to the contrary, were making themselves more and more at home. Here again American interests coincided with Chinese. Profiting by the fact that the province was still theoretically a part of the Chinese Empire, just before the outbreak of the Russo-Japanese War the United States persuaded the Peking government, in the interest of both parties, and in the face of Russian displeasure, to open two more Manchurian ports to American

[1] In 1885 the United States returned to China a sum of $453,400 for overpayment of earlier damages.

trade. When hostilities began, Secretary Hay, in a new circular, insisted on the importance of limiting their area, — a condition which was accepted by the two belligerents to the great advantage of China. Without ascribing to the United States a superhumanly altruistic motive, we may say to sum up that for many years it showed more real kindliness to the Chinese Empire and gave it more disinterested aid and protection than did any other power.[1] If the relations between the two had been confined to the western side of the Pacific, we could record them with almost unmixed praise. But, during the years when the Americans were showing themselves the honest friends of the Chinaman in his own home, their attitude toward him in theirs was something very different.

As soon as American trade with China began, a few merchants went out and settled, at first in Canton, later in other ports, forming small colonies such as have existed in other Oriental countries. That the Chinese might, in their turn, come in any considerable number across the water did not seem a contingency worth troubling about. To be sure, they had shown in their history a persistency in emigrating to the Malay Peninsula, Java, the Philippines, and elsewhere, but these had been merely migrations in Asia itself and were little known in Europe and America, where the Chinese were supposed to be a people much attached to their homes. If their relatives died abroad, did they not send them back to be buried in the sacred soil of their native land?

All this being so, when, in 1868, the American minister at Peking, Anson Burlingame, signed the treaty known by his name, it was regarded as a diplomatic triumph for his country. The contracting parties " cordially recognized . . .

[1] And yet with characteristic carelessness the United States has sometimes sent as consuls to China men who have been the laughing-stock, if not worse, of the Far East and a disgrace to the country they represented.

the inherent and inalienable right of man to change his home and allegiance, and also the mutual advantage of the free immigration and emigration of their citizens and subjects respectively from one country to the other, for purposes of curiosity, of trade, or as permanent residents."

Here was a fine repetition of the principles for which the United States had always contended, principles whose validity many European nations still refused to acknowledge, but which were now solemnly accepted by the most conservative of Oriental empires, thereby throwing open its doors to American enterprise. That the Chinese, for their part, would ever make great use of the opportunities offered to them, was not foreseen, and if it had been, it would not at the moment have aroused alarm. The first who crossed over to the Pacific coast were invaluable in the development of California; they helped in the digging of the mines, and in the building of the railways, and they made excellent servants. They were therefore heartily welcomed. Very soon, however, as they grew more numerous, the tone about them underwent a change.

We have seen what reasons have impelled many persons in the United States who bear no dislike to the Chinese to favor their exclusion from the country. It is not merely the clamor of the Pacific coast, or the influence of the labor-unions, which has led to this conclusion so much as a conviction that the Mongolians constitute an element which cannot be Americanized, cannot be amalgamated with the rest, and which, though useful in itself, will, by competition, lower the standard of living of the American workingman, and end by driving him from the field. The belief is not peculiar to the United States, it is equally strong in Canada and Australia, and would be in other places under the same conditions. And it is not necessarily a reflection on the character of the Chinese; on the contrary, we might regard it as a tribute to their sterling qualities.

It was some time before the seriousness of the problem presented was realized in the Eastern States, where the Chinese have never come in sufficient numbers to awaken much opposition, and where their virtues have been apprepreciated. A good many people in the East condemn exclusion, but they are lukewarm in the matter, whereas the Pacific coast is terribly in earnest.

The story of anti-Chinese legislation in the United States can be told in a few words. In 1878, only ten years after the signing of the Burlingame Treaty, Congress passed a first exclusion bill, which was vetoed by President Hayes as being contrary to that treaty. Two years afterward, however, the administration succeeded in concluding with Peking a new agreement, according to which the United States was given power to "limit or suspend" Chinese immigration, though not to prohibit it. On the strength of this, in 1882 Congress passed a bill forbidding Chinese immigration for twenty years. This bill was vetoed, but a similar one, fixing the period at ten years, received the President's signature. In 1888, another treaty was negotiated, but before it had been ratified by the Chinese government, Congress and the President, spurred by the near prospect of an election, passed a new exclusion bill, in violation of existing treaty rights. To quiet qualms of conscience, the authorities in Washington concluded one more treaty, by which the two countries agreed that Chinese immigration to the United States should be forbidden for the next ten years. Since 1904 this agreement has lapsed, but the exclusion law remains in force—illegally, the Chinese claim.

Not content with protecting itself against cheap labor at home, the United States has extended its policy to its tropical possessions, where the conditions are very different. Even before annexation, Hawaii had checked the inflow of Chinese, useful as they were on the plantations. Now the door has been shut against them in the Philippines, partly out of deference to the American labor-unions—though any one must know that the American can never work in the fields in the tropics—and partly because those in charge of the welfare of the islands have felt that the Filipino is no match for the Chinaman. In consequence we have the curious anomaly that though Chinese immigration on a large scale would probably be an excellent thing for the Philippines, it might be death to the Filipinos, and it is the people rather than the territory that those who are shaping American policy have at heart. On the other hand, this policy adds materially to the grievances of which the Chinese have cause to complain. Can we wonder at their indignation when the United States, while seeking unrestricted access to their territories, shuts them out of its possessions not only in its own hemisphere, but in theirs?

Whatever arguments may be urged in favor of preventing further immigration of Chinese to the United States, they do not affect the disgrace to the country of the treatment which has been meted out to some of those already settled in it. The story of the outrages which Chinese have had to suffer at the hands of mobs or of individual ruffians must make any American blush for shame.[1]

For another wrong in connection with Chinese exclusion, there can also be no defence, though there is an unsatisfactory explanation. The Chinese are born smugglers of their

[1] "More Chinese subjects have been murdered by mobs in the United States during the last twenty-five years than all the Americans who have been murdered in China in similar riots. . . . In every instance when Americans have suffered from mobs, the authorities have made reparation for the losses, and rarely has the punishment of death failed to be inflicted upon the guilty offenders. On the other hand, I am sorry to say that I cannot recall a single instance where the penalty of death has been visited on any member of the mob in the United States guilty of the death of Chinese, and in only two instances out of many has indemnity been paid for the losses sustained by the Chinese."—Speech of a former Chinese Minister quoted from *China and America To-day* (p. 165) by A. H. Smith.

persons as well as of their goods, and many have succeeded in making their way into the United States in spite of the vigilance of the government officials. On their side, the latter have received all arrivals from China with impartial brutality. Chinese gentlemen of education and refinement, provided with papers beyond suspicion, have been herded in with coolies and subjected to many indignities before being allowed to pass the customs. These barbarous proceedings for long went on unchecked. It was only when people in China began to retaliate that the Americans awoke to the necessity of mending their manners.

For many years, the Chinese government, and Chinese public opinion, such as it was, seemed extraordinarily indifferent to all these things. To an Asiatic empire of some hundreds of millions of inhabitants, the fate of a few thousand Kwantung coolies was, it appeared, not a matter of much concern. Besides, it was taken for granted in the outside world that the Chinese had no patriotism or national sentiment. Retaliation on their part was not seriously considered, and Americans cherished the comfortable belief that it was possible to have at the same time two policies in regard to them — a selfish one for home consumption and a generous one for foreign export.

The boycott of 1905 rudely shattered this illusion. We may argue as much as we will that the movement, the inner history of which we do not yet know, and perhaps never shall, was due to all sorts of influences. It may have had some foreign instigation, though there has never been any real proof to that effect. It may have been primarily a trial of strength of certain organizations which determined to show their power at the expense, as it happened, of the Americans, but might just as readily have chosen some other victim. Again, the boycott may have had something of the nature of mere chance explosion, or have been the work of a few agitators who knew how to

z

mould others to their use. Be all this as it may, the anti-American boycott has proved that, throughout China, there now exists a national resentment against the way in which the Chinese have been treated in the United States. It also gave proof of a skill in organization hitherto unsuspected, and it has revealed to Americans the disagreeable truth that, though China may be weak as a military power, her people are still in a position where they can hit back, and hit back effectually, if their rights and feelings are trampled upon.

The difficulty which faces American statesmen is a grave one. Such grievances as the ill-treatment of upper-class Chinese can be, and probably will be, easily remedied; and there is reason to hope that Chinese laborers may be better protected in the future from mob violence. But the root of the trouble goes deeper. On the one hand, there is, at present, no chance whatever that the United States will open its doors to unrestricted Chinese immigration. The Pacific coast is immovable on this point, and it is supported, not only by the laboring classes everywhere, but also by many other persons who wish America to remain "a white man's country." Every powerful independent nation will exercise as an indispensable part of its sovereignty the right of determining what strangers shall or shall not be allowed to enter and to reside within its borders; only to the weak can the privilege of shutting their doors be denied. The Americans cannot be forced to let in the Chinese if they are determined to keep them out, but this determination may cost them dear. It is perfectly conceivable that by such means as the boycott, if not by an official prohibition, Americans may be deprived of the market in the Far East to which they have looked forward with confidence. And this is no small loss in itself. If the Americans, in spite of the obvious advantage of their position, in spite of the excellence and cheapness of their manufactured goods, in spite, too, of the friendliness they have shown to China in foreign affairs, are to be denied the privilege to which their situation seems to entitle them, they will be paying a heavy price for their self-defence. And yet, even this price they will pay if need be, rather than let their country be overrun by Asiatics. It remains for their statesmen to prevent matters from reaching this extremity, and to persuade the Chinese that no hostility is intended against them; that exclusion does not imply a condemnation of their character, but it is only a recognition of the inability of white and yellow men to meet in large masses, on terms that are satisfactory to both.

There is, however, fair reason to hope that the task of maintaining good relations may not prove impossible. China, like every other state, has no motive for desiring that her children should swarm into lands where they are not wanted. Provided she receives fair and courteous treatment, which has not always been accorded her in the past, she may well think it best to submit with a good grace to restrictions which are no real injury to her. To act otherwise, to attempt to force open all doors to her emigrants, would soon bring her into disastrous conflict, not only with the United States, but with the British Empire, Russia, Japan, and probably others. And this she can by no means afford to do; for in spite of recent reforms, her military power is not yet great, nor is it likely to be, at least for offensive purposes, this many a day. Among the empires of the world she is one of those which most require internal reforms, and have most cause for keeping clear of complications with foreign powers. More than that, she is in no small need of friends.

Though friends can be had for a consideration, unfortunately, even friendship, especially when bought, may be dangerous to a weak, distracted country. Russia and Japan are both, perhaps, in a position to give China more valuable aid for the moment than is the United States, but aid from them would not be without obvious perils. The United States has a remarkably clean record in the Far East: it alone of all the powers active there has never taken, or tried to take, one foot of Chinese soil. While naturally intent on its own interests, it has shown more actual kindness to the empire than has any other nation, and it can hardly be suspected of designs against her. The Chinese know this, and they are plainly eager for at least the moral support of the Americans in their dealings with some of their neighbors. In spite of all assurances, China has not yet got back the control of Manchuria, — of either the Japanese or the Russian portion, — and the two late enemies may not improbably agree to keep her sovereignty there a nominal one. This she will not submit to tamely, if she can help herself; and still less does she intend to allow the Japanese to take her in hand and direct her footsteps as they have dreamed of doing. The reformers among the Chinese are ready to learn from Japan and to imitate her, but not at all to be dominated by her, and against her too great influence they are turning for support to the United States.

As a result of these various considerations, the prospect for American relations, though clouded, is not disheartening. The power of the United States commands respect, and its good-will is of value. The Americans can show themselves friendly to the Chinese Empire and desirous of its maintenance, without having to admit its swarms of needy laborers into their territories. And even in regard to this vexed question, their attitude now appears less offensive; for recent events have proved that they are not intent on affixing a stigma on one particular people, but are, rather, struggling with a general problem of self-defence, a problem which has brought them into difficulties with their old friend, Japan.

CHAPTER XIX

THE UNITED STATES AND JAPAN

IF the position of the United States on the Pacific Ocean offers it greater advantages, and imposes upon it graver responsibilities, in its dealings with China than fall to the lot of any European power except Russia, this is even more true in regard to its relations with Japan. Since the opening of the Empire of the Mikado to outside influences, which was brought about by the direct action of the United States, the connection between the two countries has been closer than that between Japan and any other western state. It is true that America faces, and long will face, to the east rather than to the west; for in spite of all eloquent prophecies to the contrary, there is as yet little solid ground of fact to support the opinion that a change will soon take place in this respect. Nevertheless, she already has on the shores of the Pacific a situation superior to that of her European rivals, she has just transferred, if only temporarily, the bulk of her navy to its waters, and what goes on there becomes of more vital interest to her every year. And to Japan the Pacific is all in all.

It was the famous expedition of Commodore Perry in 1854 which brought Japan into general intercourse with the rest of the world. Previous attempts to obtain this result had been made without success by Americans as well as by Europeans. Perry's expedition was a strong one, and he himself was more determined than any of his predecessors. Since he was prepared to repel attack, and firmly maintained his ground instead of complying with the requests of the Japanese that he take himself away, we may say that he triumphed by the use of physical force, however gently applied. We know now, what Perry did not, that conditions in the island empire were ripe for a revolution which must have occurred soon in any event, and that the old system of rigorous exclusion of the foreigner was doomed; but the glory of Commodore Perry loses nothing by this, any more than does that of any discoverer or inventor by his appearing when the age is ready for him. It was part of Perry's merit that he carried out his mission with singular tact, and succeeded in accomplishing his purpose without resort to actual violence, — an exploit for which there is every cause to be grateful. To-day, far from remembering with humiliation the duress once put upon them, the Japanese, in view of what they have since achieved, look back on the coming of the Americans as the beginning of their new birth, as one of the eventful, glorious dates in their history. Their feeling about it has been shown by the erection in 1901 of a monument to Perry, to which the emperor himself besides many other prominent men subscribed.

The United States was, moreover, fortunate in the choice of its first regular diplomatic representative at Tokio. Mr. Townsend Harris was not only skilful and firm in his treatment of official matters, but was also sincerely interested in the welfare of the strange people with whom he was called upon to deal. While obtaining from them concessions, which he believed would be for their own benefit as well as that of his compatriots, he took no unfair advantage of their ignorance of international usages or of their bewildered condition. His friendliness has since been gratefully recognized by the Japanese, and has helped to render them well disposed towards the country which he represented. Their first mission abroad was despatched to the United States.

In the troubled years that witnessed in Japan the over-throw of the old régime, the Americans, like others, suffered from the prevailing insecurity and the hatred of foreigners rampant in the empire. An American secretary of legation was murdered, and on another occasion the legation itself was burned to the ground, yet, in spite of all, relations continued good, and the Americans did not land troops for the protection of their ministers, as did the English and the French. The United States did, however, take a part with Great Britain, France, and Holland, in the bombardment of Shimonoseki, in 1863, and though the part was almost nominal,[1] none the less, the United States received a quarter of the indemnity exacted. But the money thus obtained weighed on the national conscience until, in 1883, by a vote of Congress, it was given back. This fair dealing, with its implied admission of a previous wrong, was not lost on the Japanese, who are quick to appreciate a chivalrous act. They were grateful, too, to the United States for being the first power to show itself favorable to treaty revision, a thing that for years they ardently desired in order to remove the badge of inferiority which the earlier arrangements, necessary at the time, had imposed upon them. In 1878, the Washington government expressed its readiness to surrender its right of exterritoriality and commercial privileges as soon as the other powers should be willing to do the same; in 1886 and 1887 it negotiated with Tokio a treaty on the subject, and when, in 1894, the British government at last acceded to the wishes of the Japanese, the American took the matter up again and brought it to a conclusion.

The far-seeing statesmen, who with marvellous success have re-made Japan, early realized the necessity of copying foreign models, and of profiting by the superior knowledge of western teachers. Among these the Americans were conspic-

[1] Owing to the Civil War at home, the Americans were represented at the bombardment by a hired Dutch vessel.

uous. They were employed as counsellors in foreign affairs
down to the most recent days; they aided in creating the
new system of public education, modelled on their own;
they organized the agricultural bureau, and assisted in the
founding of scientific institutions. By request, officials were
detached from the Treasury in Washington to establish a
modern financial system for the empire, and in many other
ways American teaching and example have exercised an
influence in its political and social transformation. Other
nations, indeed — Germany, England, France — have had
their good share in this work; but none of them, according
to the testimony of the Japanese themselves, have done as
much as the United States.

Turning now to the commercial transactions between the
two lands, we notice that for long they were very unequal.
From the first, the United States was one of Japan's best
clients. By 1871, it bought from her $5,298,153 worth of
imports (almost twelve times as much as it sold in return).
By 1893, the year before the war between Japan and China,
this total had more than quintupled, being $27,454,220, and
in 1906 it had almost doubled again, and amounted to
$52,551,520. American exports to Japan have until recently
been insignificant: as late as 1893 they were only $3,195,494,
but since that year they have grown by leaps and bounds.
In 1905, in consequence of the demands of the war with
Russia, they were twice as large as in 1904; in 1906 they
held a good part of their gain, and amounted to $38,464,952.
There is reason to expect that, in spite of protective tariffs
in both countries, trade between them will continue to
prosper, for each can furnish to the other things of which it
stands in need. Already the United States sells to Japan
more than it does to all but its largest customers, and in
return it is a far better mart for Japanese exports than is
any state in Europe.

Since Japan has been thrown open to outside curiosity,

she has exercised an extraordinary fascination on untold thousands in the western world. Visitors have returned delighted with her scenery, the monuments of her civilization, the picturesque structure of her society, and the intelligence, amiability, and exquisite courtesy of her people. Others, who have never been able to see the islands, have been carried away by the charm of Japanese art, whether in its great creations or in the dainty trifles that soon became popular abroad; their imagination has been thrilled with tales of the chivalrous ideals of old Japan and the beauty and refinement of the life there. And of foreign nations none has been more deeply interested than the Americans. They were the first to study Japanese art, as is testified by the collection of the Boston Art Museum, which is finer than any other in existence outside of the empire itself. They, the most western of modern peoples, have been peculiarly attracted by the subtle charm of the Far East. They have filled their houses with the products of its handiwork, and they have flocked over in thousands to visit it. A trip to Japan has seemed less of an undertaking to an American than to a European, and, in fact, for a citizen of San Francisco a visit to Tokio takes scarcely more time, and less trouble and expense, than one to London or Paris. No wonder that Americans have crossed the Pacific in swarms, most as mere tourists, but some for serious study, and others to aid in bringing modern knowledge to the Japanese, many of whom on their part have come as students to the United States.

It was not to be expected that these pleasant relations should be exempt from occasional discord. In the Far East, the American trading community, like the various European ones, has entertained a poor opinion of the commercial honesty of the Japanese, and has had little affection for the nation as a whole. During the war between China and Japan, American as well as European merchants in both countries, who as near observers would supposedly be well informed, not only sympathized with the former power, but were convinced that she would win. When the event turned out otherwise, though the public in the United States warmly applauded the success of its friends, the trader in the East shook his head and declared that the Japanese would now be more insufferably conceited and difficult to deal with than ever.

Few echoes of this dissatisfaction reached home; but even there enthusiasm did not go to the length of willingness to sacrifice interests. If Japan suffered from a surplus of population, let her, said the Americans, direct it somewhere else — to Korea, to Manchuria, only not in too great numbers to Hawaii, which, years before, the United States had declared would not be abandoned to any foreign power. The influx of Japanese into the little republic, and the tone which the government at Tokio took in protecting their rights, was indeed the chief reason why many people felt annexation to be urgent. When it took place, Japan handed in a formal protest at Washington, — a rather surprising act, for though it was but a mild expression of the disappointment felt at this harsh awakening from ambitious dreams of a Japanese Hawaii, still the ministers of the Mikado are ordinarily too cool and sensible to indulge in futile recriminations. They appear to have thought better of this one before long, for the protest was presently withdrawn.

When the United States took over the Philippines, whatever dissatisfaction Japan may have felt, she kept it to herself. She was not in a position to stop the transfer if she had wished to, and she desired American support in matters which concerned her more nearly.

In the various questions that agitated the Far East during the troubled years intervening between the last two wars, American and Japanese interests were usually in harmony, and the policy pursued by the two governments was much the same. They supported equally the principle of the "open door," even if the Japanese had not applied it in Formosa; and they were opposed to the partition of China, though Japan, like England, took care to provide herself by treaty with a particular sphere of influence (the province of Fukien) in case of accident. During the relief expedition to Peking, the American and the Japanese soldiers were on the best of terms, and both fraternized with the English, while the troops from continental Europe tended to form another group. The United States was throughout in sympathy with Japanese efforts to prevent the Russians from establishing themselves permanently in Manchuria, — a step which it regarded as contrary to its interests.

It is not to be wondered at, despite the surprise and anger of many Europeans, that during the recent war the American public overwhelmingly favored Japan, and gave practical proof of its good-will by its readiness to subscribe to her last loan. We must remember how much the traditional friendship between the United States and Russia had cooled down by that time. Then there was a natural sympathy for the smaller country, even if it did have the greater available resources at hand; and soon the splendid courage and patriotism shown by the Japanese in the course of the struggle, the perfection of their organization, and the skill of their conduct of affairs, elicited unstinted applause. Besides this, their triumphs flattered a certain self-satisfaction in the Americans; for nations, like individuals, are wont to be proud of their pupils, and sometimes have a closer attachment to those on whom they have conferred favors than to those from whom they have received them.

One argument which appealed to many persons in Europe, even among those who had little fondness for the Russians, — that of the solidarity of the white peoples against the yellow, — made little impression in the United States. Strong as race feeling is there, it has small influence in foreign affairs.

The American has for some time been afraid of the Asiatic as a competitor at home, and he is beginning to dread him as a rival abroad; but the "yellow peril," in a political sense, has no terrors for him. He believes that on his own continent he is able to defend himself against any armed foe; and prophecies of the future danger to the white races when countless millions of Chinese, disciplined and led by Japanese instructors, shall renew the exploits of Genghis Khan, have left him quite unmoved. He was much more affected by the comparisons drawn between the reactionary severity, then at its height, of the Russian autocracy and the liberal transformation which had made of Japan a modern civilized power. In fact, he was ready to declare that the Japanese were the more advanced and the more truly western nation of the two.

For this friendliness, the Japanese were honestly grateful. We need not always take the professions of their public men, orators, and newspapers at their face value, any more than we do those of other countries, but we should beware of distrusting Asiatics just because they are Asiatics. Even if their profusion of polite assurances may be mere figures of speech oftener than we are used to in the western world, this does not prove them to be incapable of sincerity. For instance, the extraordinary ovations to the party headed by Secretary Taft which passed through Japan while hostilities were still in progress, though doubtless stimulated and directed by political calculation, displayed, as any one present would testify, much genuine warmth of feeling. It is true that there was a sharp reaction when the terms of peace turned out less favorable than Japanese public opinion in its elation had expected, and the anger aroused by this disappointment was in part directed against the nation which had helped to end the war. But it is now recognized by unprejudiced observers that at the time the military outlook in Manchuria was far from promising for

Japan. The Russian army had never been stronger or in better condition; the cost of the siege of Port Arthur did not tend to make the prospect of the more difficult one of Vladivostok alluring; the financial strain on the Empire of the Mikado was very severe; so that, when all was said and done, the Japanese obtained as satisfactory terms as they were entitled to hope for. They have, therefore, no legitimate cause to resent the action of America in bringing about the peace of Portsmouth, especially as she put no obstacle in the way of their domination in Korea, though she was under treaty obligation to aid in maintaining Korean independence whenever her good services should be asked for. Taking advantage of the forced technical consent of the unfortunate Korean emperor to the terms imposed upon him, the government at Washington paid no attention to his private appeals, but left him and his empire to their hard, though not unmerited, fate.

To sum up, we may say that the record of the relations between the United States and Japan, from the days of Commodore Perry down to a few months ago, has been one of genuine and rather extraordinary mutual friendliness. Why, then, has a new feeling grown up of late, and why is the present outlook less serene?

In replying to these questions we may as well recognize, to begin with, that the two countries can never again be on quite the same terms that they were ten years ago. Their feelings towards one another may be of the most cordial kind, but both have changed too much for the old relation, which was almost that of benevolent teacher and eager pupil, to be possible in the future. The Americans are no longer the mildly interested spectators in the Far East that they once were, and Japan has outgrown the need of their tutelage. In the past they have applauded her successes, sometimes without stopping to consider whether these would in the end be to their advantage, and now they can claim no grievance if her altered position gives her new interests and inspires her with new ambitions which are not invariably in accord with their own desires. America, who has grown to be the rival of so many older states, cannot complain when she in her turn is confronted by the rivalry of a younger one. The world is still large enough for many nations to compete without quarrelling, but when the aspirations of one conflict with those of another, it serves no good purpose to blink the truth.· It is saner to accept the situation frankly, and to try to see what can reasonably be expected on both sides, for without such an understanding, a fair adjustment cannot be arrived at.

For the sake of convenience, we may divide the questions which threaten to produce friction between Japan and the United States into two groups: the first to include those which relate to the coming of the Japanese into the New World, and the second those pertaining to the rivalry between the two powers in Asia and in the waters of the Pacific. The line of demarcation between these sets of questions is not distinct, — it is hard to say to which of them Hawaiian matters belong, — but in the main they are separate, though they react on one another and combine to make a much involved problem.

On taking up the first group of questions, we note at the start that for some time the Japanese have been less popular on the Pacific coast than in other parts of the United States. Merchants of California have had unpleasant experiences in trading with them, and the laboring classes have looked on Japanese immigrants with the same hostility that they have felt towards the Chinese. Different as these two Asiatic peoples are, the effect of their presence from the point of view of the white laboring man is the same, — it exposes him to a competition against which, as long as he maintains his present standard of living, he is unable to hold his own. In California, the Japanese have found a climate

which suits them perfectly, occupations which are conge-
nial, — indeed, owing to their intelligent carefulness they are
particularly well adapted to the important industry of fruit-
growing, — and they can get wages far above what they can
hope for at home. It is true, the cost of living is greater
in America, but it leaves a large margin of profit for people of their simple, economical habits. To many of them a
preliminary sojourn in Hawaii has served as an introduc-
tion to American ways and conditions.

If the movement of immigration were a small one, it need
not excite alarm, but though still young, it has rapidly
taken on large dimensions. The annual surplus of births
over deaths in Japan, already an overcrowded country, is
some seven hundred thousand, and a yearly immigration of
half this number into the United States — a thing by no
means inconceivable — would soon flood the Pacific coast
with an Asiatic population that would certainly displace
white workmen and shopkeepers, and perhaps whole communities. Already there are Japanese capitalists there who
own industrial enterprises of importance, which employ
many of their compatriots and attract others from Japan.
No wonder that the labor-unions are up in arms against the
danger, and that they find popular support, to the surprise
of many good people in the eastern states who cling to their
old pro-Japanese sentiments. The exclusion of Japanese
children from the California schools was but the chance
occasion of the raising of the whole broad issue.

Some persons maintain that the ideals which have made
America great in the past are above mere differences of race
and color, and rest on fundamental truths applicable to all
mankind. They declare that the treatment and influences
which make good Americans out of Italians, Hungarians,
and Russian Jews will be equally efficacious with the Japanese; that no one can doubt their mental capacity, or deny
their eagerness to learn, not only the language of their new

home, but everything it has to teach them, and to copy its ways; that nothing, indeed, but the unjust law which forbids the naturalization of Asiatics prevents the Japanese immigrants from becoming good citizens within a few years after their arrival in the United States. It may be answered that all this is unquestionably true of individuals, and were the Japanese coming over in small numbers only, it would be invidious and wrong to impose restrictions on them, even if we might regret the addition to the American population of another ethnic element, which, whatever may be its own virtues, would not, in the opinion of many, blend well with the rest. But the question at issue is different; it is that of checking such an influx of the yellow race as will swamp the whites on the Pacific coast. We may doubt, too, whether the Japanese, though desirous of obtaining citizenship, are as willing as most other immigrants to divest themselves of their former nationality; whether for them naturalization would not be merely a means of gaining influence and power, and whether they would not use the advantages the vote confers to build up on American soil a great community of the Shin Nihon (the New Japan), which their enthusiasts have dreamed of, and some of their writers have discussed with a frankness that, if known, would make men stare in the United States. It is not easy to believe that a people who hold such views think of their emigrants as lost to their old home for the benefit of a new one: on the contrary, they appear to regard them as pioneers in a movement of national colonization. But national colonization of the sort is an obvious menace to the integrity of the country to which it is directed. While we need not take unauthorized patriotic fancies too seriously, it would be unwise to ignore them altogether.

The late violent outburst against the Japanese on the Pacific coast was primarily due to their rapid increase of numbers in the last two years. The incident placed the government at Washington in a very uncomfortable situation. Owing to the nature of the American Constitution, federal control over any state in such matters is feeble enough at best, as was clearly shown at the time of the New Orleans massacre in 1891. Now, while unable to bring much pressure upon California, the administration has had to soothe the legitimate wrath of a proud, sensitive nation, aglow with triumph. The assumption that their compatriots were to be treated as an inferior race whose children must be parked for infectious moral disease in separate schools, seemed an intolerable insult. The Japanese, except when they are trying to win popularity with the Chinese, resent being classed with them or being termed Mongolians at all, and they will never submit to the same unceremonious treatment. They ask for no privileges, but only for the equality granted to twenty other peoples and assured to them by solemn treaty. No wonder that they were fierce with anger at the news that reached them from San Francisco, and that the unscrupulous howling of the American yellow press provoked equally wild outbursts in reply.

Happily for all parties, the cool, clear-sighted statesmen who are at the head of affairs in Tokio have remained unmoved by popular clamor. They realize the difficulties under which the American government labors, and they have shown themselves willing to help it out to the best of their ability, provided only the dignity of their country be respected. To have insisted uncompromisingly on their treaty rights without doing anything to make the situation easier for the Americans, would have been to move directly towards war; for we may accept it as beyond doubt that, if Japanese immigration to the United States were to keep on growing at its recent rate, some means would be found to stop it, treaty or no treaty, peacefully or by force, at any risk and at any cost. This may well have been appreciated at Tokio.

2 A

Another consideration which, we may feel sure, has been weighed there by men who have not been led astray by dreams of the Shin Nihon, is whether it is for Japan's real interest, not to speak of her dignity, that her children should leave her in this manner. Few countries view with pleasure the permanent departure of their citizens for foreign climes. It is true that colonies, even under alien rule, help to stimulate the national trade; and many Japanese emigrants to America send or take back the money they have made there, to the enrichment of their native land. But will they not all in the end be lost to their old home, as so many Europeans have been? Would it not be better for the Empire, in any case, that they should colonize Formosa, Korea, Manchuria, where they would remain under the control of their own authorities, and could use their strength and skill for the benefit of the Empire?

The United States on its part may take comfort in the fact that the Pacific coast of Canada, as the troubles at Vancouver have shown, shares its dislike to Asiatic competition. This is but natural in view of the similarity of conditions. There is also sufficient evidence that the same feeling obtains in Australia; all of which is exceedingly awkward for Great Britain, the sworn ally of Japan. Since it is hardly conceivable that the mother country should attempt to coerce her great self-governing colonies, it appears that, like the United States, she is in the rather humiliating position of having to rely chiefly on the prudence and moderation of another country to get her out of a bad predicament. Probably she will not be disappointed; for the Japanese, whatever may be their feeling towards the Americans, are not going just now to rush into a quarrel with the English. But concessions made to Canada cannot well be refused to the United States. The anti-Japanese movement is the same in both places, and its spread into the dominions of Japan's close friend proves that its character is not specifically American. After all, Japan herself has just been ruthlessly expelling Chinese and Korean laborers from her territory.

We must lament that the very desire to exclude people from a territory serves as an advertisement of its attractions, and leads to determined efforts to smuggle themselves in, a thing hard to check in the United States because of its thousands of miles of open frontier toward Canada and Mexico. The measures taken to suppress this smuggling cannot help leading to incidents not conducive to international good feeling.

It is fortunate that the whole situation appears to be well understood by the governments concerned, who have preserved cordial relations. The Japanese one has earned a claim to gratitude by its spirit of concession, as shown in a willingness to restrict the number of its emigrants to the United States, as also to Canada. On their side, most Americans still entertain a lively admiration for Japan; they are fair-minded enough to appreciate her side of the question, and they have sufficient respect for her military strength to appreciate that, even if they would, they could not settle matters off-hand without regard to her wishes. Under these circumstances, as long as they gain their main point, the checking of immigration, they are not likely to indulge in wanton provocation of a great and friendly power. For the moment, at least, the danger of serious complications seems past.

Nevertheless, it would be idle to pretend that the outcome is wholly satisfactory. An unpleasant feature of the controversy for Americans has been that, however much they may be in the right on the larger issues, the fact remains that, owing to formal treaty stipulations, and to their own inability to suppress mob violence with due promptness, they have been in an awkward quandary from which they owe their release chiefly to the wisdom, not to say the magnanimity, of Japan. And the arrangement which will give the United States the protection it demands, will rest, not on the efficiency of its own laws, but on the fulfilment of obligations voluntarily assumed by a foreign state. This may be making the best of a bad job, but it is not ideal. Whatever course wisdom may dictate to the Mikado and his counsellors, a great nation like the American cannot depend indefinitely on the generosity, real or presumed, of a neighbor. The Japanese people as a whole will not regard even their partial exclusion from the United States with anything but bitterness; and if they should ever wish for war with their former friends, they will have no trouble in finding a plausible pretext. As long as the Americans make a distinction between nations in the opening of their doors to strangers, so long will those who are discriminated against feel that they have a grievance hard to forgive. This consideration may strengthen the growing opposition in the United States to the present enormous immigration from all quarters. Such a measure as the imposition of a property qualification, which many advocate on its own merits, would have the additional advantage that it would at the same time put an end to the invasion of Asiatic laborers, and remove the most serious complaint of China and Japan. It may be that the solution of the whole problem lies in this direction.

The present rapid increase of population in certain parts of the world threatens to raise troublesome questions. On the one hand, the peoples herded together in poor, small areas will strive to break down all barriers erected by the selfishness of those who possess thinly settled tracts with rich natural resources. On the other, those who by the kindness of nature or by their own efforts are well provided for, will not lightly consent to be swamped by a horde of famished strangers; they will not see why they should sacrifice their own comfort and standard of life just because their needy neighbors choose to have big families. Communism among states will not soon prevail, especially as it is unattractive to the very men who favor it among individuals; for the laboring classes are those who suffer most from unrestricted immigration, and are, in consequence, most hostile to it.

Now the Japanese, perceiving that their islands have already about as large a population as they can well contain, and that the tide is still swelling, are anxious to find a good outlet for their overflow. For the moment Korea may do; but Korea is not very spacious, and it has people of its own, who may be expected to multiply under improved conditions. If, in addition it were to receive for a generation the surplus of births from across the strait, it would become as crowded as is Japan to-day. Manchuria is larger, but Manchuria already has some twenty million Chinese inhabitants, with many more coming. There is room enough there for Japanese enterprise, but the Chinese trader is not easy to surpass, and the Chinese day laborer, under fair competition, has yet to find his equal. Looking further, we see vacant land in the tropics; but the Japanese have so far not shown themselves well adapted to field work in a hot climate; in Formosa, for instance, they have been none too successful. It would seem that, like the whites, they can live as officials, merchants, and employers of labor everywhere, but only within the temperate zone can they emigrate in such numbers as to relieve the congestion at home. Among the comparatively empty temperate regions, Siberia, Canada, and Australia will assuredly be closed to any great immigration on their part, for the reasons that have been operative in the United States, and that would be equally so in any country of Europe. There remains only Latin America.

Most of the Latin-American republics are the happy possessors of splendid natural resources still waiting to be developed. In order to develop them, and it is desired to do so at once, there is need of both capital and labor. The former can be furnished by Europe or the United States, and will be forthcoming, provided it can enjoy security. The latter is also to be had; but so far only a few of the Latin-American countries have attracted any considerable European immigration. The others may have their turn in time, but they are unwilling to wait while their rivals pass them in the race, and if they cannot get European laborers, they are ready to take Asiatic. They made their first experiments in importing Chinese in the days of the infamous coolie traffic; but not many of these Chinese have remained, and few have come since. Here, then, is an opening for the children of Japan,— broad, fertile, thinly settled lands, fine climates, natural wealth of divers kinds, and in some cases indolent, unprogressive populations, who with their mixture of white, black, and Indian blood can hardly entertain the race haughtiness of the Anglo-Saxon. Neither governments nor peoples seem to have any fear of the Japanese; nay, in some quarters a desire has already been expressed for growth of their influence in the New World to prevent the too great preponderance of the United States.

The existence of these favorable conditions is already known in Japan, where a movement towards Latin America has actually started, and bids fair to proceed rapidly. For some years there has been a Mexican colonization society in the empire, whose activity did not altogether cease even during the late war with Russia. But in Mexico the conditions are peculiar, for if immigrants should flock there only to make their way across the border into the United States, as they have already begun to do, the latter may, in self-defence, be obliged to ask of Mexico and Tokio that the same restrictive measures be applied to Mexican immigration as to its own. At last accounts, something of the kind had been conceded, but, judged by international law, it is a curious demand to make, and it might be hard to persist in if it were refused. And now the Japanese are appearing in South America. They have begun coming to Peru and Chile, where they have been welcomed, and recently their government signed a treaty with Brazil providing for the establishment there of agricultural immigrants, to whom lands are to be allotted. Direct communication between the Empire of the Mikado and the chief ports of the Southern republics is to be assured by a Japanese line of steamships. In view of all these facts it seems highly probable that immigration will soon set in on a large scale, to the immediate advantage of all concerned.

At present this does not matter in any way to the United States, and we may hope that it never will; yet we cannot be too confident. If the plan of having European capital coöperate with Asiatic labor in the development of the South American countries for the particular benefit of the natives is attractive, it is not without its dangers. We have considered elsewhere some of the difficulties connected with the investment of capital from Europe; those springing from the influx of laborers from Asia are certainly not less.

Even in the sparsely settled territories of Latin America, the presence of a considerable number of Japanese may provoke agitation. This will be more likely to happen if the newcomers are successful and get control of affairs to an extent that will alarm the rest of the population, — a not impossible contingency, for the Japanese have shown their ability to meet more severe competition than that of the ordinary Latin American. And they need not be expected to disarm hostility by excessive modesty or by prompt assimilation with those about them. In the United States, where the Japanese have freely acknowledged that they have had much to learn, one of the charges commonly brought against them is that of intolerable conceit. How will it be in lands where they will feel themselves superior at all points to their neighbors? If it is difficult to think of the Japanese as being converted into "good Americans," it requires a wider stretch of the imagination to conceive of them as turning promptly into typical Peruvians or Brazilians; and they have proved that they will not submit tamely to ill-treatment, such as, for instance, the Chinese formerly endured in Brazil. We may rest assured that the government at Tokio will not leave its citizens unprotected in any part of the world; nor will it sit by with folded hands while one door after another is slammed in their face, — an insult which no high-spirited nation could bear with equanimity. It is one thing to show moderation in dealing with the United States, and readiness in helping its government out of a quandary; it is another to put up with an affront from, let us say, Ecuador. Can we imagine that in every case Japan would submit to an exclusion act directed against her people?

Questions like the above may some day have to be taken into earnest consideration by the United States; for it is certain that, if the Japanese should threaten to use force against any Latin-American republic, that republic, even if it harbored no friendly feeling towards its Anglo-Saxon sister, would speedily appeal to her for protection in the name of the Monroe Doctrine. The Americans might then find themselves in a bad dilemma. They would not wish to protect a delinquent against deserved punishment, and could remain tranquil if the punishment were not pushed too far, but the case might not be so simple. If, for instance, the Japanese were to increase to such an extent in Peru that the native population, in fear of losing control of their own country, were to forbid further admission of Asiatics, and were to turn to the United States for support against coercion from Japan, what then? Could the Americans be expected to accept all the fearful responsibilities of war solely that the people of Peru, not one-seventh of whom are of the white race, might shut out at their good pleasure the immigrants who could best develop the country? It would be still more absurd if the United States, while excluding the Japanese from its own borders, should insist that a sister republic admit them. And yet, to stand aside and abandon that republic to its fate would be hazardous, besides being quite out of keeping with the present practice of the Monroe Doctrine. We must remember, too, that while the Japanese may respect the Monroe Doctrine as the corner-stone of the foreign policy of a powerful nation, there is no reason why they should like it any more than many Europeans do. As applied to them, it cannot be defended on the same moral ground as when enforced against Europe; for then, in theory at least, it rests on the idea of reciprocity. The United States holds no land in the Old World, takes no part in its political affairs, and in return will not tolerate that any European power should intervene in the affairs of the New, or extend its domination there. But this theory breaks down when applied to Japan, for the United States not only takes part freely in the affairs of the Far East, — witness its championship of the "open door," — it also has acquired extensive territories, territories much nearer to Japan than is most of South America to the United States. To any insistence on the Monroe Doctrine the Japanese can therefore reply, "Why not Asia for the Asiatics?"

No people, of course, ever lets itself be prevented by a logical dilemma from defending what it believes to be its rights and its legitimate interests; and the Americans will not change their long-established policy, even if the Japanese are able to prove in argument that it is one-sided. But they will do well to appreciate the Japanese point of view. Fortunately, the perils of a large immigration into Latin America are not immediate, and the movement itself may not come to anything, — prophecy in such matters is most uncertain. If the present problem of the Japanese influx into the United States can be satisfactorily settled, Americans will not borrow trouble about the future in their own part of the world.   They must, however, pay attention to their relations with Japan in the Far East, for in that region, too, though there is no crisis, there are causes of discord which will require watching to prevent them from becoming serious.

To begin with, it is, alas, true that the Japanese, in addition to their resentment about the immigration question, have other grievances, the existence of which is barely known in the United States, but which are not forgotten by the jingo party in Japan.   These same jingoes also entertain ambitions not reconcilable with American interests.   To be sure, there is as yet no valid reason for taking these ambitions tragically, or for supposing that they are shared by public men; every country has its irrepressible chauvinists, who often attract more attention abroad than at home. Their aspirations cannot, however, be entirely overlooked in a study of international politics, for the jingoes are sometimes merely an advance guard, — men who give indiscreet expression to hopes that others cherish in secret and may some day, if circumstances are favorable, try to carry out.

The first Japanese grievance of this kind relates to Hawaii. Although the useless protest made at the time of annexation was soon officially withdrawn, the disappointment to which the protest gave expression has not disappeared, nor can we expect it to as long as the Japanese in the islands outnumber all the other elements put together and are several times as numerous as the Americans.   Geographically, Hawaii is almost as much a natural outpost of Japan as it is of the United States, and would be invaluable to her for either defensive or offensive purposes.   Since it will hardly be pretended that the Japanese there are inferior to the natives, they cannot in justice remain indefinitely deprived of the vote; but, if they get it, they may profit by their numbers to agitate in favor of union with their former country. We need not wonder, then, that there are patriotic subjects of the Mikado who still hope to see his authority extended over this, the first conquest of Japanese colonization.

In the Philippines the situation is different. Few Japanese are to be found there, and, though their number is increasing, it will never be formidable, as the tropical climate is no more suited to them than to white men. In the past, Japan has had some slight connection with the islands, and in the sixteenth century even meditated a military expedition against them. In recent years she has been accused of eyeing them covetously, of encouraging native revolt against Spain, and, now that the United States has taken the place of Spain, of biding her time until she is ready to snatch at this splendid spoil.

As far as we know, there is little foundation for this supposition. Admitting that Japanese imperialists of the usual type are animated by a desire to get the Philippines, there is no reason to think that their feeling is shared by responsible statesmen in Tokio. Nor is there evidence that the latter ever had designs on the islands when they were under Spanish rule, although this spectre was made use of by malcontent Filipinos, and troubled men's minds in Madrid.[1] A few Filipino insurgents at the time of the last rising against Spain sought refuge in Japan, where the movement in which they were engaged awakened a certain amount of sympathy, and suggested tempting possibilities, but never received real help. Japan was just then taken up with plans in another direction, and at the moment of

[1] In 1895 when Russia, Germany, and France forbade a Japanese acquisition of the Liaotung Peninsula, Spain wished to have the same prohibition extended to Formosa, in order to avoid having Japan the nearest neighbor to the Philippines.

the transfer of the Philippines to the United States she gave no sign of resentment. The desire of the Japanese for the islands, such as it is, and their objection to the presence of the Americans there, date rather from the last war, which so mightily stimulated their national self-confidence and ambition. Their successes were indeed enough to turn weak heads, but the men who direct their destinies cannot be accused of weakness.

Many of those who accuse Japan of longing for the Philippines forget that since she is rich in children and poor in capital, what she really needs is vacant lands in the temperate zone, and not unprosperous territory in the tropics peopled by seven million Christian inhabitants who prefer to govern themselves. Still, we must admit that the ardent expansionist will not be stopped so easily. He believes that his country, like others, should have tropical colonies, and he points out that the Philippines should obviously be the first, not only because they are close at hand, but because they have been forcibly acquired by their present owners at so recent a date that possession is not consecrated by time. To crown all, they are inhabited by a discontented population, possibly of distant kin to the Japanese, who, he is convinced, will be welcomed as liberators. If he is an enthusiast for Pan-Asiatic ideals, his zeal will be the more inflamed against the Americans, the most western of western nations.

Without attaching too much importance to fancies of this sort, we must recognize that they exist and may need watching. We must remember too that, though the Japanese said nothing when the Philippines were taken over by the Americans, no people, be it ever so innocent of covetousness, enjoys seeing the territories in its vicinity, those which are the most obvious field for possible future expansion, pass from the hands of a weak nation into the grasp of a strong one. Ten years ago the United States had no designs on the Spanish West Indies, but it had long announced that it would never allow them to be transferred from Spain to another European power. If Japan at that date had been in a position to enforce her views, she would have been justified in maintaining a similar doctrine about the Spanish East Indies, albeit against the United States. To-day, when she is strong enough to take such a stand, it is too late, but the thought will rankle.

Another thing which Americans must be prepared to accept is that their policy, however justified, of debarring the Japanese from the western world, will surely impel them towards the eastern. In recent years the Japanese have been almost morbidly desirous of not being regarded as Asiatics in the ordinary western sense of the term. It has been their heart's dearest wish to be accepted as one of the great civilized peoples, the equal of any other. And now the United States, with Great Britain shamefacedly concurring for her colonies, says to them, "We welcome Europeans of every nationality to our shores, we throw open our gates to Jews and Armenians, but you are not wanted, you are Asiatics." If the Japanese are forced to acquiesce in this decision, we may expect to see them bending their energies the more strenuously to the work of securing and extending their position in Asia, where they have been told that they belong. There is limitless room for their ambitions, and, after all, why are not Pan-Asiatic dreams as legitimate as Pan-American?

In the general politics of the Far East, complete harmony, as we have seen, prevailed for a time between the interests of the United States and those of Japan. We may doubt, however, whether the situation is still the same. Both powers were opposed to a partition of China; but this danger is no longer menacing, — indeed, it is less so than Japanese predominance, which would hardly be to the advantage of the United States. Both were hostile to a Russian absorption of Manchuria; but if Russia should now keep any part of Manchuria, it would only be in collusion with Japan, who herself threatens to absorb the southern and more thickly settled portion, the chief field for American trade. Already accusations have been made that the Japanese are aiding the sale of their own goods by underhand methods, and we may expect to hear of more such charges in the future. If, as seems likely, the United States and Japan are to be two of the most active commercial rivals in this part of the world, perhaps the most active, we need not be surprised if wherever one is in political control it is tempted to put obstacles in the way of the other, which, in return, will be ready on the slightest provocation to complain of unfair play. What adds to the displeasure of Americans is that the Japanese imitate, not to say counterfeit, their productions with inferior ones of their own, a way of underbidding, and at the same time discrediting a rival that has more than once been followed by nations as well as by individuals. If now the Japanese make use of their position in Korea and southern Manchuria to violate the principle of the "open door," — a principle so much easier to support with enthusiasm when you yourself do not control the door, — American resentment is sure to be keen.

On the side of the Japanese, it will not be conducive to good feeling if people get the impression that the United States is not only a troublesome competitor in the Chinese markets, but is also the power which does most to hinder the fulfilment of their political ambitions. Already they have one grudge on this score, which, however unwarranted, none the less exists. Though the wiser heads among them may recognize that at the peace of Portsmouth Japan obtained as many advantages as she had any right to expect in view of the military situation and of her own financial condition, to the Japanese public, the terms of the treaty came as a bitter disappointment; and there is danger of the survival of a belief that just as Russia, Germany, and France combined to rob Japan by force of the fruits of her earlier victories, so the United States, actuated by the same jealousy, but in the guise of a friend, managed to deprive her of the full reward of her triumphs over Russia. False as is this interpretation of what took place, it is the sort of legend which, owing to its appeal to national passion, is everywhere too readily accepted. The whole story points out some of the perils of even the friendliest mediation.

Towards China, the position of the Japanese is, in their own eyes, that of magnanimous liberators who have saved her from servitude to the Europeans, of wise teachers who have imparted to her the lessons necessary for her regeneration, of kindly guides who will direct her footsteps along the paths that lead to future greatness. The Chinese look at the matter differently: it was Japan, they say, that first exposed their weakness to the world, that robbed them of Formosa, and deprived them of their ancient suzerainty over Korea, which state she has now seized for herself; her action in repelling the Russians was due to selfish motives, and in any case it will be time enough to talk of gratitude when Manchuria has been restored without restriction to its sole legitimate possessor. Accordingly, their attitude, far from being docile, is rather one of distrust not unmixed with fear. Taught by experience, they are suspicious of disinterested professions, but they feel the need of foreign aid, and there is but one country to which they can well turn. Great Britain, France, Russia, have all recently signed treaties with Japan; Germany, though doubtless sympathetic, is not in a position to run the risk of openly opposing her for their sake; there remains, then, the United States, whose interest still is, as it has been, to maintain the integrity of the Chinese Empire, including Manchuria, and to uphold the policy of the "open door."

This is all very well, and it may be sound policy as well as generosity for the United States to assume a benevolent attitude, but whatever it gains in thanks from China it will assuredly lose in good-will from Japan. The mere suggestion that the Chinese look upon it as their natural protector against the ambitions of the Japanese is enough to irritate the latter, whether they cherish designs or not, — a fact of which the Chinese are perhaps quite well aware.

There remains one last set of reasons for which many people in Japan as well as in the United States, and perhaps still more outside, believe that the two must some day come to blows. The inevitable contest between them is to be either a "conflict between eastern and western civilization" or for the less ideal, but scarcely more tangible, "dominion of the Pacific." Now it is safe to say that the vast majority of the persons who use these high-sounding terms have very little idea of what they mean. The differences between eastern and western civilization, though often profound, are not easy to define with accuracy, and the phraseology is misleading. There is more difference between the Turk and the Japanese, for instance, than between the latter and the European. But, whatever the differences may be, it is not clear how Japanese and Americans, by destroying each other's persons and possessions with the aid of the latest improved implements of warfare, are going to promote civilization of any kind. If the Americans triumph, they will scarcely impose on their adversaries, by the articles of peace, the use of the Roman alphabet or baptism into the Methodist Church, and even a complete Japanese victory would do little to further the study of the Chinese classics or to spread the tenets of Shintoism in the New World. If there is to be a conflict of civilizations between the East and the West, a point about which one may remain sceptical, it will not be settled in this simple, forcible manner.

Again, the grandiloquent expressions "dominion of the seas," "mastery of the Pacific," and the like, are mere claptrap. What does this "mastery" signify, and how is either America or Japan to obtain it by victory over the other? Does it mean building up the larger navy? But Britannia continues to rule the waves by having more ships of war than any other power, and she can send them all to the Pacific, if she so pleases. As long as she retains this superiority, American or Japanese "mastery" can last only so long as the English kindly keep out of the way. Or, suppose that one country possesses the stronger fleet and the other holds most of the trade: which will then enjoy "dominion"? Theoretically, perhaps, the one with the more vessels of war, as being able to plunder its neighbor; but piracy is out of date, and while peace is preserved, there is no doubt which will have the more valuable asset. And why should a war between the United States and Japan settle any question of commercial supremacy between them? Great loss might be incurred, and certain industries be crippled, but the day is past when the victors could prohibit the vanquished from manufacturing what they wished to, and disposing of their produce as best they could in neutral markets. If the American fleets were to sweep the Pacific, this would not prevent Japanese cotton goods from underselling American ones in the shops of Shanghai, or, when peace returned, Japanese ships from charging lower freight rates than those of their American competitors. *Per contra*, the loss of the Philippines and Hawaii, grievous as it might be, would probably not seriously affect the sale of Standard oil in the Far East. The United States and Japan may, indeed, be rivals in the waters of the Pacific to-day, and rivalry of this sort is accompanied by some friction, but the supposition is monstrous that they must therefore enter into a desperate struggle with each other in order that one of them may obtain an undis-

2 B

puted primacy, which depends on other things than force of arms.

Unfortunately, the use of even meaningless phrases may be dangerous in itself. Vague and intangible as "dominion" and "mastery" are, they appeal to men's imagination; and before now people have fought for abstractions. We may think that a war for the "dominion of the Pacific" would be absurd, and wicked, but if a large number of persons in the United States and in Japan are convinced that this "dominion" properly belongs to their own country and not to the other, and that there must some day be a war between the two to settle the point, — an opinion in which many outsiders noisily concur, — a situation and a state of mind are created which are perilous to the peace: nations have not quite lost the temper of the game-cock ready to do battle for the privilege of having the roost to himself and crowing undisturbed. And the widespread impression that the United States and Japan are inevitable rivals for the "mastery" of the Eastern seas renders friendship between them more difficult, and familiarizes both with the idea of a possible conflict. Even when the adjective "peaceful" is attached to the word "domination," and it is explained that only commercial supremacy is meant, the reiteration of the claim by leading men in both countries is not likely to improve international relations.[1]

[1] The first number (October, 1907) of the new review of *The Pacific Era*, contains articles by President Roosevelt and Baron Kaneko. Here are two extracts : —

"The extension in the area of our domain has been immense; the extension in the area of our influence even greater. America's geographical position on the Pacific is such as to insure peaceful domination of its waters in the future if we only grasp with sufficient resolution the advantages of that position." — PRESIDENT ROOSEVELT, revised version of speech in San Francisco, in 1903.

"What then should be the attitude of our imperial country in the face of all this American activity? It cannot possibly be otherwise than this: That we must do our utmost in disputing this command of the Pacific

To sum up, when we come to consider the factors, large and small, which have contributed in the last three years to the estrangement of Japanese and Americans, we need not marvel at the change in their feeling towards one another. How far it has gone, whether the angry vaporings of a part of the press or the cordial utterances of public men represent more exactly the popular temper in the two countries, it is not easy to say, though we may remember the general truth that an angry man talks louder than a contented one. There are people in both who expect war; there is distrust on the American side, a suspicion that Japan having triumphed, first over China, then over Russia, has now picked out the United States as her third antagonist, and that when she thinks the moment come, she will strike as suddenly and as fiercely as she did in her last conflict. In return, there are Japanese who look on the United States as the chief obstacle to the future greatness of their country. But in both lands there are also men, men high in authority, mindful of the old friendship between the two, convinced that there is no valid reason why it should not continue, and certain that a war between them would be not only a folly but a crime.

If Japan were to plan an attack, she would have to act soon. She cannot build as many ships as the United States, and when the Panama Canal is dug, — a task which some might compare, in its military significance, to the construction of the Trans-Siberian land route for Russia a few years ago, — the Americans will no longer suffer from their worst disadvantage, the dispersion of their naval strength, and it is not likely now that they will be caught napping as the Russians were.

It is also not very evident where Japan could find the resources for a prolonged contest, especially as there is

with the United States, and also do our best in the control of the Far Eastern markets." — BARON KANEKO KENTARO.

little chance that she could obtain financial or other aid from outside. Alliance or no alliance, Great Britain will never take up arms against the United States in Japan's sole behalf. No treaty obligations could stand the strain, for such a course of action would not be tolerated by the English public, and would be enough to drive some of the colonies into rebellion.

The glib prophets of future conflicts usually overlook the many forces that are working to prevent them. Nations are capable of losing their heads and of beginning to fight before they know what they are doing, but the consequences of modern war are enormous, and the uncertainties so fearful that few public men will deliberately plan one. It may not take two to make a quarrel, but one at least has to be willing for it. Now there is no reason why the United States should wish for a war with Japan: it has no desire for her territory, no grudge to vent, and no grave danger to fear from her in the future. The trade rivalry between the two is not dissimilar to other commercial rivalry all over the world. We may confidently affirm that it is beyond the bounds of probability that the Americans should go out of their way to seek a conflict with the Japanese. For Japan the temptation may be greater. The chance of getting the Philippines and Hawaii, of adding another to the list of Japanese victories, of giving to the empire of the Mikado a still prouder position among the nations of the world and vindicating the claims of the Japanese race to equality with others, — all these may well appeal to the instincts of an ambitious, warlike people flushed with success. But if Japan has more to gain by a war than the United States, the risks she runs are more formidable. The American navy is the stronger of the two; but even supposing it to be defeated, and the Americans to be deprived of their insular possessions in the East, the mass of their territory would remain invulnerable, and they have given in the past sufficient evidence of their pride and determination to make it probable that they would persist in the struggle till it terminated in their favor, as it should do ultimately, owing to their superior resources.[1] When it did, they would exact heavy retribution for whatever humiliation they had undergone. In war with the United States to-day, victory would bring to Japan glory and power, but scarcely much permanent gain; defeat would mean crushing disaster, the end of her high hopes, and the loss of the splendid position she has won for herself by her two brilliantly successful appeals to the decision of the sword.

It was only with extreme reluctance that several of the Japanese statesmen consented to the war with Russia, although they believed that the vital interests of their country were imperilled; and it is hard to imagine their plunging light-heartedly into a perilous conflict with a country from which otherwise they have little to fear. Of course, if their safety were threatened or their honor were affected, the Japanese would fight, and fight to the bitter end, or if the Americans were to neglect reasonable precautions for defence, this might subject the virtue of their neighbors to too severe temptation. There is no especial reason to expect either of these contingencies, but when all is said and done, the best guarantee for continued peace between the two nations is the earnest desire of the wisest men in both that they should remain friends.

The moral for Americans of the various international complications in which they find themselves involved is, after all, the old one that greatness brings responsibilities. These they will have to face, for it is now too late for them to return to the simple life of their earlier history.

[1] Russia, who was in a much more disadvantageous position, might have fought on indefinitely if she had not been weakened by internal discontent.

They will do well, therefore, to take to heart the words
of the President : —

"We have no choice, we people of the United States, as
to whether or not we shall play a great part in the world.
That has been determined for us by fate, by the march of
events. We have to play that part. All that we can
decide is whether we shall play it well or ill."

INDEX

Adams, J. Q., and Monroe Doctrine, 96, 99 n.

Aërial navigation and Canadian-American relations, 266.

Aguinaldo, Emilio, and American officials, 152–155.

Alabama claims, 232.

Alaska, government, 30; purchase, 38, 216; status, 138; boundary tribunal, 241; effect of acquisition on Canada, 251.

Alexander I of Russia, and United States, 214.

Alexis, Grand Duke, visit to United States, 215.

Algeciras Conference, United States and, 119; "open door," 183.

American Revolution, cause, 29; French aid and attitude, 184–186; German interest, 197; attitude of Catherine II, 213; of French Canadians, 247, 248; Canada and peace negotiations, 248; loyalists in Canada, 249.

Americans, character, and immigration, 40, 43; English as language, 44–46, 58; future, 60; French opinion of, 193–195; and Russians, 216; English opinion of, 235, 242. *See also* Nationality, Political ideas.

Annexations. *See* Territory.

Anti-imperialists, origin, 134; and Hawaii, 134; and Porto Rico, 135, 143; arguments against annexation of Philippines, 135; and Philippine Insurrection, 156; and government of Philippines, 159; and protectorate, 167; and naval base in Philippines, 322.

Anti-Semitism in United States, 52. *See also* Jews.

Arbitration, San Juan Island, 102; Venezuela-Guiana boundary, 104; and Monroe Doctrine, 111; Behring Sea, 232; Geneva, 232; Alaskan tribunal, 241.

Argentine Republic, not a world power, 7; future, 17; and Falkland Islands, 283; future American relation, 308. *See also* Latin America.

Armed neutrality, 213.

Armenian massacres, 226.

Army, American, negroes as soldiers, 73; attitude towards regular, 89; in Philippine Insurrection, 157.

Assimilation. *See* Immigration.

Australia, anti-Japanese agitation, 354.

Austria-Hungary, as European power, 2; not a world power, 7; and United States, 224.

Bahama Islands, strategic position, 267.

Balkans, Russian intervention (1877), 128.

Baltimore incident with Chile, 284.

Beaconsfield, Earl of, and expansion, 5.

Behring Sea controversy, 232.

Belgium and Congo, 5.

Bermuda, strategic position, 267.

Bismarck, Fürst von, and expansion, 5; on Monroe Doctrine, 107.

Blaine, J. G., and New Orleans Mafia lynching, 235; and isthmian canal, 274; and Pan-Americanism, 298, 300.

Bohemians as immigrants, 54.

Bolivar, Simon, and Washington, 282.

Boundaries, character of United States, 20; disputes with England, 230; Alaskan, 241; Canada and disputes over, 250.

Boxer troubles, attitude of United States, 332.

Brazil, not a world power, 7; future, 17; German colonists, 49; and German expansion, 208–211; past American relations, 284; future American relations, 308; Japanese immigration, 359. *See also* Latin America.

Bureau of American Republics, utility, 300; enlarged scope, 301.

Burlingame, Anson, Chinese treaty, 333.

California, annexation and development, 35, 316, 334. *See also* Chinese, Japanese.

Canada, and treaty of 1783, 27, 248; England and American relations, 244; physical divisions, 245; geographical relations with United States, 246,